With illustrations by
T Brittain
P Endsleigh Castle ARAeS
·T Hadler
D Johnson
A Sturgess
M Trim

Aircraft in Profile

Volume 14

General Editor   **Charles W Cain**

Profile Publications Ltd Windsor Berkshire England
Doubleday & Company Inc Garden City New York

© Profile Publications Limited 1974

Doubleday & Company Inc edition 1975

First published in England 1975
by Profile Publications Limited
Coburg House Sheet Street Windsor
Berkshire England

ISBN 0 85383 023 1

ISBN (USA) 0 385 01089 3

Uniform with this volume
Aircraft in Profile Series *3rd Edition*
AFVs of the World Series *1st Edition*
Locomotives in Profile Series
Warship in Profile Series
Small Arms in Profile Series
Cars in Profile Series

Errata

Martin B-57 Night Intruders
Page 2, column 2: Second pattern aircraft
Canberra B.2 (WD940) assigned USAF serial
"AF:51-17351" to read as AF:51-17352.
Page 4: Lower of two big photos lacks caption
to read as: *Like the B-57B above (individual letter
'H' but serial no./Buzz no. not visible), this
individual letter 'L' (AF:53-3888/BA-888; see also
page 21) was assigned to the 13th Bomb Squadron
(Tactical) on temporary duty in the Republic of
Viet Nam. (Photo: USAF 94693)*
Pages 6 & 11: "Table VI" read as Table III and
"Table III" read as Table IV, respectively.
Page 23, Table II: B-57E "55-4243 through
55-4301" read as 55-4234 through 55-4301.
Page 24, Table IV: Serial 63-13286, rebuild of
"B/B 52-1599" read as B/B 52-1558 (vertical
stabilizer Obsolescent prefix AF:0-21558). In
storage, MASDC, as 'BM-066'.
Page 24, Table VIII, Misc. units: The 4713th
DSES known as 'The Roving Ravens'.

de Havilland D.H.9A (RAF 1918–30)
Page 48, column 2: Digby "18489" read as
J8489.

Douglas R4D variants
Page 59, bottom photo: R4D-5 (BuNo.17246)
"Korara II" read as Korora II

Aérospatiale/BAC Concorde
Page 77, column 2: Douglas D-558-2 with Scott
Crossfield at the controls exceeded Mach 2 not
in "February 1948" but on November 20, 1953,
in a M.2.04 dive from 72,000 ft.

Note to readers
Authenticated additional or corrected
information, together with appropriate
photographic or other material evidence, will
be welcomed by the Editor; the specific author
will be notified accordingly.—CWC.

Acknowledgements
Credit where credit is due. The authors, artists,
the general editor and the publishers, Profile
Publications Ltd., take this opportunity of
acknowledging with sincere and grateful thanks
the immense amount of invaluable assistance
rendered unstintingly by government
departments, military bureaux, the aerospace
industry, learned bodies, historical associations
and museums—not least, people as people who
have opened up their own private archives
simply because of their real affection for
aviation in one form or another. In the case of
the more recent parts of *Aircraft in Profile*,
authors have been invited to make
'Acknowledgements' an integral facet of their
overall work. To everyone who has helped in
the past and will feel free to do so in the
future. . . . Thank you! from the team that
makes up *Aircraft in Profile*.—CWC.

Printed in England by Mears Caldwell Hacker Limited, London

Foreword

With this latest volume of *Aircraft in Profile*, a proud record of sorts has been achieved. In something over 1,150,000 words, this unique aircraft library has encompassed 250 separate monographs, civil and military, ancient and modern. And you can't get more modern than the Concorde featured within these hard covers.

Veteran readers of this series do not need to be reminded of the wealth of detail which is packed into each *Profile*. But the new-comer might care to browse through the novel reference section with the self-explanatory title of Aircraft Profile Finder. Each *Profile* has its own identifying part number. The 'first generation' is numbered from No. 1 to 204 (12–16 pages each) and the 'second generation' from No.205 onwards (20–24 pages) is now well beyond the 250 mark.

Volume 14 opens the door to a broad aeronautical horizon; from the tribulations of the 1920s to the trials of the 1970s. Between the hard covers are more than 50,000 words of text, over 250 black and white photos and 80 individual full-colour artwork views of aircraft variants and sub-variants. To the newcomer with discerning tastes, this is a volume which will be richly satisfying. To the owners of the existing library, Volume 14 will not disappoint.

We've said it before and no doubt we'll say it again: No *Profile* can ever be total perfection. But we do try to improve on the improve-ments. This is a team effort that really works. Read on and judge for yourself!

January 1975   **Charles W Cain**

Contents

Legend

(1) ■□□□ World War 1 :1914-18	(3) □□■□ World War 2 :1939-45
(2) □■□□ Post-W.W.1 :1920s-1930s	(4) □□□■ Post-W.W.2 :1950s-1970s

Austria-Hungary (1914-18)

Ö. AVIATIK (BERG)
151 ■□□□ Berg D I
PHÖNIX
175 ■□□□ Scouts (D I-IV)

Australia

COMMONWEALTH
178 □□■□ Boomerang
154 □□■□ Wirraway

Canada

CANADAIR
186 □□□■ Sabres (Mks. 1-6 ; see also U.S.A./North American F-86 Sabre)

Czechoslovakia

AVIA
152 □■□□ B-534

France

AEROSPATIALE/BAC
250 □□□■ Concorde
BLOCH (see M. BLOCH)
BREGUET
157 ■□□□ †Breguet 14 (Type XIV)
DASSAULT (M. DASSAULT)
230 □□□■ †Mirage III-5 (& Milan)
143 □□□■ M.D. 450 Ouragan
DEWOITINE
135 □□■□ D.520
HANRIOT
109 ■□□□ †HD-1
LIORE ET OLIVIER
173 □□■□ LeO 45 Series
MARCEL BLOCH
201 □□■□ (M.B.) 151 & 152
MORANE SAULNIER
147 □□■□ M.S.406
NIEUPORT
49 ■□□□ †N.17C-1
79 ■□□□ †N.28C-1
POTEZ
195 □□■□ Potez 63 Series
SPAD
17 ■□□□ S.P.A.D. XIIIC.1
SUD-AVIATION
180 □□□■ Caravelle 3 & 6

Germany

ALBATROS
127 ■□□□ †D I-D III
9 ■□□□ †D V
ARADO
215 □□■□ Ar 234 Blitz
AVIATIK (see Ö. Aviatik: Berg D I, Austria-Hungary)
BÜCKER
222 □■□□ Bü 131 Jungmann
DORNIER
164 □□■□ †Do 17 & 215
FIESELER
228 □□■□ †Fi 156 Storch
FOCKE-WULF
3 □□■□ †FW 190 A
94 □□■□ FW 190 D/Ta 152 Series
99 □□■□ FW 200 (Condor)
FOKKER
25 ■□□□ †D VII
67 ■□□□ †D VIII
55 ■□□□ †Dr I (Triplane)
38 ■□□□ †Monoplanes (Eindeckers)

GOTHA
115 ■□□□ G I-G V
HEINKEL
15 □□■□ He 111 H
203 □□■□ †He 162 (Salamander)
234 □□■□ He 177 (Greif)
219 □□■□ He 219 Uhu
HENSCHEL
69 □□■□ Hs 129
JUNKERS
177 □□■□ Ju 52 Series (Ju 52/3m)
76 □□■□ Ju 87 A & B ('Stuka') ('A'—'Anton' ; 'B'—'Berta')
211 □□■□ †Ju 87 D Variants ('Stuka') ('D'—'Dora')
29 □□■□ Ju 88 A
148 □□■□ Ju 88 Night Fighters
187 ■□□□ Monoplanes ('Blechesel')
L.F.G. (see ROLAND)
MESSERSCHMITT
40 □□■□ †Bf 109 E ('E'—'Emil')
184 □□■□ Bf 109 F ('F'—'Friedrich')
113 □□■□ Bf 109 G ('G'—'Gustav')
23 □□■□ †Bf 110 (Day Fighters)
207 □□■□ Bf 110 (Night Fighters)
225 □□■□ †Me 163 Komet
161 □□■□ †Me 210/410 Series
130 □□■□ †Me 262 (Schwalbe/Sturmvogel)
PFALZ
43 ■□□□ †D III
199 ■□□□ †D XII (& D XIV)
PHÖNIX (see AUSTRIA-HUNGARY)
ROLAND (L.F.G.)
163 ■□□□ †C II ('Walfisch')
SIEMENS-SCHUCKERT
86 ■□□□ †D III & IV
UDET
257 □■□□ U-12 Flamingo

Great Britain

AIRSPEED
227 □□■□ Oxford Mks. I-V
ARMSTRONG WHITWORTH
153 □□■□ Whitley (Mks. I-VII)
AVRO
†Avro 707 (see Avro Vulcan)
65 □□■□ †Lancaster I
235 □□■□ Lancaster Mk. II
243 □□□■ Avro (Hawker Siddeley) Shackleton Mks. 1-5
162 □□□■ †Vulcan (& Avro 707)
168 □□■□ York (Mks. I & II)
BAC/AEROSPATIALE
250 □□□■ BAC/Aerospatiale Concorde
B.E.
133 ■□□□ B.E.2, 2a & 2b
BOULTON PAUL
117 □□■□ Defiant (Mks. I-III)
BRISTOL
193 ■□□□ Bristol M.1 (M.1A-M.1D)
137 □□■□ Beaufighter Mks. I & II
93 □□■□ Blenheim I
218 □□■□ Blenheim Mk. IV (& R.C.A.F. Bolingbroke Mks. I-IV)
6 □□■□ †Bulldog (Mks. I-IV)
21 ■□□□ †Fighter ('Brisfit')
237 □■□□ F.2B Fighter (see No. 21) (RAF: 1918-30s)
139 ■□□□ †Scouts C & D
DE HAVILLAND
91 ■□□□ †D.H.2
26 ■□□□ †D.H.4 (see also AMERICAN DH-4)
181 ■□□□ †D.H.5
62 ■□□□ †D.H.9
248 □■□□ D.H.9A (RAF:1918-30)
145 ■□□□ D.H.10
108 □□□■ †Comet Srs. 1-4 (now Hawker Siddeley Comet)
174 □□□■ Hornet (& Sea Hornet)
52 □□■□ †Mosquito I-IV
209 □□■□ Mosquito Mk. IV
144 □□■□ †Rapide (Dragon Rapide)

132 □□■□ †Tiger Moth
48 □□□■ †Vampire Mks. 5 & 9
ENGLISH ELECTRIC/BAC
54 □□□■ †Canberra Mks. I & IV
114 □□□■ †P.1 & Lightning 1
FAIREY
44 □■□□ Fairey III F
240 □□■□ Barracuda Mks. I-V
34 □□■□ †Battle Mks. I-V (and Trainer)
56 □■□□ Flycatcher
254 □□■□ Fulmar Mks. I & II
212 □□■□ Swordfish Mks. I-IV
GLOSTER
33 □■□□ †Gamecock (Mks. I-III & Grebe Mk. II)
10 □■□□ Gauntlet (Mks. I & II)
98 □□■□ †Gladiator (Mks. I & II, also Sea Gladiator)
179 □□□■ †Javelin 1-6
78 □□□■ Meteor F.IV (F.4)
12 □□□■ †Meteor F.8
HANDLEY PAGE
11 □□■□ Halifax B.III, VI, VII
58 □□■□ Hampden (Mks. I & II, also Hereford)
182 □■□□ †Heyford (Mks. I-III)
HAWKER
198 □□□■ P.1127 and Kestrel (now Harrier)
140 □■□□ Audax & Hardy
18 □■□□ †Fury
57 □■□□ †Hart (& Hart Trainer)
4 □□□■ Hunter F.6
167 □□□■ Hunter Two-Seaters
111 □□■□ Hurricane I (& Sea Hurricane Mk. IA)
24 □□■□ †Hurricane IIC (& Sea Hurricane Mks. IC & IIC)
126 □□□■ Sea Fury (& Fury)
71 □□□■ †Sea Hawk
197 □□■□ Tempest I-VI
81 □□■□ †Typhoon
HAWKER SIDDELEY (see AVRO & DE HAVILLAND)
MARTINSYDE
200 ■□□□ Elephant
R.E.
85 ■□□□ †R.E.8
S.E.
103 ■□□□ S.E.5
1 ■□□□ †S.E.5a
SHORT
74 ■□□□ Short 184
84 □■□□ Empire Boats ('C' & 'G'-Class ; also 'Mercury-Maia' Composite)
142 □□■□ Stirling (Mks. I-V)
189 □□■□ Sunderland (Mks. I-V)
SOPWITH
121 ■□□□ †Sopwith 1½ Strutter
31 ■□□□ †Camel F.1
169 ■□□□ †Dolphin (5.F.1)
13 ■□□□ †Pup
50 ■□□□ †7F.1 Snipe
73 ■□□□ †Triplane
SUPERMARINE
39 □■□□ †S.4-S.6B (Schneider Trophy Racers)
221 □□■□ Seafires (Merlins) (Mks. I-III)
41 □□■□ †Spitfire I & II
166 □□■□ †Spitfire V Series
206 □□■□ †Spitfire Mk. IX (& Mk. XVI)
246 □□■□ Spitfire (Griffons) Mks. XIV & XVIII
224 □□□■ †Walrus I & Seagull V (RN variants)
VICKERS (-ARMSTRONG)
66 □□□■ †Valiant (Mks. 1 & 2)
5 ■□□□ **F.B.27 Vimy (Mks. I-III)**
72 □□□■ †Viscount 700
229 □□■□ Warwick Mks. I-V
256 □□■□ Wellesley Mks. I & II
125 □□■□ Wellington I & II
WESTLAND
159 □□■□ †Lysander (Mks. I-III)
32 □■□□ Wapiti (Mks. I-VII)
191 □□■□ Whirlwind (Mk. I)

Italy

ANSALDO (see S.V.A.)

CAPRONI REGGIANE
- **123** □□■□ **Re. 2000 (Falco I)**
- 244 □□■□ Re 2001 (Falco II), Re.2002 (Ariete) & Re.2005 (Sagittario)

FIAT
- 110 □□■□ B.R.20 (Cicogna)
- 22 □■■□ C.R.32
- **16** □□■□ †**C.R.42 (Falco)**
- 188 □□■□ G.50 (Freccia)
- 119 □□□■ G.91

MACCHI
- 64 □□■□ M.C.200 (Saetta)
- **28** □□■□ **C.202 (Folgore)**

S.V.A (ANSALDO)
- 61 ■□□□ Scouts (S.V.A 4-10)

SAVOIA MARCHETTI
- **89** □□■□ **S.M.79 (Sparviero)**
- 146 □□■□ S.M.81 (Pipistrello)

Japan (*Allied code names)

AICHI
- 241 □□■□ D3A ('Val') & Yokosuka D4Y ('Judy') Carrier bombers

KAWANISHI
- 233 □□■□ Four-motor Flying-boats: H6K 'Mavis' * & H8K 'Emily' *
- 213 □□■□ Kyofu; Shiden & Shiden KAI Variants ('Rex' * ; 'George' *)

KAWASAKI
- 105 □□■□ †Ki-45 Toryu ('Nick' *)
- 118 □□■□ Ki-61 Hein ('Tony' *)

MITSUBISHI
- 129 □□■□ A6M2 Zero-Sen ('Zeke' * & 'Rufe' * floatplane)
- 190 □□■□ A6M3 Zero-Sen ('Hamp' *)
- 236 □□■□ †A6M5/8 Zero-Sen ('Zeke 52 *') (see Nos. 129 & 190)
- 160 □□■□ G3M ('Nell' * & Yokosuka L3Y 'Tina' *)
- 210 □□□■ G4M 'Betty' * (& Ohka Bomb — 'Baka' *)
- 172 □□■□ Ki-21 ('Sally' * & Ki-57/ MC-20 'Topsy' *)
- **82** □□■□ **Ki-46 ('Dinah' *)**

NAKAJIMA
- **141** □□■□ **B5N 'Kate' *
- 46 □□■□ Ki-43 Hayabusa ('Oscar' *)
- 255 □□■□ Ki-44 Shoki ('Tojo' *)
- 70 □□■□ Ki-84 Hayate ('Frank' *)

YOKOSUKA
D4Y ('Judy') (see AICHI D3A)

Netherlands

FOKKER
- 87 □□■□ C.V
- 63 □□■□ D.XXI
- 134 □□■□ G.1 ('Faucheur')
- 176 □□■□ T.VIII

Poland

LUBLIN
- 231 ■□□□ R.XIII Variants

P.Z.L.
- 75 □□□□ †P.11 ('Jedenastka')
- 104 □□□□ P.23 Karas
- 170 □□■□ P.24
- 258 □■□□ P.37 Los

Sweden

SAAB
- 138 □□■□ J 21 A & R
- 36 □□□■ †J 29

Yugoslavia

- 242 □■□□ IK Fighters (IK-1 to IK-3, & IK-5)

U.S.A.

AMERICAN DH-4
- 97 ■□□□ DH-4 ('Liberty Plane')

BELL
- **165** □□■□ **P-39 Airacobra**

BOEING
- 192 □□□■ Boeing 707 (& 720 ; C-135/ VC-137)
- 77 □□■□ B-17E & F Flying Fortress
- 205 □□■□ B-17G Flying Fortress
- **101** □□■□ **B-29 Superfortress**
- 83 □□□■ †B-47 (Stratojet)
- 245 □□□■ B-52A/H Stratofortress
- 27 □■□□ †F4B-4
- 2 □□■□ P-12E
- 14 □□■□ †P-26A ('Peashooter')

BREWSTER
- 217 □■□□ Buffalo (Brewster F2A & Export Models 239-439)

CHANCE (& LTV) VOUGHT
- **47** □□■□ †**F4U-1 Corsair (also as Brewster F3A, Goodyear FG)**
- 150 □□■□ F4U-4 to F4U-7 Corsair (also AU-1 & Goodyear F2G)
- 239 □□□■ LTV A-7A/E Corsair II
- **90** □□□■ **F-8A to E Crusader (now LTV F-8)**
- 251 □□■□ OS2U Kingfisher (Vought-Sikorsky OS2U & NAF OS2N)

CONSOLIDATED
- **19** □□■□ **B-24J Liberator**
- 183 □□□■ PBY Catalina ('Dumbo' ; also PBY-5A/6A Amphibian Canso)

CURTISS
- 37 ■□□□ †JN-4 ('Jenny')
- 45 □□□□ †Army Hawks (P-1 & P-6)
- 116 □□■□ †Navy Hawks (BFC & BF2C ; F6C & F11C & F11C-2 Goshawk)
- **80** □□■□ **Hawk 75 (R.A.F. Mohawk)**
- **136** □□■□ †**P-40 Kittyhawk (Mks. I-IV ; R.A.F. only, U.S.A.A.F. Warhawk)**
- **35** □□■□ **P-40 Tomahawk (Mks. I-II)**
- **124** □□■□ **SB2C-1 Helldiver (also U.S.A.A.F. A-25 Shrike)**
- 194 □□■□ SOC Seagull
- 128 □■□□ Shrike (A-6, A-8 & A-12)

DOUGLAS
- 102 □□□■ †A-4 Skyhawk
- 202 □□■□ A-20 (7A to Boston III) (also R.A.F. Havoc ; not U.S.A.A.F. models)
- **96** □□■□ †**DC-3 (to Dec. 1941 only)**
- 220 □□■□ †Dakota Mks. I-IV (1941-,70 ; R.A.F. & Dominion/Common-wealth air forces only)
- 249 □□■□ †R4D variants (U.S.N's DC-3/ C-47s)
- 196 □□■□ †SBD Dauntless
- 171 □□■□ TBD Devastator
- **60** □□■□ **Skyraider (ex-AD-1 to AD-7 now A-1E to A-1J)**

FORD
- 156 □■□□ Tri-motors ('The Tin Goose' series)

GEE BEE (GRANVILLE BROTHERS)
- 51 □■□□ †Racers

GRUMMAN
- 252 □□□■ A-6A/E Intruder, EA-6A & EA-6B Prowler
- 92 □■□□ †F3F Series
- **53** □□■□ **F4F-3 Wildcat (British R.N. Martlet I only)**
- **107** □□■□ **F8F Bearcat**
- 214 □□■□ TBF Avenger (also Eastern TBM Avenger)

LOCKHEED
- 120 □□■□ Constellation (L-049/C-69 ; L-1049 Super Constellation/ C-121/R7V/WV-2 ; L-1649 Starliner)
- 223 □□□■ C-130 Hercules
- 253 □□■□ Hudson Mks. I-IV (also U.S.A.A.F. A-28/A-29, AT-1 & U.S.N. PBO-1)
- **106** □□■□ **P-38J-M Lightning**
- 131 □□□■ †F-104G/CF-104 (U.S.A./ Canadair : Starfighter)
- 204 □□□■ P2V Neptune (now P-2, also Kawasaki GK-210 Turboprop version)

LTV (see CHANCE VOUGHT)

MARTIN
- 247 □□□■ B-57 Night Intruders & General Dynamics RB-57F (U.S.A.F. Canberras)
- **112** □□■□ **B-26B & C Marauder R.A.F. Mks. I-II, AT-23/TB-26 & U.S.N. JM-1)**
- 235 □□■□ Maryland & Baltimore (R.A.F. Maryland Mks. I-II, Baltimore Mks. I-V, U.S.A.A.F. A-30)

McDONNELL DOUGLAS
- 208 □□□■ †F-4 Phantom

NORTH AMERICAN
- **59** □□■□ **B-25 A to G Mitchell (R.A.F. Mks. I & II, U.S.N. PBJ-1, U.S.A.A.F. AT-24, RB/TB-25)**
- **100** □□■□ **P-51 B & C Mustang (R.A.F. Mk. III, also U.S.A.A.F. F-6)**
- **8** □□■□ †**P-51D Mustang (R.A.F. Mk. IV, F-6/-51D, TP/ TF-51D)**
- **20** □□■□ †**F-86A Sabre (see also CANADAIR Sabre)**
- **30** □□□■ †**F-100 Super Sabre (F-100A to F & TF-100)**
- 42 □□□■ FJ Fury (FJ-1 to FJ-4)
- 155 □□□■ T-28 (Trojan, also in U.S.A., Nomad & Nomar, France as Fennec)

REPUBLIC
- **7** □□■□ †**P-47D Thunderbolt (R.A.F. Mks. I-II, also P/TP-47G)**
- 95 □□□■ †F-84F Thunderstreak (Also RF-84F Thunderflash)
- 226 □□□■ †F-105 Thunderchief

RYAN
- 158 □□■□ PT/ST Series (PT-16 tö PT-25 ; Sport Trainers)

THOMAS-MORSE
- 68 ■□□□ †Scouts (S-4 to S-9)

VOUGHT (see CHANCE VOUGHT)

U.S.S.R.

ILYUSHIN
- 88 □□■□ †IL-2 ('Shturmovik')

LAVOCHKIN
- 149 □□■□ †LA-5 & 7

MIKOYAN
- 238 □□□■ †MiG-21 variants ('Fishbed'/ 'Mongol')

PETLYAKOV
- 216 □□■□ PE-2

POLIKARPOV
- 122 □□■□ †I-16 ('Mosca' or 'Rata')

YAKOVLEV
- 185 □□■□ †YaK-9

---

†Line drawings, with cross sections for accurate model making, are available for these types from 'Plans Service', Model and Allied Publications Ltd, 13-35 Bridge Street, Hemel Hempstead, Herts, England. Send 3p/25c S.A.E. for their full price list of 'Scale Aircraft Drawings'.

In early 1954, the Martin B-57 assembly area in Plant 2 was crammed with aircraft; about 20 are shown here in final assembly, plus a large number of fuselages in jigs to the left. Aircraft 5, B-57A (52–1422) is at the forward position on the line to the left; the aircraft under tow is presumed to be B-57A No 4. (Photo: Martin, ref. P-50228)

The Martin B-57 Night Intruders & General Dynamics RB-57F

by David A. Anderton, B of AeE, AFAIAA

The Martin B-57 was born out of one war, grew to fill a requirement spawned by a second war, and lived to fight in a third.

It began as the British-conceived English Electric Canberra jet bomber,[1] developed from design requirements that had originated in the latter days of World War Two. The characteristics that made the Canberra a superb high-altitude bomber gave it amazing manœuvrability in low-level flight. That, coupled with its internal volume, led to its selection to fill a Korean war requirement for an 'off-the-shelf' replacement for the Douglas B-26, with a design mission of night interdiction.

The Korean war faded into memory, and hundreds of B-57s in their seven models were built, flown, crashed, scrapped and modified. And then came the conflict in Viet Nam and the final days of glory for the old war horse. There and then it was used to do the night interdiction job it had been chosen for almost two decades earlier.

The Martin B-57 Night Intruder—for that was and is its official name—has been respectfully called the 'gooney bird of the jet fleet' by one pilot who spent more than 4,700 hours flying various models of the B-57. What he meant was that the B-57—like the Douglas C-47 'gooney bird'—was a versatile aircraft that could be modified to do almost any job well. The Air Force Logistics Command has said that the B-57 has been modified to more effective configurations than any other USAF aircraft in the inventory.

'It will be around in some shape or form for some time,' the pilot said, 'And I hope you can get others to appreciate it as much as the guys did who flew the B-57.'

This is an attempt to do just that.

Requirement for the B-57

'I believe that the paramount deficiency of the USAF today . . . is our inability to effectively seek out and destroy the enemy at night.' When Lieutenant General Earle E. Partridge, USAF, said that in April 1951, he was speaking from the bitter experiences of his Fifth Air Force in night operations in Korea. Only one available unit—the 731st Bombardment Squadron (Light-Night Attack)—had been trained for the job. They were equipped with the ageing Douglas B-26 (born A-26 Invader in World War Two).

But there were never enough trained crews or B-26s available, and repeated requests to Headquarters brought only partial satisfaction. Finally the experience and requests materialized

Contrasts in cockpits are shown by this pair of photos of the left side of the Martin B-57A and the English Electric Canberra B.2. Part of the Canberra clutter may be attributed to the fact that it was early in production for that particular mark. But the layout and colour contrasts in the US aircraft cockpit show a remarkable improvement in cockpit accommodations, and indicate the result of considering human engineering principles in the redesigned layout.
(Photo: Martin via Air Force Museum)

[1] Aircraft Profile No 54: Canberra Mks. 1–4

in the form of a requirement for a new 'night intruder' aircraft, intended to be a replacement for the B-26, 'off-the-shelf' because time was so short and the need so urgent.

Colonel Frank Allen, USAF, worked on the requirements and was a member of the group of senior USAF officers who evaluated and tested five airplanes for the job. They narrowed the available contenders down to the Martin XB–51, a tri-jet bomber which had been flying for more than a year; the North American B-45 Tornado four-jet bomber and AJ-1 Savage two-motor carrier attack aircraft; the Avro Canada CF-100 Canuck twin-jet fighter; and the English Electric Canberra.

Allen wrote later that the most serious deficiency then was the lack of poor-weather and night sensors and weapon-release systems. The Board concluded that only the Canberra had the available volume to accommodate those sensors and systems when they became available, and selected the Canberra as the B-26 replacement.

It received the designation of B-57 Night Intruder and arrangements were made to fly two pattern aircraft over from England for use by the Glenn L. Martin Co., chosen to build the B-57.

The first of the pattern aircraft was also the fourth production B.2 (Royal Air Force serial no. WD932). Loaned to the USAF from February 20 1951, it was flown the following day from Aldergrove, Northern Ireland, to Gander, Newfoundland, a distance of 2,060 miles, in four hours and 40 minutes. On February 24 it continued to Andrews Air Force Base, near Washington, DC, and a few days later was flown by R. P. Beamont, English Electric's Chief Test Pilot, in a competitive demonstration against the Martin XB-51.

On March 5, WD932 was handed over to Martin and used by the company for performance verification, evaluation and test work. It was transferred to USAF ownership after several months, and assigned the United States Air Force serial number (Fiscal Year 1951) 51–17387. In the event, the aircraft was never so marked.

Nine months later, on December 21, WD932 disintegrated in a tight turn at 10,000 ft. and crashed. The pilot escaped, but the second crew member was killed when his parachute failed to open. Investigators concluded the crash was caused by flying the aircraft with its centre-of-gravity aft of its prescribed limit. In a tight turn, this unstable configuration wound up into a tighter and tighter turn with rapidly increasing loads until the port wing failed near the nacelle.

Second of the pattern aircraft was WD940, which was the 12th production Mk. 2. On August 31 1951, it was flown from Aldergrove to Gander by an English Electric crew headed by Beamont, setting an official record time of four hours and 18 minutes, for an average speed of 481.1 mph.

This Canberra was handed over to Martin on September 4 and about one year later was marked with US insignia and the serial no. 51–17351. It retained the RAF colour scheme of light grey upper surfaces and black under surfaces.

Used in flight testing of proposed features of the B-57—including underwing pylons for weapons—WD940 was later modified to test the

The eleventh RB-57A (52–1428) flies low over the Kansas countryside near Forbes AFB. Now in storage at MASDC, 1428 served with the 4677th DSES, Hill AFB, and the Kansas ANG, based at both Forbes and Hutchinson AFB.
(Photo: KanANG via Sgt. Ron Loewen)

The first Martin B-57A (52–1418), in the bare metal finish characteristic of early production aircraft, cruises on a test flight near the company's Middle River, Maryland, plant. Aircraft made its first flight July 20 1953. It was later assigned to the Lewis Research Center of NASA at Cleveland, Ohio, as a testbed aircraft.
(Photo: Martin)

'Blackbird' RB-57A (52–1470), the 53rd production aircraft, in gloss black finish standardized for the night intruder mission. Markings and codes are in gloss red. Aircraft was lost later, sometime before 1957, for unexplained reasons.
(Photo: Martin via N. E. Taylor)

RB-57A (52–1427), the tenth
production aircraft, is shown
in September 1961 in the
colourful markings of the
Arkansas Air National Guard.
The aircraft had earlier been
assigned to duty on Taiwan;
in 1963 it was designated to
to be rebuilt as RB-57F (63–
13300) and currently is on
active duty at Yokota Air
Base, Japan, with Detach-
ment 3 of the 9th Weather
Reconnaissance Wing.
(Photo: Duane Kasulka)

EB-57A (52–1464) waiting
final disposition in storage
at MASDC, Davis-Monthan
AFB. The 47th production
aircraft, it served with the
Arkansas ANG during the
early 1960s and with the
Aerospace Defense Com-
mand in the late 1960s,
operating out of Holloman
AFB, NM.
(Photo: Ben Knowles)

new canopy design for the tandem seating arrangement that was introduced with the B-57B model.

B.2 and B-57A Differences

Comparing the Canberra B.2 and the B-57A would reveal no outward changes at first glance. But closer scrutiny would turn up more than a dozen fundamental differences between the two types of aircraft.

The US mission was different, calling for the ability to hit moving targets at night. That meant manoeuvrability at low altitudes, range to strike at distant targets, and endurance to loiter in the target area.

The RAF's three-man crew was reduced to two in the USAF version. In the B-57A, it was a pilot and a navigator, but later models would have a second pilot, an electronic warfare officer, or an observer.

The unarmed Canberra became the 'gun-toting' B-57 with the addition of forward-firing guns installed in the wings outboard of the nacelles. Fire-control systems and gunsights were installed, and the wings were fitted with hardpoints for external weapons.

The Canberra cockpit was, at that stage of development, most kindly described as clut-tered. The USAF specified a complete cockpit redesign with improved, standardized lighting. The B-57 cockpit was air-conditioned. Toe brakes were fitted to the rudder pedals, replac-ing the hand brakes of the B.2.

The engines were changed from Avons to licence-built Armstrong Siddeley Sapphires, built by Buick Motors for early aircraft and later by the Wright Aeronautical Corp., the original licensee. Because the USAF used JP-3 and later JP-4 jet fuel instead of kerosene, the fuel system had to be altered upstream of the engine. The hydraulic system was standardized as a 3,000 lb/sq. in. system, necessitating complete rede-sign. The hydraulic pump and the engine-driven generator were mounted directly on the B-57's engines; in the B.2 they had been mounted in the wing stub and driven by an extension shaft.

A major improvement was the development and installation of the Martin rotary bomb door. This design idea, patented by Martin engineers Werner Buchal and Albert T. Woollens (US Patent 2,634,656), used a pre-loaded bomb door which rotated instead of hinging open. Fully rotated, the door sealed what would normally be an open bomb-bay, which often subjected the aircraft to buffeting and the bombs to ex-traneous aerodynamic forces before and during drop.

In addition to its performance advantage, the rotary bomb door can be pre-loaded at a remote site, and then towed to the aircraft for installa-tion. Different weapon arrays can be pre-loaded, to minimize the turnaround time between sorties and to give the maximum flexibility in mission planning.

The Martin engineers developed the door for their Model 234 which became the Air Force XB-51. It was designed in two forms, one for ex-tremely large bombs, which bulged the belly contour of the B-57, and the second for all other types of bombs. Rockets could also be carried on the door. In later models, cameras, tow-target winches, electronics countermeasures equipment, and other armament were carried on the rotary doors.

Finally, the doors themselves had external strong points to hold two additional stores, but as far as can be determined, this feature never was routinely used operationally in the B-57.

B-57A Description

The B-57A retained Canberra characteristics and geometry. Its wing area was 960 sq. ft.; and the aspect ratio a low 4.27. RAE (Royal Aircraft Establishment) aerofoil sections were used at the root (12%) and tip (9%).

Power was provided by two Sapphire turbo-jets, redesignated J65-BW-5, or J65-W-5, de-pending on whether they were built by Buick or Wright. Early B-57s had the Buick engines; later

RB-57A (probably 52–1438)
operated by the then US
CAA (Civil Aeronautics
Authority) for high-altitude
flight inspection. Aircraft was
finished in white, with Dayglo red blaze outlines in
black.
(Photo: via G. S. Williams)

production was entirely Wright-powered. The J65 was rated at 7,220 lb thrust at sea level, military and maximum power.

Fuel was carried internally in fuselage and wing tanks, and externally in wingtip droppable tanks. Total capacity was 2,892 US gallons.

Armament was 8 × .50-cal. (0.50-in.) M-3 machine-guns, each with 300 rounds of ammunition.

The RB-57A was essentially the same aircraft equipped for reconnaissance. Later, some RB-57A aircraft were modified for electronic warfare missions, and redesignated EB-57A. They carried a bomb-bay full of ECM equipment; the bomb door naturally was inoperative when the aircraft was airborne.

Weapons Delivery
Bomb release was done either by manually dropping on known coordinates, or automatic-

ally by the Shoran computer. Either the pilot or the navigator could release the bombs, but the pilot had to select the specific weapon and release sequence.

The rotary bomb door is actuated just before bomb drop. It opens in four seconds and closes in six. The door is loaded in three bays, each with seven bomb stations mounting S-2 bomb racks. There are two alternate bomb racks between the middle and rear bays for larger stores, and there is also a second-layer suspension system when smaller bombs are carried.

Typical bomb loads include 52- and 80-lb. flares, and 220- and 260-lb. fragmentation bombs, which can be loaded at all 21 stations. Nine are used to carry either the 500-lb. general-purpose (GP) or the 500-lb. fragmentation bomb; the 500-lb. intermediate bomb is loaded on five of the stations. Heavy weapons—a 750-lb. store and a 1,000-lb. GP—are carried at four stations only.

There is no airspeed limit on operation of the bomb door, but some stores—such as the box-finned 500-lb. GP bomb—do carry jettison speed limits.

Performance
Early US press reports said that careful aerodynamic overhaul of the B-57 had given it a major increment in top speed compared to the

EB-57A (52–1461) banks to reveal a bomb bay full of ECM equipment. Note the large number of external antennas, and the podded chaff dispensers. This aircraft served with the Arkansas ANG before going to Aerospace Defense Command for ECM missions; it is now in storage at MASDC. (Photo: USAF)

Four 500-lb. general-purpose bombs on wing pylons, plus an internal weapons load, arm this B-57B taking off on a sortie against Viet Cong forces in central Viet Nam. (Photo: USAF 94690)

This JB-57B (52–1540) was one of several used for support missions at the Air Force Missile Test Center during the early 1960s. Specific test missions included calibration of missile tracking-camera lenses, done by photography of the test pattern on the forward fuselage. (Photo: Jimm Dorrance via Aardvark Art)

B-57B (probably 51–1497) with Bomarc missile nose, modified by Temco Aircraft Corp. in 1956 for flight tests of guidance systems. Aircraft was subsequently flight-tested by Temco, Boeing—as shown in the photo—and the Air Force. Changes included separate missile electrical, hydraulic, cooling and pressurizing systems, and strengthened primary structure.

(Photo: via G. S. Williams)

Canberra. This was supposed to have been largely the result of gap-sealing between fixed and movable surfaces. As much as a 30-kt. speed differential was reported, corresponding to nearly 1/10th of a Mach number at altitude.

In fact, all the work done on sealing by Martin produced at the most a five-kt. gain in true airspeed. The quoted higher figures later were found to have been due solely to position error in the airspeed indicator system. English Electric had found that the static vent position on the Canberra was critical and needed close production control to maintain accuracies.

Some miscellaneous pilots' notes on the B-57A will characterize that aircraft, and the behaviour of the other similar models—B, C and E—in the fleet.

Both the B-57 and the Canberra are noted for good handling qualities at low speed. The controls are effective down to the stall, and there is good response to control deflections. They have extremely safe stall characteristics.

Stalling speeds for B-57s varied from a maximum of about 130 kt. (at 53,400 lb., take-off configuration, landing gear down and zero flap deflection) to a minimum of 85 kt. (at 28,000 lb., landing configuration, landing gear down and 60° flap deflection).

There was a slight tendency to tuck at Mach 0.88, and sharp pitch-up could occur around Mach 0.87. A modification in the longitudinal control system on all B-57 aircraft made it easier to pull 'g'; the elevator forces were decreased at all weights and centre-of-gravity (c.g.) positions. The B-57A, according to the pilots' notes, was normally operated close to the aft c.g. limit, approaching the neutral point, so there was little feel in the elevator controls. The pilots were cautioned that they could apply destructive load factors with no effort, and that the airplane then would become unmanageable.

With wingtip tanks 'on', the B-57A had a never-exceed speed of 444 kt. indicated; tanks 'off', the speed limit was 513 kt.

B-57B, C and E Descriptions

These three models were sisters under the skin, and almost identical triplets. They all used the same basic airframe, which had been modified from the earlier B-57A and RB-57A design to use tandem seating. Pilot and second crewman were enclosed in a pressurized cockpit under a

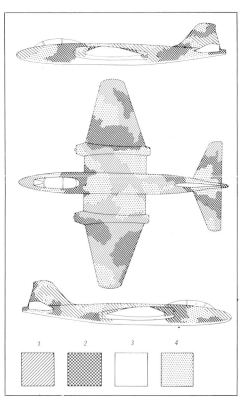

| 1 | 2 | 3 | 4 |

B-57 Aircraft camouflage
pattern
1. Green No. 34079
2. Green No. 34102
3. Grey No. 36622
4. Tan No. 30219

Wingtip pods for capture of airborne debris from nuclear weapons tests are carried by this RB-57C (53–3832) of the Air Weather Service photographed in May 1965. Pods have removable paper filter elements, were developed by the Los Alamos Scientific Laboratory. Aircraft is now designated WB-57C and was still assigned to the 58th WRSq in April 1972.
(Photo: via Gordon S. Williams)

clamshell canopy. Additional changes included a second set of speed brakes, triangular in shape and mounted on the aft fuselage, augmenting the finger type of brakes retracted into the upper and lower wing surfaces.

The J65 engines were retained, and the fuel capacity remained a total of 2,892 gallons. An additional 548 gallons could be carried on the bomb door in ferry tanks.

The basic differences between the models were the inclusion of dual controls on the B-57C for training missions, and removable tow-target installations on the B-57E for that mission. The C could be converted quickly to the B configuration, and the E could be converted to either the B or C model.

Armament on the B-57B was initially 8×.50-cal. machine-guns. On the 91st and all subsequent aircraft, they were replaced by four 20-mm. M-39 cannon, each with 290 rounds.

External pylons under the wing outer panels gave the B-57B and C much additional weaponry to load, including the cluster stores developed during the mid-1950s.

Combat performance was somewhat decreased because of the reduced fuel and higher weights of later models (Table VI compares the design missions of the various B-57 models).

RB-57D Description

The RB-57D is, even at this late date, a mystery aircraft. Its principal mission, and its reason for being, was high-altitude photo-reconnaissance in daylight. To do that, it needed new powerplants and larger wings. The guns and other armament provisions were removed.

The D models originated with a reduction in the contract for B-57B aircraft. Twenty airframes

in two batches—one of 13 and the other of seven—were earmarked for separate use under a different contract. That use came from a design study issued by Wright Air Development Center in June 1953.

Martin received a letter contract dated June 29 1953 for a design study, and subsequent contracts and amendments over the next five years, covering the design, development, construction, testing and support of what were to become the RB-57D aircraft.

Preliminary engineering established the first D configuration, designated as Model 294 by Martin. At the same time, Martin engineers were studying the best equipment for radar photography, simultaneous day and radar photography, and electronic ferret missions.

On February 4 1955, Martin received a letter contract to build 14 B-57Ds. One B-57D would be built according to Contractor's Model 796; seven to Model 744; and six to Model 797. Note that Model 294 is not mentioned in this contract, that three new Contractor Model numbers are introduced, and that the aircraft were specified as B-57D and not RB-57D.

On March 29, an approved contract called for Martin to build six B-57Ds at a total cost of $18,825,780. There was no mention of different configurations, and eight aircraft had been dropped from this contract.

The final word came in an approved document dated December 21 1955, by which time the first of the modified aircraft had flown and been accepted by the USAF. That contract awarded Martin $24,795,640 to build seven RB-57Ds (Model 744); one RB-57D (Model 796); and six RB-57Ds (Model 797). The contract also called for six aircraft to be changed from B-57D

The unusual markings on this RB-57D at Wright-Patterson AFB were done to test the quality of lenses and film emulsions in Project APRE (Aerospace Photographic Reconnaissance Experiments). Neutral grey area on left horizontal tail is photographic standard for color reproduction. A dozen convex mirrors are positioned on fuselage and wing upper surfaces. Aircraft was flown below a balloon carrying the camera on test, and photographed as it passed within the camera's field of view.
(Photo: USAF)

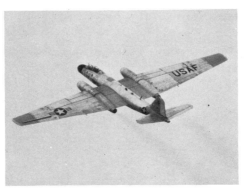

This photographic study of B-57D (53–3965) was taken at Otis AFB, Mass., where the aircraft was on the strength of the 4677th DSES. Originally one of the six RB-57D-2 models, 3965 was placed in storage at MASDC where it currently waits its final disposition.
(Photo: Picciani Aircraft Slides)

Climbing out, uses its spoilers (near left wingtip, the deflected surface is thrown into relief by the shadow area) to bank into the left-hand pattern around the field. Then, using both spoilers for flight-path drag control, the aircraft comes in . . .

over the fence, with gear down and locked. This rare sequence of a D model in flight was photographed by Ron Picciani.
(Photos: Picciani Aircraft Slides)

to RB-57D models. The total was 20 aircraft, the number eventually built.

In the same contract there was an item for six airborne semi-automatic 'ferret' equipment systems, presumably intended either for the ex-B-57D aircraft, or the six built to Model 797 specifications.

By the time the bills were all added up, these 20 aircraft cost more than $60 million. The first RB-57D flew in November 1955 and was accepted that same month. The last was accepted in March 1957. The first official mention of the RB-57D identified it as a high-altitude testbed for the J57 engines, and thus skirted mention of its true role.

There were four production batches of RB-57D models. The first six to be built, presumed to be of the original Model 294 configuration, carried the serial Nos 53–3977 through 53–3982. They were designated RB-57D, and carried a one-man crew.

Serial numbers 53–3970 through 53–3976—the 7th through 13th airframes—were also designated RB-57D. They carried a one-man crew also, but had aerial refuelling systems. These are presumed to be the Model 744 aircraft.

Serial No 53–3963—the 14th airframe—was the only one of its kind. Designated RB-57D–1, it carried a one-man crew and had aerial refuelling. This was Model 796.

Serial numbers 53–3964 through 53–3969 were the 15th through 20th airframes built, and were designated RB-57D-2. They carried two-man crews and had aerial refuelling. These are presumed to have been Martin Model 797.

All the D aircraft were powered by two Pratt & Whitney J57-P-27 turbojets, each rated at 10,500 lb t. at sea level. They carried 2,740 gallons of fuel in internal wing tanks.

The major external change was in the wing, which was enlarged to 1,505 sq. ft. area, and spanned 106 ft. The original RAE aerofoil sections were retained.

The RB-57Ds were ill-starred aircraft. There were some losses due to wing failures, and the fleet was grounded for repair. Martin got a contract to modify nine; while another four served as the basis for rebuilds as RB-57F models.

However, they continued to serve until recently in the role of high-altitude 'fakers', as EB-57D aircraft of the USAF Aerospace Defense Command. Nine—the ones modified by Martin —were assigned to the 4677th Defense Systems Evaluation Squadron at Hill AFB, Utah.

By then, USAF pilots had learned a lot more about flying these high-altitude, over-powered gliders. They learned that take-off was made at less than full throttle, because the rudder could not handle an engine-out situation. The RB-57D would roll for less than 2,000 ft. on the runway and become airborne at 106 kt. The initial climb angle was 25° and they seldom took more than 15 minutes to attain 50,000 ft. from brake release.

Airframe limitations kept the speeds down below 190 kt. indicated. So the RB-57D was flown in climb, cruise and letdown at 180 kt. At

50,000 ft., that corresponds to a true airspeed of 450 kt.

Pilots wore MC-3 pressure suits for flights above 50,000 ft., but oil contamination made the suits unsafe, and the aircraft were restricted to altitudes below 50,000 ft. until a new pressure suit came along.

Endurance was about five and one-half hours, unrefuelled. Descent for a normal landing began about 70 miles out, because the RB-57D lacked any speed brakes. The landing gear and spoilers were extended for the entire letdown, which was made at 180 kt. Final approach was at 120 kt. and there was always a tendency to 'float' because of ground effect.

The last of the RB-57Ds are in storage at the Military Aircraft Storage and Disposition Center (MASDC), Davis-Monthan AFB, Ariz.

Pre-Production Preparations

Martin sent a team of design and production engineers to the United Kingdom for a month's stay at English Electric early in 1951. They familiarized themselves with the problem, and then headed back home to form the nucleus of B-57 design and production teams. By July, more than 200 engineers were working on the programme, and the manpower curve was expected to peak at about 350 by that autumn.

Late in July, the Air Force Board of Inspection saw the finished mock-up of the wing and cockpit. The final design of the aircraft was approved by the end of the summer.

There were problems in production, caused by the differences in production methods used by both countries. Initially, Martin engineers wanted to break the structure into components of a size that could be handled by automatic riveting machinery. For example, the top aft section of the Canberra fuselage was made in a single, hand-riveted piece, too large for US automatic riveting equipment. This section was redesigned to use shorter pieces, automatically riveted. The redesign meant extra weight, but saved production time and cost.

British practice called for hand-finishing late in assembly, fitting sheet-metal parts to tolerances as close as ±0.005. Martin engineers, redrawing all the B-57 structure, specified sheet-metal tolerances of $\pm1/32$ in. The change was accomplished while maintaining the outside mould lines of the aircraft. The end result was the same, without the cost of working to unjustifiably close tolerances.

The main spar bulkhead—called the 'garden gate' by British production engineers—had to be made at Martin from two slabs of 3-in. thick high-strength aluminium alloy, about $3\frac{1}{2}\times8$ ft. in size. After hogging out much of the metal, the two pieces were assembled in the 'garden gate'. Martin engineers had hoped to forge the fitting as was done in England, but the size was too large for contemporary US forging capacity.

By early 1952, tooling was well along, with more than 12,000 separate tools developed by Martin, and another 13,000 or more tools built by subcontractors. Originally, more than half the airframe by weight was subcontracted. Major producers were Kaiser Metal Products, responsible for the outer wing panels and rotary bomb doors; Hudson Motors, who built the complete aft fuselage and empennage or tail assembly; and Cleveland Pneumatic Tool Co., who supplied the landing gear. Kaiser failed to meet wing deliveries; Martin took that contract back and built the panels in its own facilities.

Martin also subcontracted the engine nacelles, the nose cone, the pilot's canopy, all fuel cells, the tip tanks and much of the aircraft equipment. The company retained the main fuselage nose and centre section, the carry-through structure and wing centre section as its share of production, and did the final assembly and flight testing.

The B-57s were built in Martin Plant No 2, a facility used since World War Two by the Signal Corps. Martin got the plant back, rehabilitated it and laid out a line with 19 positions for B-57 production.

Contract Summary

The first B-57 development and production contract, designated AF33 (038)–22617–FPI–FY1952, was approved September 3 1953, long after the programme had started. It originally totalled $217,151,281.00, and included the construction of eight B-57As at a unit price of $5,920,381.50; 67 RB-57As at a unit price of $835,751; and 102 B-57B at a unit price of $679,100. The contract also covered the purchase of two Canberra B.2 pattern aircraft at a total cost of $901,061 plus $100,000 for spare parts. A mobile trainer and 103 special weapon bomb doors were included in the price.

Production schedule stretches and engineering changes raised the final cost of this first contract to $276,276,361.51, almost $60 million higher than the first contract price.

The follow-on production contract, designated AF33 (600)–22208–FPI–FY1953, was approved November 4 1953. It totalled $114,119,575, and called for the production of 191 B-57B models at a unit billing price of $500,991.11. In addition to the usual spare parts, tools and ground handling equipment, technical data, training and development work, the contract covered the cost of 191 special weapons bomb doors.

This second contract was revised in June 1955 to cover 38 B-57Cs and 120 B-57Bs, with 138 bomb doors. The 120 B-57B models were further reduced to 100 in October 1955, and the remaining 20 airframes were earmarked for the construction of the B-57D. The final total of this second contract was $115,477,008.66.

The third production contract, AF33 (600)–25825–CPFF–FY1953, covered the RB-57D series.

Key to Colour Illustrations

1 Martin RB-57A (US Air Force serial 52-1490) of the Arkansas Air National Guard.

2 B-57A Canberra (AF: 52-1419) is a Miami-based 'hurricane hunter' with civil registration N1005.

3 NRB-57B (AF: 52-1581) was used as *Tropic Moon III* TV system test bed for the B-57G variant.

4 B-57B mid-1960s, operating in the Republic of Viet Nam with RVNAF military markings.

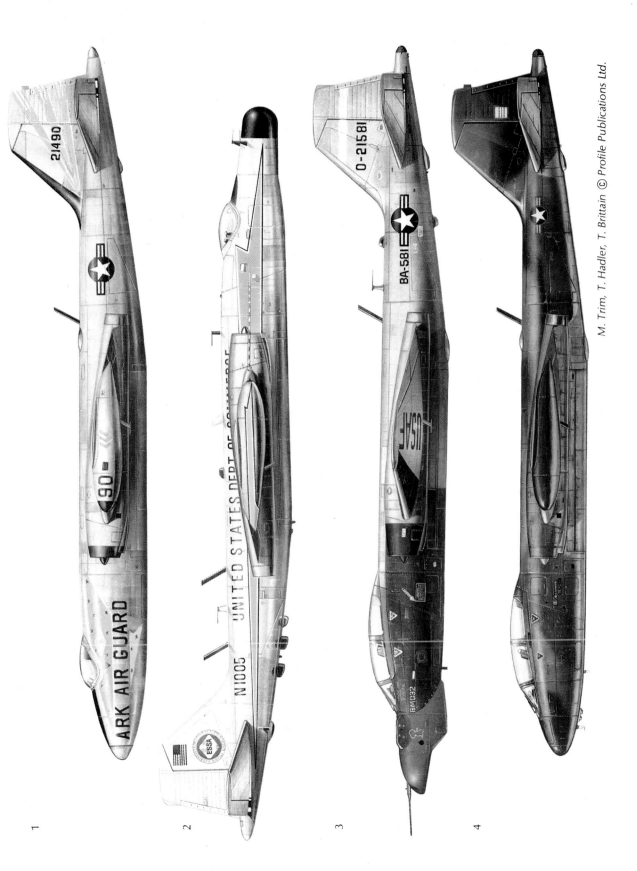

21490

ARK AIR GUARD

190

1

N1005

UNITED STATES DEPT OF COMMERCE

ESSA

2

0-21581

BA-581

USAF

BM032

3

4

M. Trim, T. Hadler, T. Brittain © Profile Publications Ltd.

Final cost of the contract totalled more than $60 million, for a unit price of about $3 million per aircraft, including spare parts and other items in the contract.

Final contract in Martin's production of the B-57 series was AF33 (600)–29645–FPI–FY1955, and it covered the production of 68 B-57Es at a unit price of $816,840. At the close of B-57E production, the total contract price was estimated at $58,210,073, only a slight over-run on the original contract price of $55,545,120.

These four production contracts came to a grand total of $510,572,148, and paid for design through flight-testing of 403 Martin-built B-57s.

Production and Acceptance Schedules
There were 11 basic acceptance schedules during the life of the B-57 programme. The first, in March 1951, was built around an envisioned production of 250 B-57A models at a rate reaching a peak of 50 per month.

This never happened. That particular schedule gave way to later ones specified by firm contracts, and actual final acceptances were stretched over a period from July 1953 to March 1957. For the record, the first B-57A was accepted in August 1953 by the Air Force; the last was delivered in February 1954. The first RB-57A was accepted in January 1954, and the last in May 1955, delayed for a 'garden gate' modification programme.

For the B-57B, the first and last acceptance dates were August 1954 and September 1956; and for the C model, January 1955 and May 1956. The first RB-57D was accepted in November 1955; the last in March 1957. First B-57E acceptance was in May 1956; the last in March 1957.

The maximum number accepted in any single month was 26—one RB-57A, 23 B-57B and two B-57C aircraft—in January 1955. But in no way does this acceptance figure reflect production rates. In February 1955, none was accepted. In March, April and May, acceptances were 24, 6 and 16 respectively. These fluctuations are why one should always question quoted production rates of 'X aircraft per month'. The important number is acceptances by the customer, not aircraft shoved out the door by the manufacturer.

Modifications and Rebuilds
Although production of original B-57 airframes terminated in 1957, Martin and others have since received subsequent contracts for rework, modification and rebuild of large numbers of the B-57 fleet.

In June 1965, Martin was awarded $2 million to modernize nine of the RB-57D aircraft to extend their service life by an estimated eight years. Whether the estimates or the modernizing went wrong is not known; the service life of those RB-57Ds ended short of the target by several years.

In October 1956, Martin delivered the last of a number of B-57s which had been sent back to the factory for conversion to tactical bombers for duty in Viet Nam. They had been used for non-tactical missions such as reconnaissance. Under a $4.2 million contract with Air Force Logistics Command, Martin installed the wing-mounted guns, added the rotary bomb doors, and attached rocket pylons to the undersides of the wings. Fire-control systems also were installed, and the aircraft were camouflaged in the now-familiar two-tone green plus tan finish.

At the same time, Martin was completing its RB-57D modernization programme and installing special electronic equipment in a dozen RB-57As. This latter work was later expanded to include installations in 51 aircraft for a total contract amount close to $10 million. These modified aircraft probably became the EB versions used in electronics countermeasures training and missions.

Current USAF B-57 aircraft are managed, logistically speaking, by the Warner Robins Air Materiel Area (WRAMA), Robins AFB, Georgia. WRAMA plans and provides all the support needed for all B-57s, including all communications and electronics equipment, and airframe and engine overhaul and repair. Routine maintenance above the field level, repair, overhaul and modification are done at WRAMA, or by specialist teams around the world working out of WRAMA.

General Dynamics RB-57F
The RB-57F programme started with a requirement for high-altitude sampling aircraft. The result was a major rebuild of the B-57, done by

Carrying the red nose, drop tanks and tail colours of Alaskan Air Command, this EB-57E (55–4247) of the 21st Operations Squadron cruises above the overcast in February 1969. Note podded chaff dispensers and ECM antennas on belly, nose and tail. Aircraft was lost on 13 June 1969 after a mid-air collision with an F-102A. (Photo: via N. E. Taylor)

General Dynamics at Fort Worth, Texas. Under *Project Peewee*, GD/FW received an October 1963 contract to modify two aircraft. Subsequent contracts were issued to cover the modification—actually more of a complete rebuild—of 21 aircraft.

Candidate airframes were drawn from RB-57A, B-57B, and the then-grounded RB-57D fleet. General Dynamics salvaged not much more than the fuselage centre and aft sections, the horizontal tail and the landing gear. Everything else—plus the cockpits of the RB/A aircraft—was new construction.

Basic to the RB-57F design was the huge wing, almost doubling the span of the standard B-57s, and stretching 122 ft., tip to tip. The wing area was more than doubled, to 2,000 sq. ft.

Existing powerplants were replaced by new Pratt & Whitney TF33-P-11A turbofan engines, each rated at 16,500 lb t. at sea-level. Auxiliary jet engines, two Pratt & Whitney J60-P-9 turbojets producing 2,900 lb t. each, were podded under the wings in removable packages.

A completely new, larger vertical tail was designed to handle the asymmetrical thrust problem of the increased power, but the horizontal tail, main landing gear and fuselage were only changed in minor ways. Most of the aircraft systems also were changed, to accommodate the more rigorous requirements of high-altitude flight.

Seventeen RB-57F aircraft were built, using the RB/A and B/B airframes as a basis. The last four RB-57F models were built on the fuselages of the RB-57Ds, and were intended for high-altitude reconnaissance rather than air sampling missions. The two batches differed in detail and equipment.

The basic characteristics of the RB-57F—now officially redesignated WB-57F—are presented in Table I. Incidentally, the RB-57F now WB-57F has never been named either Night Intruder or Canberra. Serial numbers of the F models and their predecessor airframes, as well as the status of each aircraft at August 1 1972, are presented in Table III.

The enormous wing of the F model uses a unique control system. No flaps are installed, or required. Instead, inboard ailerons are fitted, with both fixed and movable trim tabs on their trailing-edges. Large retractable spoilers, located outboard and forward of the ailerons, add to the lateral control power.

Another view of EB-57E (55–4247) shows it coming in for a landing at Elmendorf AFB, Alaska.
(Photo: N. E. Taylor)

The wing was designed with $-1\frac{1}{2}°$ anhedral in the outer panels, for added stability during take-off and landing. The wingtip leading-edges are shaped to reduce trim drag; by drooping the tips, they act as rudimentary end plates to prevent the airflow over the wing from moving spanwise and requiring extra elevator trim—and therefore drag—to compensate.

To avoid the wing problems caused by the single-spar construction of the basic models, General Dynamics engineers designed a three-spar wing for the B-57F, using honeycomb sandwich structure for upper and lower panels. There are few internal ribs. This construction technique produces an aerodynamically smooth wing, which is refined still further by careful fitting of the control surfaces and sealing of the gaps between them and the wing structure. Hardpoints incorporated in the wing structure are available to mount external stores.

The fuselage nose was enlarged to carry specialized radar and other equipment; consequently, the fuselage forward section was reworked to increase its diameter about three inches. The internal fuel tank was removed from the fuselage, and other clean-up work freed a large volume for the installation of special equipment. Fuselage dive-brakes also were removed.

All fuel is carried internally in the wing, outboard of the TF33 turbofan nacelles. Total fuel capacity is 3,870 US gallons, or about 25,150 lb., of JP-4.

The original B-57 landing gear was designed for a high sink rate and hard landings characteristic of tactical use. Consequently, it was rugged enough to be used—essentially unmodified—on the F, even though the maximum landing weight had been increased to 61,500 lb.

Typical equipment installed for an air-sampling mission includes four air samplers with paper filter elements, four gas samplers, three radiation rate meters, a wing pod ion chamber, a cosmic ray spectrometer, an F-415P vertical

One of the Patricia Lynn aircraft, B-57E (55–4249), returns to Tan Son Nhut AB, Viet Nam, after a mission on December 14 1970. Note the elongated nose which housed a forward-looking Fairchild KA-1 camera. Aircraft is in flat black finish with flat white tail codes; it was assigned to Det. 1, 460th Tactical Reconnaissance Wing.
(Photo: N. E. Taylor)

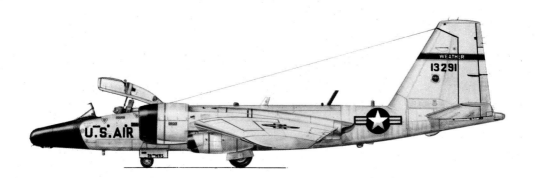

General Dynamics WB-57F (ex-RB-57F; AF serial 63-13291A) of the 58th Weather Reconnaissance Squadron, Air Weather Service, Military Aircraft Command. The 58th WRS operates from Kirkland Air Force Base, Albuquerque, New Mexico. Growth of RB/WB-57F over conventional planform is indicated by the small sketch on the facing page.

M. Trim, T. Hadler, T. Brittain © Profile Publications Ltd.

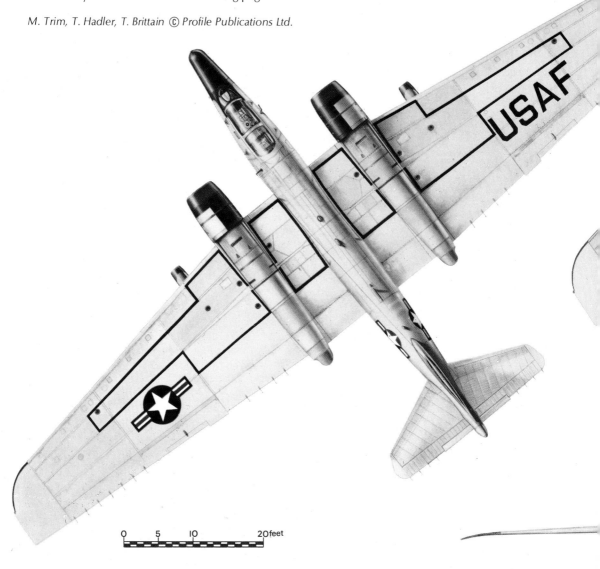

0   5   10   20 feet

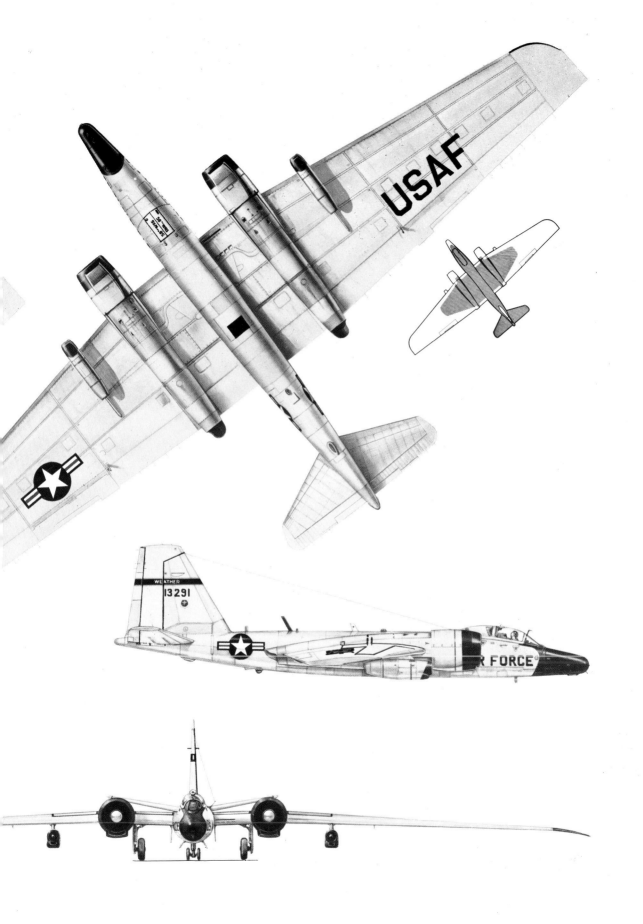

panoramic camera for particulate photography, and data and voice recorders. Three special equipment sections house this mass of installations: The new nose, the bomb bay area, and the second cockpit, designed to carry both operator and equipment.

Official performance data for the WB-57F shows it to have an altitude capability of 65,000 ft. with the J60s operating in conjunction with the TF33 turbofans. This number is conservative.

The first converted RB-57F flew in April 1964, and the USAF accepted its first aircraft in June of that year. Production continued through March 1967.

All RB-57F aircraft delivered went to the 55th, 56th or 58th Weather Reconnaissance Squadrons, Air Weather Service, under the Military Air Transport Service (MATS). Now only the 58th WRS operates the WB-57F; and MATS is now MAC—Military Airlift Command.

Convair Aerospace Division of General Dynamics still repairs and overhauls WB-57F aircraft under a continuing contract with USAF. The company also does special modifications, such as installations used on the WB-57F supporting NASA's Earth Resources Technology Satellite programme.

With more than 30 different agencies and

friendly foreign governments now stating requirements for high-altitude data, the WB-57F appears assured of continuing operations for years to come.

B-57G for Night Interdiction

Last of the major modification programmes for the B-57 produced the aircraft that was able to tackle the job for which the B-57 had been chosen 20 years earlier.

Specifically, the B-57G was developed to detect, track and strike targets in total darkness. Under a prime contract to Westinghouse Electric Corp. for about $49 million, the Martin company modified 16 B-57B airframes to include a nose section packed with electronics and electro-optical equipment.

In the G nose were Texas Instruments' AN/APQ-139 forward-looking radar and AN/AAS-26 forward-looking infra-red (IR) detection system. Westinghouse low-level light television, laser rangefinder and AN/AYK-8 weapons delivery computer completed the nose package. In the belly was a 20-mm. Emerson Electric cannon turret.

The radar and IR systems were used for target detection, and the laser for ranging. Weapons were fired by reference to the cockpit TV monitor, which displayed both the electronics and electro-optical information simultaneously.

The low-level light TV systems had been developed during the USAF *Tropic Moon* programme, and the belly turret with laser rangefinder was an outgrowth of the USAF *Pave Gat* programme.

The reshaped nose of the B-57G houses the APQ-139 radar, which has an effective range of about 10 miles. At this distance, it can detect and track slow-moving targets such as trucks at speeds as low as 3–5 mph. The radar also has the ability to gather terrain-following and ground-mapping data. The low-level light TV, laser rangefinder, and forward-looking IR systems are carried in chin housings which bulge the nose contours of the B-57G.

Underwing pylons are carried for external weapons, three on a side, and Mk.82 laser-guided bombs have been mounted in those positions.

One of the 16 finished aircraft crashed during single-engine tests at the Martin factory. Four were stationed at MacDill AFB, Florida, for crew training. The remaining 11 were deployed to Ubon Air Base, Thailand, with the 13th Bomb Squadron (Tactical) in September 1970 for night operations against moving targets on the Ho Chi Minh Trail. One aircraft was lost in these operations, reportedly to ground fire. Later indications were that it was lost in a mid-air collision with a Cessna O-2A FAC—Forward Air Controller—aircraft.

The B-57G did not have an impressive combat record. Reports said the aircraft was under-

This B-57E of the 8th Tactical Bomb Squadron made it to Ubon AB, Thailand, after absorbing ground fire during a bomb run over Viet Nam in September 1968. Owl under the US insignia is the marking of the 497th Tactical Fighter Squadron of the 8th Tactical Fighter Wing, and how it got on a B-57E of the 8th TBS is one of those mysteries. Clue: The 8th TFW was based at Ubon in 1968.
(Photo: Capt. Al Piccirillo via N. E. Taylor)

Suit checklist is final step before engine starting on a WB-57F flight. Here Sergeant Jesse Harris reads the checklist to navigator Major Edwin Hull before takeoff.
(Photo: USAF/AWS)

Last RB-57F built, this aircraft is shown in the markings of the Air Weather Service, which operated all the F models. Redesignated as a WB-57F by USAF in 1971, this aircraft (63–13503) was transferred to NASA in 1972, and is operated by the Manned Spacecraft Center.
(Photo: USAF/AWS)

The camera pallet under the fuselage of this WB-57F was developed for the corn blight experiments, and is typical of the installations that will be used in support of NASA's ERTS (Earth Resources Technology Satellite) programme.
(Photo: NASA)

powered for its mission. There were some regrets that the Air Force had not accepted the alternate proposal from General Dynamics, which included re-engining the B-57G with Pratt & Whitney J57 turbojets. Since this had been done earlier for the D models, there were no expected problems in making that engine change.

After less than two years of operations, the B-57Gs were withdrawn from SEA—Southeast Asia—and assigned to the 190th Tactical Reconnaissance Group, of the Kansas Air National Guard, Forbes AFB, Kansas.

Serial numbers for the complete B-57G programme are presented in Table IV.

Patricia Lynn Modifications

Two B-57E aircraft (USAF serial Nos 55–4243 and 55–4245) were modified in early 1963 by the special projects section of General Dynamics at Fort Worth. These aircraft were assigned to a highly classified project under the code name of *Patricia Lynn*, and sent to South Viet Nam. Based at Tan Son Nhut Air Base, they were used for in-country reconnaissance by day and night.

The reshaped nose of these aircraft housed a Fairchild KA-1 forward oblique camera with a 36-in. lens, and a Fairchild KA-2 vertical camera. A Fairchild KA-56 panoramic camera, whose lens sweeps from horizon to horizon, was mounted vertically in the bomb-bay for ground photography at altitudes below 200 ft. Also in the bomb-bay area was a Fairchild F-477 split vertical camera for night photography.

Within a year, two more B-57Es (55–4237 and

55–4249), now painted matt black, were added to the force. Later still, two more (55–4257 and 55–4264) received the same modifications at GD/FW.

In 1965, 55–4243 and 55–4245—and possibly other *Patricia Lynn* aircraft—were sent back to GD/FW for systems updating. Reports from Viet Nam in 1967 identified special reconnaissance aircraft using, in addition to the camera gear cited earlier, a Texas Instruments AN/AAS-18 infra-red reconnaissance system. That equipment may have been installed during the updating in 1965. The AAS-18 suffered from marginal resolution above 2,000 ft. altitude, and low reliability in bad weather. The equipment also required a good deal of maintenance and, in general, was regarded as not satisfactory for those missions.

The unit responsible for operating these few special B-57s, the 460th Tactical Reconnaissance Wing, was deactivated in Viet Nam in September 1971. Four of the *Patricia Lynn* aircraft were returned to the USA and re-assigned to the 4677th DSES, Hill AFB, Utah. One of the four (B-57E: 55–4249), still in its original external configuration and finish, was sent to storage in MASDC in May 1972.

B-57 Testbed Aircraft

Complete details on the many B-57 aircraft used for test and development programmes are far beyond the scope of this *Profile*. The following brief mention of some of the programmes and projects with which B-57 aircraft have been associated emphasizes this:

Operation Redwing, with the Defense Atomic

5

6

7

8

Support Agency (1960); high-resolution low-level light television systems (1966–1968); *Compass Eagle* infra-red reconnaissance system (1967); Hughes QRC-341 infra-red warning system (1967); radar camouflage techniques (1967); high-level aerial cloud photography (1969); *Pave Gat* system with Emerson Electric belly turret and laser range-finding (1970); Mk.82 laser-guided bomb (1970).

Additionally, B-57 aircraft were used to aid the development of pump-fed liquid-hydrogen fuel systems, to calibrate solar cells, to measure the spectra of reflected solar energy, and for at least 19 of the *Coldscan* flights to measure atmospheric turbulence and temperature gradients at SST—supersonic-transport—altitudes.

At least one B-57B (51–1497) was modified by Temco Aircraft Corp. in 1956 for tests of the Boeing IM-99A Bomarc guidance system. The modification added a 17-foot section of the missile nose to the B-57 forward fuselage. Separate hydraulic and electrical systems, and ammonia and nitrogen tanks, for cooling and pressurizing the missile, were added, too.

The B-57 structure was strengthened to take the extra loads, and the weight increase. After static and flight tests at Temco, the B-57B was delivered to Boeing for further testing, and then turned over to the Air Force Missile Test Center for flight research on the Bomarc guidance system.

Two B-57B aircraft (52–1539 and 52–1562) were fitted with the nose sections of the Goodyear Aerospace Corporation's TM-76 Mace missile, and used to simulate the missile's tracking capabilities in flight paths which closely corresponded to programmed paths for the TM-76.

NRB-57B (52–1581), now in storage at MASDC,[1] began its versatile test career when the Air Force loaned it to CAL—Cornell Aeronautical Laboratory—for flight research with the Autoflite terrain-following system that had been developed at CAL. Flight tests were run between 1958 and 1962. The aircraft was then assigned to Westinghouse for tests of another type of terrain-following system and, still later, for tests of the *Tropic Moon* systems. It was eventually developed into the *Tropic Moon III* configuration, basis for the B-57G.

An RB-57D was used in 1964 on Project APRE (Aerospace Photographic Reconnaissance Experiments), marked with a lens-resolution test pattern on its upper surfaces in sharply defined shapes of flat white against a flat black background. A single neutral grey area, for verification of colour rendition, was marked on the left horizontal tail. A number of convex mirrors also were part of the test array.

In the experiments, a test camera was carried in a balloon gondola to altitudes near 100,000 ft. The RB-57D was vectored to pass within the field of view, at pre-determined altitudes below the balloon. The resulting photographs helped evaluate the camera lens and the film emulsions used, and undoubtedly contributed to later successful reconnaissance by high-altitude aircraft and satellites.

Several JB-57B aircraft, based at Patrick AFB, Florida, and assigned to support the Air Force Missile Test Center, were also used for lens-resolution tests. Carrying a test pattern painted on the forward right fuselage, these JB-57Bs were used in calibration of missile tracking cameras.

Allocations

The first eight B-57A aircraft were committed to test programmes and were never assigned to operational units. The first RB-57A units equipped were part of the 363rd Tactical Reconnaissance Wing, based at Shaw AFB, South Carolina. The first B-57B units were with the 461st Bomb Wing (Light), based at Hill AFB, Utah, and the 345th Bomb Wing, based at Langley AFB, Virginia.

During subsequent years, B-57s served with a large number and variety of units. Known B-57 allocations are summarized in Table VIII.

Pakistan received a quantity of B-57s under the US Military Assistance Programme (MAP). Their serial numbers are listed in Table V, but reliable data on their present status is not available.

Military Operations

The first large-scale operation in which B-57 forces participated was *Exercise Sagebrush*, conducted in 1955 across the lower eastern quarter of the US. More than 140,000 US Army and USAF personnel and 800 USAF aircraft were based on more than seven million acres of Louisiana, with 17 'aggressor' and 24 'defender' air bases stretching across the arc from Langley AFB, Virginia, to the Texas-Mexico border.

The aim of the exercise was to find out whether an aggressor, hitting suddenly with nuclear weapons, could win a quick victory over defending forces that were well dug in.

It was no contest. The B-57s struck on November 15, the first day of the exercise, and within two hours had 'knocked out' 18 defender bases. At daybreak on November 16, both sides launched air strikes against opposing air bases. During that day the B-57s 'knocked out' 19 of the defender's 24 air bases, while the aggressor forces lost six. The remaining five defender air bases were clobbered that night by repeated B-57 strikes.

The B-57s, moving fast and striking with speed and accuracy, had outmoded the time-honoured schedules for conventional warfare, and had proved that an aggressive attack could knock out well-established forces in the field.

The aggressor forces were drawn from the 461st Bomb Wing and the 363rd Tac Recon Wing, both part of Tactical Air Command (TAC).

---

[1] MASDC—Military Aircraft Storage and Disposition Center, Davis-Monthan AFB, Ariz.

The next year, aircraft from the 461st flew a goodwill tour of Latin America, under the code name of *Vista Able*. Other TAC B-57s were part of *Mobile Charlie*, a deployment to support *Exercise Counterpunch* in Europe.

These deployments were the routine sort that characterize peacetime duty. But, in July 1958, there was a threat—real or imagined, historians still argue—in Lebanon. On July 15, TAC went on a war footing, and ordered the 19th Air Force to deploy Composite Air Strike Force (CASF) 'Bravo' to Incirlik Air Base, Turkey. Within three hours of the alert, a dozen B-57Bs were out over the Atlantic headed for Turkey—and 100 days of waiting for nothing to happen.

But during the 100 days, something happened on the other side of the world: Another crisis, this time centred on Taiwan. On August 29 1958, the 12th Air Force sent the 399th Bomb Squadron, equipped with B-57Bs, to Taiwan as CASF 'X-Ray Tango'.

TAC kept two wings—the 461st and 345th—equipped with B-57s until both wings were deactivated, the 461st on April 1 1958 and the 345th on June 25 1959. One squadron of B-57E tow-target aircraft stayed on TAC strength until June 1962.

By then, the action in Southeast Asia was heating up, and the first combat deployment was not far off.

LABS Manœuvre

From 1956 through mid-1965, the B-57 was one of the USAF aircraft assigned to the special weapons delivery mission—strikes with nuclear weapons. The characteristics of tactical nuclear bombs demanded new and different methods of dropping them. The Low-Altitude Bombing System (LABS) was developed for that kind of mission.

What it was like to make such a delivery from a B-57 is well described by Robert C. Mikesh, Major USAF, (Ret.), who spent a lot of time in B-57 cockpits.

'In inter-unit LABS competitions with other aircraft types including the F-100, the B-57

crews would win hands down with a wide margin in score. The B-57 was a very responsive and stable bomb delivery platform.

'This was a challenging manœuvre; the run-in to the target was right on the deck to avoid detection. At 425 kt. this was usually a rough ride due to surface wind turbulence, like riding a steel beam down a corduroy road. It made my left arm flail around when not hanging on to the throttles and when attempting to actuate the bomb door switch and the bombing system. When the door rolled open, only a little extra power would hold 425 kt. precisely.

'When right over the target, or at an offset point to compensate for wind, the 'pickle button' on the control wheel was depressed and held, throttles opened to full power, and a pull-up of 3.5 g. was immediately begun, starting a half-loop. Wings had to be kept level relative to the vertical plane, and a constant back pressure was necessary on the controls. Special instrumentation was provided for this delivery, but it still required considerable practice to execute it accurately.

'At somewhere near the 120-degree point of the pull-up, the bomb was automatically released at the point which was preset into the instrument before takeoff. The release of a three-quarter ton bomb at this point with these g. forces applied resulted in a shocking and sudden jolt. The bomb continued up to about 15,000 ft. while the airplane was topped out of the loop at about 9,000 ft. Back pressure was relieved to about 1.5 g. or even less after release, as the speed could decrease to as low as 160 to 140 kt. This reduced the possibility of snapping at the top prior to the intended roll-out, or stalling which could result in an inverted spin.

'Once the bomb was away, the manœuvre became essentially a visual recovery. The horizon was picked up as a reference by looking straight overhead. After the nose passed well through the horizon at an inverted dive angle of about 40°, a half roll set things upright again. It took the full strength in both arms, and one knee wedged against the side of the cockpit, to

Carrying the tail code letters for the 13th Bomb Squadron Tactical ('Grim Reapers'), this B-57G sits between missions at Ubon AB, Thailand.
(Photo: USAF 107539)

Ominous look of this Thailand-based B-57G is accentuated by its squat posture and the black under-surfaces standardized on all B-57G aircraft.
(Photo: USAF 107538)

twist the control wheel enough for a coordinated and smooth roll-out. Even the seat was felt to shift to the side because of the body forces. But aside from this, the B-57 responded well throughout the manœuvre.

'We needed all the speed possible in the escape, so we closed the bomb door and didn't retard the power. The dive toward the ground at full throttle gained back the lost speed very rapidly. With level-off right on the deck at maximum speed, the B-57 was well down the road before impact.'

Combat Operations

Two B-57E aircraft, originally built to tow targets but converted for reconnaissance, pioneered the combat operations. They were sent to South Viet Nam in May 1963, under the code-named *Patricia Lynn* project. One of the two—B-57E (55–4243)—was the first B-57 to sortie against a live enemy. Captain William Scott was pilot and Lieutenant Leo Otway was his navigator. The date was May 7, 1963.

For two months, these two aircraft were the sole representatives of the B-57 fleet to hear guns fired in anger. In July 1963, two more *Patricia Lynn* aircraft were added, and the four-plane unit was designated as Det. 1, 460th Tac Recon Wing.

The Tonkin Gulf incident was the ultimate cause for the 'mass' combat deployment of the B-57. On August 4 1964, Secretary of Defence Robert S. McNamara ordered 36 B-57s to South Viet Nam. They arrived on August 7. Later reports said that one crashed on final approach, killing the crew. An additional three were reported damaged in landing accidents.

From August on through most of the year, there were no references to combat by the B-57s. They may have been committed cautiously, or on recon missions to gain familiarity in the area.

But on November 1 1964, Viet Cong mortars found the range of the Bien Hoa flight line, pounded five of the B-57s to bits and damaged as many as 22 of the remainder. Those losses, added to the one that crashed and the three that were damaged on arrival, never were made good. The total reported strength of the entire B-57 fleet in Southeast Asia never exceeded 21 aircraft from then on, and frequently was less.

The first interdiction strikes and the first combat for the B-57s came February 19 1965, when a combined force of B-57B and North American F-100 Super Sabres aircraft struck targets in Phuoc Tuy province, about 40 miles east of Saigon. There were no details of the raids, either at that time or later.

In fact, the exploits of the B-57s in that tragic theatre of war probably never will be described adequately, except in the afterglow of later years at crew reunions. The missions involved no mass raids, no massive strikes, no air-to-air combat against enemy pilots. Their job was interdiction. They bombed up, went out and dropped their weapons, fired their rockets and cannon, came back to base, and repeated the entire procedure. That kind of work is unsung in any war, and there were no special heroes. They were all heroes.

In April, reports gave the total B-57 strength as 16 B-57B and three RB-57—model suffix unspecified—based at Bien Hoa. In May 1965, hard luck struck again. During a bombing-up before a strike, a 500-lb. bomb with a delayed-action fuse exploded on the flight line among ten B-57s parked wingtip to wingtip. All were destroyed. The only reason the other six on

Factory-fresh three-tone and grey camouflage finish marks this B-57B as a recently modified aircraft about to head into combat in Southeast Asia. Work was done during 1966.
(Photo: Martin Co.)

A sunshade shields the cockpit from the desert sun on the flight line at NASA's Flight Research Center, Edwards, Calif. This B-57B, registered NASA 809, is used for tests of the Viking Mars-lander parachute, and for probing the upper atmosphere for clear-air turbulence.
(Photo: NASA)

strength were not destroyed is because they were off on a strike.

This time the losses were replaced, and strength was brought back up to about 20 aircraft before the end of the year. Meantime, the Republic of Viet Nam in the person of Air Vice Marshal Nguyen Cao Ky complained loudly because its air force was not operating jets. The gripe was heard and, in August 1965, four B-57B aircraft were 'transferred' to the RVN Air Force. The white bars on the US insignia were over-painted with yellow, short horizontal yellow identification bars were added on the rudders, and the RVNAF was, overnight, a jet force. The only problem was that there were then no rated jet pilots in the RVNAF, and so USAF crews continued to fly the RVNAF B-57Bs, sometimes giving an RVNAF officer a ride in the back seat after telling him to keep his hands the hell off the controls.

In October 1965, B-57Bs were part of a strike force that lifted the six-day siege of Plei Me. More than 700 sorties were flown against targets in that area by a mixed air component of B-57s, A-1, F-100 and F-8 aircraft.

By January 1966, there was a total strength of 20 B-57s in South Viet Nam, and by July that year, it was reported—perhaps optimistically—that the RVNAF was flying combat in their B-57 aircraft. One observer who was there said that there never was a fixed complement of B-57s assigned to the RVNAF. Whatever aircraft were not busy that day had their insignia overpainted and called the RVNAF.

Whoever made the count in August 1966 saw six aircraft marked with RVNAF insignia, and it was duly reported that the strength of the

RVNAF had been increased substantially.

Both 1966 and 1967 were quiet years, as far as any notice being taken of B-57 operations. They were not quiet years for the crews, but war never is. The B-57s soldiered on, making their strikes against selected targets day after day, and exhibiting the staying power of the aircraft.

Finally, in September 1970 the 13th Bomb Squadron (Tactical) arrived at Ubon Air Base, in Thailand, with the B-57G, ready for night inter-diction missions. These G models, crammed with special radars, infra-red detection systems, laser rangefinders, cannon, rockets and laser-guided bombs, were sent against targets on the Ho Chi Minh Trail. Aircraft worth several millions of dollars, plus two invaluable crewmen, were flying against individual targets worth only a few hundred or thousand dollars. Clearly the game was not worth the candle, and the B-57Gs were pulled out of action after less than two years, and returned to the USA where they are flying above the level plains of Kansas with the 190th TRG, Kansas Air National Guard.

Being sent to Kansas is a fairly hard end for an expensive combat aircraft, but it is better perhaps than going to the 'boneyard', the USAF term for MASDC. It's a misleading term; aircraft are, in fact, scrapped there, but more often the storage area serves as a gigantic spare-parts warehouse that keeps the aircraft flying long after the company that built them has stopped making parts.

In the late spring of 1972, 40 B-57s of different models were in storage at MASDC. A few were scheduled to be scrapped, but by far the larger number waits for re-activation, perhaps even

back to tactical uses. Eight B-57Bs, for example, were taken out of storage in mid-1972 to be replacements for ADC's EB-57A ECM aircraft. They presumably will be re-equipped as EB-57B models and assigned to defense systems evaluation missions.

DSES Operations

Two Defence Systems Evaluation Squadrons (DSES) are the 'enemy' to US air defences. Simulating an enemy bomber force, the specially-modified EB-57s strike without warning, day or night, at low level or high altitude, trying to get past the defence systems.

The aircraft are assigned to the 4677th DSES, at Hill AFB, Utah, and the 4713th DSES, at Otis AFB, Mass., units of the Aerospace Defence Command (ADC). B-57s modified to do this mission bristle with antennas protruding from their bellies. Their bomb-bays are filled with the latest electronic countermeasures and warfare systems to confuse the defence.

Typically, a DSES force—one B-57 to several types—flies to a remote staging base in Canada, Bermuda, or the US and waits to attack. Crews get last-minute weather briefings and takeoff to strike. They fly clear of the known Air Defence Identification Zones (ADIZ) and to their assigned mission penetration points.

On the attack, the second crewman—an electronics warfare officer (EWO)—drops chaff to begin the confusion. As soon as the crew detects defence action against them, the EWO brings out the full panoply of countermeasures. He jams, sends spurious intercept information, discharges more chaff, and tries to confuse the defence forces. Pre-arranged signals end the encounter.

Reconnaissance Missions

A more dangerous game than playing enemy is the game of high-altitude reconnaissance, the kind of job that led to the requirements for the RB-57D and the RB-57F. These operations are highly classified, and very little information is available.

Two RB-57Ds were reported to have been operating out of Formosa some years back, marked with the insignia of the Nationalist Chinese Air Force. The mainland Chinese made a loud outcry about the overflights, specifically identifying the RB-57D as the culprit. The US made no comments at the time, or later.

Other reports said that the Pakistan Air Force was operating one or more RB-57F aircraft. It is likely that the aircraft were marked with Pakistani insignia, but that the crews flying them were USAF.

A detachment of WB-57F aircraft currently is stationed at Yokota Air Base, Japan, operating as part of the 9th Weather Reconnaissance Wing. And detached DSES aircraft occasionally are seen on duty in Europe, where they can be used not only to simulate attacking forces, but to annoy enemy defenders of air space in the continuing battle of electronic wits over the borders.

Hurricane-Hunting and Other Jobs

Certainly the oldest B-57 now flying is B-57A 52–1419, the second production aircraft. Now registered N1005, the aircraft is operated by the Research Flight Facility of the National Oceanographic and Atmospheric Administration (NOAA). Based at Miami International Airport, Florida, along with several other NOAA aircraft, it has been flying with the unit since January 1960 when it was transferred from USAF.

N1005 is used for chasing and seeding hurricanes, for investigating high-altitude weather phenomena, and for specific studies in clear-air turbulence (CAT). CAT is also a concern of NASA and the Dept. of Transportation. They jointly operate a B-57B (52–1576) registered NASA 809 out of the NASA Flight Research Center, Edwards, Calif. The B-57B is flown in areas of potential CAT, and flies a 30-minute recording pattern when it encounters any.

This NASA aircraft also is being used for drop

B-57B (53–3888) of the 13th Bomb Squadron, 3rd Bomb Wing, unloads a pylon against a target in the highlands of Central Viet Nam in February 1965. Diagonal red stripe on fuselage identifies 13th Bomb Sq., with yellow the band colour for the 8th Bomb Sq., 3rd Bomb Wing. The two squadrons did alternate combat tours in Viet Nam following the Tonkin Gulf incident. Units were based at Clark Air Base in the Philippines and rotated to Viet Nam. (Photo: USAF 94507)

The first RB-57D, serial 53–3977, was accepted by the USAF in November 1955. Assigned to Strategic Air Command for day photo reconnaissance, the aircraft was one of a batch of six designed for the job. Note the break in the belly contour under the cockpit, where cameras were mounted. This aircraft later served with the Air Weather Service and then was converted to an EB-57D and assigned to ADC for defence systems evaluation, where it was based at Hill AFB, Utah. It was in storage at MASDC in May 1972.
(Photo: Martin Co.)

tests of the Viking parachute decelerator that will be used to soft-land an experimental package on Mars in 1976.

An RB-57F and other aircraft were used to detect corn blight from the air in 1971. The F photographed more than 45,000 sq. miles during the corn-growing season, recording on colour infra-red film the spread and extent of the plant disease.

Two WB-57F have now been loaned by USAF to NASA's Manned Spacecraft Center, at Houston, Texas, to operate in support of the Earth Resources Technology Satellite (ERTS). The support programme is intended to establish base-line data to which later satellite photos will be compared. Flying at altitudes of about 60,000 ft., the WB-57Fs have been used to obtain 'leaves-off' and 'leaves-on' photos in portions of both the visible and invisible spectrum.

Weather Reconnaissance

Aircraft of the 58th WRS, Kirtland AFB, have supported many such experiments for agencies of the government. But, flying WB-57Fs, their primary task still is weather reconnaissance and, in the official statement of their mission, '...the Air Weather Service provides or arranges ... airborne atmospheric sampling (gathering particulate or whole air samples of the atmosphere) and reconnaissance operations for the Department of Defence and other Federal agencies ...'

Weather reconnaissance missions last up to seven hours, and both crew members are confined in their pressure suits for that entire time. This suit, which can maintain a 35,000-ft. internal pressure level up to ambient altitudes of 75,000 ft., is a $12,000 garment that has to be fitted carefully, and tended lovingly. Each crew member has two suits available.

The crews are all volunteers; they train at the 4756th Psychological Training Unit, Tyndall AFB, Florida, in an altitude chamber that takes them to 75,000 ft. in simulated flights.

Routine flights in the WB-57F are made above 60,000 ft., and specialized crew training is very necessary. Each flight is preceded by a complete medical exam for both crew members and the back-up crew. A special meal follows, featuring high protein and low residue. The crews then dress, checking their pressure suits once before

getting into the aircraft and once again after they are seated inside. The back-up crew has given the aircraft its pre-flight inspection, so that the prime pilot starts the engines as soon as the suit check is complete. The reason for this routine is that the suits get very uncomfortable on the ground; they are inefficient before the airplane is airborne. Taxi and takeoff clearances get priority.

The second crew member is the navigator on weather flights. Primary navigation is done by dead-reckoning and celestial navigation means, using the Baird-Atomic system and a dead-reckoning kit made up before the flight. The navigator carries at least two of these, because if he drops one, he can't bend over to locate it in the cockpit.

Even though the WB-57F carries Doppler radar, VOR, Tacan and ADF equipment, most of the flights are in remote areas over the Poles where radio navigation is highly marginal. The Doppler does give ground speed and drift with good accuracy to aid the dead-reckoning calculations. But winds above 60,000 ft. are completely unpredictable, change quickly and can blow as fast as 100 kt. or more.

External Markings and Colours

Early B-57 models were finished in the gloss black paint standardized for the night intruder mission. Markings and codes were in gloss red. Some of the B-57B models in service with USAFE carried distinctive markings on their vertical tails, but this practice was not widespread.

Aircraft assigned to the Air National Guard were stripped to bare metal and operated that way. The markings varied from state to state, both in size and location. The closest approach to standardization was the use of a 24-in. diameter ANG decal insignia on the vertical tail.

Most B-57 types not in a theatre of war retained the bare metal finish. Some of the RB-57D aircraft sported the white upper surface and black belly combination in the late 1950s.

B-57s operating in South Viet Nam at first were unpainted and carried only their standard codes and markings. Later they were all camouflaged in the standard three-tone arrangement called for in TO 1–1–4: Under surfaces in FS 36622 grey, upper surfaces in FS 30219 tan, FS 34079 dark green and FS 34102 green. Pacific Air Forces was granted special authority to use FS 17038 black as an under-surface colour in special cases. Some B-57s did use that scheme.

Jettisonable wing or pylon tanks were specified with grey or black bottoms, with 34079 green tops.

Tow-target and DSES aircraft carried large areas of Dayglo paint markings on their nose and vertical tails. All tip tanks on these two classes of B-57s were also painted with Dayglo red (FS 38905) or orange (FS 38903).

Aircraft assigned to the Air Force Missile Test Center were refinished with aluminium lacquer to protect them from the salt spray.

B-57 Valedictory

The Night Intruder carries on, out of combat now, but still playing the deadly game of war. Its crews still probe defences here and abroad, still monitor the upper atmosphere, still photograph and record the earth from 70,000 ft.

Perhaps a hundred of the fleet remain, with half that number in service.

Twenty years is old for an airplane, and the B-57 is approaching that mark. Newer aircraft have taken over some of its missions. War finally is becoming unpopular. Military budgets are feeling the pinch of inflation and the escalating costs of new technology.

But don't write off the B-57 quite yet. It has been a versatile performer, coping readily with the jobs for which it was designed, and equally readily with missions unimagined at its birth.

It may well turn out to be the 'gooney bird of the jet fleet'.

TABLE I: B-57 SPECIFICATIONS (ALL MODELS UNLESS NOTED)

Dimensions: Span, 64.0 ft.; 106.0 ft. (D); 122.5 ft. (F); overall length, 65.5 ft.; 64.8 ft. (D); 68.3 ft. (F); 68 ft. estimated (G); height, three-point 15.5 ft.; 14.8 ft. (D); 20.5 ft. (F).

Weights: Empty, 24,290 lb. (A); 27,091 lb. (B&C); 27,275 lb. (D); 34,099 lb. (E); 36,876 lb. (F); combat mission, 35,750 lb. (A); 38,689 lb. (B&C); 35,335 lb. (D); 37,300 lb. (E); 49,500 lb. (F); maximum take-off, 51,547 lb. (A); 56,965 lb. (B&C); 45,507 lb. (D); 54,072 lb. (E); 61,500 lb. (F).

Powerplant and maximum rated thrust: 2 × J65-W-5 at 7,220 lb. each; 2 × J57-P-27 at 10,500 lb. each (D); 2 × TF33-P-11A at 16,500 lb. each plus 2 × J60-P-9 auxiliaries at 2,900 lb. each (F).

Fuel system capacity (US gallons): Internal, 2,252 gal.; 2,740 gal. (D); 3,870 gal. (F); external, 640 gal. in wingtip drop tanks (A, B, C, E & G).

Communication equipment: ARC-27 or -34 UHF command set; AIC-10 interphone; AIC-18 interphone (F); APX-6 or -25 IFF radar; VHF-101 VHF command set (F); 618T-3 HF command set (F).

Bombing/navigation equipment: ARN-12 marker beacon; ARN-6 radio compass and ARA-19 remote tuning group; S-2A or S-4 Shoran; ARN-21 Tacan; APW-11A radar beacon and APA-90 indicator group; APN-69 radar beacon (D); ARN-14 omni-range receiver; ASN-6 navigation computer; ARN-18 ILS receiver; M-1 toss bomb computer; MA-1 fire control system; MA-2 LABS (Low-Altitude Bombing System).

Bombing/navigation equipment installed in modification programmes: APG-31 ranging radar; APN-22 radio altimeter; APN-59 navigation radar; ARD-9A detection and homing device; APS-60 search radar; ARA-25 UHF direction-finder; APN-69 rendezvous equipment; ARN-30 navigation receiver.

Navigation equipment on WB-57F: VOR-101B VOR/ILS system; APN-102 Doppler radar; ARA-25 UHF direction finder; ID-663/U bearing distance heading indicator; ID-387 course indicator; 51Z-2 marker beacon; C-12 gyro compass; ARU-4A attitude indicator; Lear-Siegler MC-1 autopilot; Baird-Atomic 511F sextant and viewer.

Electronic countermeasures or reconnaissance equipment: ALE-2 or -6 chaff dispensers; ARA-3 modulator; APR-9 radar receiver; APG-30 tail-warning radar, later replaced by APS-54 tail-warning equipment; ALT-6 jamming transmitter; ANH-2 wire recorder (D); APA-54 reconnaissance recorder; APR-14 panoramic reconnaissance radar receiver; ALQ-71 and -72 noise jammer transmitters. Much other classified and unidentifiable equipment.

TABLE II: MARTIN B-57 CONTRACT SUMMARY

Model	Serial Numbers	Quantity
Contract AF33(038)-22617		
B-57A	51-17352 (was B.2 WD940)	1
	51-17387 (was B.2 WD932)	1
	52-1418 through 52-1425	8
RB-57A	52-1426 through 52-1492	67
B-57B	52-1493 through 52-1594	102
Contract AF33(600)-22208		
B-57C	53-3825 through 53-3858	34
B-57B	53-3859 through 53-3935	77
B-57C	53-3936	1
B-57B	53-3937 through 53-3939	3
B-57C	53-3940	1
B-57B	53-3941 through 53-3943	3
B-57C	53-3944	1
B-57B	53-3945 through 53-3947	3
B-57C	53-3948	1
B-57B	53-3949 through 53-3962	14
Contract AF33(600)-25825		
RB-57D	53-3963 through 53-3976	14
	53-3977 through 53-3982	6
Contract AF33(600)-29645		
B-57E	55-4243 through 55-4301	68

TABLE III: B-57 MISSION PERFORMANCE

Item	B-57A	EB-57A	B-57B	B-57C	RB-57D	EB-57D	B-57E	RB-57F
Take-off weight, lb.	51,547	48,600	53,721	53,721	45,085	46,000	54,072	63,000
Weapons payload, lb.	5,460	None	5,260	5,260	None	None	4 trgt	None
Fuel load, lb.	19,318	18,798	18,798	18,798	17,810	16,800	18,798	23,000
Take-off distance, ft.	4,315	3,860	5,000	5,000	2,300	2,000	5,050	2,600
SL rate of climb, ft./min.	4,340	4,000	4,320	4,320	6,700	—	3,825	2,725
Service ceiling, ft.	40,500	40,500	40,100	40,100	55,000[1]	—	28,600	60,800
Combat radius, naut. mi	662	725	514	514	1,354	—	—	1,280
Av. cruise speed, kt.	423	390	417	417	413	—	—	411
Speed at target, kt.	434	390	500	500	413	—	371	411
Altitude at target, ft.	SL	37,000	SL	SL	59,700	—	35,000[1]	63,200
Landing weight, lb.	27,726	32,302	31,528	31,528	29,056	—	38,287	42,587
Ground roll, ft.	1,192	2,425	2,350	2,350	1,500	—	2,875	2,800
Total mission time, hr.	4.2	3.8	3.5	3.5	6.6	—	2.7	6.1

Notes: [1] =Estimated; all other data from official USAF sources, based on design mission parameters. Actual aircraft performance will vary from these numbers depending on mission loadings, aircraft configuration and condition.

TABLE IV: GENERAL DYNAMICS RB-57F CONTRACT SUMMARY

Serial	Rebuild of	Status, August 1 1972
63–13286	B/B 52–1599	In storage, MASDC
63–13287	B/B 53–3864	Lost
63–13288	B/B 52–1539	58 WRS, Kirtland AFB, NM
63–13289	B/B 52–1527	In storage, MASDC
63–13290	B/B 52–1562	58 WRS, Kirtland AFB, NM
63–13291	B/B 52–1574	58 WRS, Kirtland AFB, NM
63–13292	B/B 52–1594	58 WRS, Kirtland AFB, NM
63–13293	B/B 52–1583	In storage, MASDC
63–13294	B/B 53–3935	58 WRS, Kirtland AFB, NM
63–13295	B/B 53–3918	58 WRS, Kirtland AFB, NM
63–13296	B/B 53–3897	58 WRS, Kirtland AFB, NM
63–13297	B/B 53–3900	Lost
63–13298	B/B 52–1536	58 WRS, Kirtland AFB, NM
63–13299	B/B 52–1573	58 WRS, Kirtland AFB
63–13300	RB/A 52–1427	Det 3, 9 WRW, Yokota AB, Japan
63–13301	RB/A 52–1432	Det 3, 9 WRW, Yokota AB, Japan
63–13302	RB/A 52–1433	Det 3, 9 WRW, Yokota AB, Japan
63–13500	RB/D 53–3972	58 WRS, Kirtland AFB, NM
63–13501	RB/D 53–3975	NASA 925 at MSC/Houston
63–13502	RB/D 53–3970	58 WRS, Kirtland AFB, NM
63–13503	RB/D 53–3974	NASA 926 at MSC/Houston

TABLE V: MARTIN B-57G SERIALS

Martin B-57G aircraft all were rebuilt from B-57B models and carried the same serial numbers before and after the rebuild. The 16 aircraft in the programme were:

52–1578	53–3886
52–1580	53–3889
52–1582	53–3898
52–1588	53–3905
53–3860	53–3906
53–3865	53–3928
53–3877	53–3929
53–3878	53–3931

TABLE VI: MAP AIRCRAFT

In late 1959, Pakistan received a number of B-57 aircraft under the US Military Assistance Program (MAP). The following list of serial numbers is believed to be complete.

B-57B 53–3885	B-57B 53–3951
53–3891	53–3952
53–3938	53–3954
53–3941	53–3955
53–3942	53–3956
53–3943	53–3957
53–3945	53–3958
53–3946	53–3959
53–3947	53–3960
53–3949	53–3961
53–3950	B-57C 53–3846

Additionally, a B-57B (53–3939) was in the MAP listing at that time, on loan to Autonetics Corp., and based at Palmdale, Calif.

TABLE VII: PRODUCTION CHRONOLOGY, FIRST B-57A

1951:

January:	First meeting between Martin and English Electric, Company.
February:	Initial licence discussions with US Air Force.
February 24:	First B.2 Canberra pattern aircraft arrived at Martin.
March:	Letter contract for 250 aircraft plus one static article.
May:	First engineering data received from English Electric; licence agreement signed, first payment made to EEC.
July:	First details released to shop for fabrication.
August:	USAF approval of Hudson & Kaiser subcontracts.

1952:

August:	First centre-section completed by Martin.
September:	First nose section completed by Martin.
December:	First aft section received from Hudson.

1953:

February:	First J65 engine received from Buick for test; first wing received from Kaiser for static test.
June:	Final assembly completed.
July 20:	First flight, first B-57A.

TABLE VIII: B-57 ALLOCATIONS

The following operational units are known to have used one or more models of the Martin B-57:

1st Tactical Fighter Wing:
4424th Combat Crew Training Squadron

3rd Bomb Wing:
8th, 13th and 90th Tactical Bomb Squadrons

10th Tactical Reconnaissance Group:
1st, 32nd, 38th and 42nd Tactical Reconnaissance Squadrons

13th Reconnaissance W

17th Bomb Group:
34th, 37th, 73rd and 95th Bomb Squadrons (Tactical)

26th Tactical Reconnaissance Wing

33rd Tactical Group:
Detachment 1

35th Tactical Fighter Wing

38th Bomb Wing:
71st, 405th and 822nd Bomb Squadrons

66th Tactical Reconnaissance Group:
30th, 362nd and 303rd Tactical Reconnaissance Squadrons

345th Bomb Group (Tactical):
498th, 499th, 500th and 501st Bomb Squadrons (Tactical)

363rd Tactical Reconnaissance Wing:
9th, 17th, 160th and 161st Tactical Reconnaissance Squadrons
4416th Technical Evaluation Squadron

405th Fighter Wing

460th Tactical Reconnaissance Wing:
Detachment 1

461st Bomb Group (Tactical):
764th, 765th and 766th Bomb Squadrons (Tactical)

Air National Guard:
110th Tactical Reconnaissance Group, Michigan
123rd Tactical Reconnaissance Group, Kentucky
189th Tactical Reconnaissance Group, Arkansas
190th Tactical Reconnaissance Group, Kansas
Unidentified units, Nevada

Air Weather Service:
55th, 56th and 58th Weather Reconnaissance Squadrons
9th Weather Reconnaissance Wing: Det. 3

Miscellaneous units:
17th Tow Target Squadron
21st Operations Squadron
317th Fighter Interceptor Squadron
556th Reconnaissance Squadron
4677th Defense Systems Evaluation Squadron
4713th Defense Systems Evaluation Squadron
4758th Defense Systems Evaluation Squadron
6250th Combat Support Group: Det. 1
6550th Operations Squadron
7406th Combat Support Squadron
7407th Combat Support Squadron

Acknowledgments

The author gratefully acknowledges the help of the following people in supplying research data or photographs or both:
Colonel R. D. Bartholomew, Michigan ANG; Roger F. Besecker; Captain G. Knox Bishop, USAF; Kenneth W. Buchanan; E. J. Bulban; Captain Michael I. Burch, USAF; William S. Callahan, NOAA; Lieutenant Colonel Ralph B. Campbell, Jr., Michigan ANG; Lieutenant Colonel Ralph B. Cochrane, Jr., USAF; Edward J. Cottrell; Harold E. Daubert; David Davidson; Jimm Dorrance via Aardvark Art; Edward V. Duggan, DNA; John F. Fuller, AWS; Malcolm H. Holloway; Ralph B. Jackson, NASA; Colonel Bruce Jacobs, National Guard Bureau; Alexander Johnston; Duane A. Kasulka; Charles J. Kay, Jr.; Ben Knowles; Major Robert L. Lince, USAF; Sergeant Ron Loewen, Kansas ANG; John F. Loosbrock; R. H. Maltby, AFSC; David W. Menard, AAHS; Robert C. Mikesh; Barry Miller; Kurt Miska; Dave Musikoff; Gerald J. McAllister; Don McDowell; Walter J. McGinnis; John E. McLeaish, NASA; John T. O'Brien, AFSC; John J. Orris; Robert Pandy; Arthur Pearcy, Jr., ARAeS; Ron Picciani and Picciani Aircraft Slides; Lawrence C. Railing, MASDC; Ed Richardson; Lieutenant John F. Sander; USAF; Frank F. Smith; N. E. Taylor; Harold S. Tolley; Captain Thomas S. Waller, USAF; Ira Ward; Gordon S. Williams; Norman B. Wiltshire; Andrew J. Wood, AFSC; Fred L. Wolff; Charles G. Worman; Major Stanley A. Worsham, Kentucky ANG and John Zimmerman.

Series Editor:
CHARLES W. CAIN

Ninaks of B Flight, No. 47 Squadron, based at Helwan, Egypt, 1926. Nearest, J7086, was piloted by Flight Lieutenant S. D. Macdonald (later AVM, CB, CBE, DFC), whose pet bull mastiff, Monty, is seen braving the slipstream with the gunner. (Photo: C. A. Sims)

de Havilland D.H.9A (R.A.F. 1918–30)
by Chaz Bowyer

The de Havilland D.H.9A, like the doughty Bristol F.2B[1] was born in war, proven on operations and then soldiered on for a further 12 years in frontline service with the Royal Air Force, helping to maintain the uneasy 'peace' throughout the British Empire. Known to all as the 'Ninak',[2] its genesis was circumstantial, being a reasonably hasty improvisation on an existing discredited design—a situation which was to have its parallel over 20 years later when the superb Lancaster bomber emerged from the chrysalis of the condemned Avro Manchester.

The Ninak's origin can be said to have been one result of the German daylight bombing raid on London on Wednesday, June 13 1917 when the Air Board, pressured by public and political agitation, decided that emphasis for future aircraft equipment of the Royal Flying Corps (RFC) must be placed on bombers capable of deep (sic) penetration into the German homeland.

A Cabinet decision of July 2 1917—to increase the existing RFC strength of 108 squadrons to 200—implied that a majority of these units would have such bombers; and one 'new' design mooted was the de Havilland 9, a redesigned version of the successful D.H.4 already in operational use. Fully detailed histories of

these aircraft—by J. M. Bruce—have appeared in earlier *Profiles*; the D.H.4 as *Profile* No. 26 and the D.H.9 as No. 62.

Apart from relocating the crew positions of the D.H.4, a major difference in the proposed D.H.9 concerned the latter's nominated engine —the 300 h.p. BHP 'Beardmore-Halford-Pullinger'), later known as the Siddeley Puma. For a variety of reasons, mainly that of inadequate development, the BHP finally emerged with a mere 230 h.p. rating; inferior to the more powerful D.H.4 it was intended to replace. Geoffrey de Havilland, then chief designer for the Aircraft Manufacturing Company at Hendon, privately informed the RFC's Commander, Major-General Hugh Trenchard, of his misgivings over the Puma-engined D.H.9, stressing that it would give a lower ceiling and shorter operational range than the D.H.4. On November 16 1917, Trenchard complained forcefully about the whole matter to Major-General John Salmond, Director General of Military Aeronautics, and requested that 'every endeavour' be made to halt production of the D.H.9 and more important, that a replacement be provided '...with a performance equal at least to the D.H.4'. In the event Trenchard was told bluntly that circumstances decreed little choice—he could have the D.H.9 or nothing. In support of Trenchard, General Douglas Haig had requested on November 14 that D.H.9 production should at least be

[1] See *Profile* No. 237 by Chaz Bowyer.
[2] From contemporary usage of a phonetic alphabet whereby the letter A became 'Ac', 'Ack' or 'AK'.—Editor

reduced and limited to equipping a maximum of 15 squadrons.

Seemingly providential, on August 12 1917, in the United States of America, lavish publicity was initiated about a 'revolutionary' new engine, a 400 h.p., liquid-cooled 12-cylinder Vee, jingoistically titled 'Liberty' which had just been 'perfected' by a USA design team. With thousands of these much-vaunted powerplants promised from the American production lines—and considering the contemporary short supply of Rolls-Royce engines in Britain—the Liberty appeared to be a solution to the D.H.9 dilemma. Because of the existing pressure from the Air Board for the D.H.10 (see *Profile* No. 145), the Aircraft Manufacturing Company found it necessary to contract out the official request for a Liberty-powered D.H.9 to the Westland company at Yeovil, Somerset. To assist in the initial production stages, they 'loaned' a draughtsman, Mr J. J. Johnston, who was already involved in preparation of necessary modifications for acceptance of a Liberty into a D.H.9 airframe. Johnston, in close cooperation with Westland's Robert A. Bruce, set to work without delay and the first 'converted' D.H.9 (military serial no. B7664) was fitted with a 375 h.p. Rolls-Royce Eagle engine as a trial installation, pending the arrival of the promised Liberty engines from the USA.

Although nominally a conversion, in fact the so-named D.H.9A was almost a complete redesign; having greater span, greater chord, increased wing area (this factor being the reason for the 9A designation, not the change in engine) and a heavier all-up weight. General construction was conventional for the period and differed from the D.H.9 mainly in details. Extra strengthening was mandatory for support of the heavy Liberty engine and included a 1-inch thick plywood bulkhead built into the fuselage top, plus two bays of bracing wires under each engine bearer. Two 50-gallon fuel tanks were situated behind the engine with an additional 7-gallon gravity-feed tank let into the upper wing centre-section. The most easily-recognized external feature was the 9A's large and flat-fronted radiator, providing a neater profile to the nose which dispensed with the clutter of 'ironmongery' so evident in the D.H.9 design. Using a four-blade propeller (two two-blade units bolted together), B7664 was first flown at Yeovil in March 1918 by the renowned B. C. Hucks. At almost the same time a second Eagle-powered 'prototype' D.H.9A (C6350) was built and flown by the parent firm at Hendon.

In March 1918, the first 10 Liberty engines arrived in the United Kingdom and the first four production contracts for D.H.9As were placed on March 20 and 21, totalling 75 aircraft. The first 9A to be fitted with a Liberty (C6122) was initially air-tested on April 19 1918 at Yeovil by Captain A. R. Boeree. With Robert Bruce in the rear cockpit, Boeree took off smoothly; but soon

B7644, built by Westland Aircraft of Yeovil, one of the two Eagle powered prototypes. (Photo: G. S. Leslie/ J. M. Bruce)

C6350, the other Eagle Ninak, seen here at Hendon. (Photo: G. S. Leslie/ J. M. Bruce)

ran into trouble. Instead of the estimated gliding speed of 70 m.p.h., he found himself 'hurtling down' for the landing at 120 m.p.h. Finally getting the nose-heavy D.H.9A down safely, Boeree immediately instructed the maintenance crew to insert 21 lbs. of lead ballast into the rudder post for counter-balance. He then accompanied C6122 to Martlesham, although he refused to fly the aircraft until it had been fully rerigged. At Yeovil, Westland arranged for the top wing to be staggered a further two inches forward and C6122 then completed its trials without undue trouble. Production of D.H.9As soon commenced and by the end of June 1918, 18 had been delivered. During the next three months 288 Ninaks passed their acceptance tests; while in the following three months, 579 more were accepted for service.

Operations, 1918

The first operational unit to be equipped with D.H.9As was No. 110 Squadron, Royal Air Force. Formed on November 12 1917, this squadron was originally intended to have D.H.4s and D.H.9s for bombing duties on the Western Front in the spring of 1918. Instead, No. 110 moved to Kenley on June 15 1918 and began receiving D.H.9As; quickly reaching its full 18-aircraft establishment. Each of the first 18 Ninaks allocated to 110 was suitably inscribed to indicate that they had been paid for and 'presented' by His Serene Highness, the Nizam of Hyderabad.

On August 31 1918, 110 Squadron flew to Bettoncourt in France to join the Independent Force, RAF, and flew its first operations on September 14 when a dozen 9As attempted to bomb Boulay aerodrome, near Metz. Only six Ninaks found the target but all returned un-

F993, a Westland-built production D.H.9A in factory finish. Allocated to 110 Squadron in the unit's initial 18-aircraft batch, this Ninak was named 'Hyderabad No. 6'.

F1000, another of No. 110's original aircraft. Its presentation inscription read 'Presented by His Serene Highness, The Nizam of Hyderabad' 'Hyderabad No. 7'.

Fine side elevation of E9665, a Ninak of typical 1918-19 construction—in this case by Mann, Egerton of Norwich.

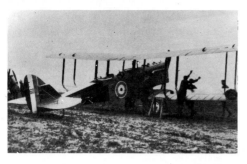

scathed. Their apparent immunity to enemy reaction did not last long. Eleven days later, 12 Ninaks set out to raid Frankfurt and lost five in the trying; while a sixth 9A aborted the mission early with engine trouble. Four more 9As were lost on October 5 during a sortie to Kaiserlautern. Then, on October 21, a further seven of a formation of 12 aircraft failed to return. By the Armistice a total of 17 of 110's 9As had been shot down and a further 28 written-off-charge as 'Wrecked'—a 'wastage' equivalent to $2\frac{1}{2}$ times the normal squadron establishment in a mere eight weeks of operations. The reasons for this apparent vulnerability was due not to any intrinsic fault of the Ninak design, but to a combination of inexperienced crews, unfamiliar

territory and, by no means least, a bitterly intensive opposition in the closing weeks of the war from the German *Jagdstaffeln*. Compared to other units of the Independent Force, the losses of 110 Squadron were relatively small.

The only other Independent Force unit to receive D.H.9As was No. 99 Squadron which flew its first example on September 4 1918 and had six on charge by the end of that month. Continuing to fly an impractical mixture of D.H.9s and D.H.9As until the Armistice, this squadron next received twelve 9As on November 11 and 12 and was fully re-equipped by November 16. The few operations accomplished in Ninaks by 99 Squadron pilots showed emphatically the superiority of the 9A over its predecessor, lifting almost twice a D.H.9's war-load to a higher ceiling and reaching that ceiling faster.

Other RAF units to receive D.H.9As during the war included Nos. 18 and 205 Squadrons. The latter squadron began replacing its D.H.4s in September 1918, and flew its first Ninak operations on September 29; being fully re-equipped by October 1. No. 18 Squadron received its first 9A on September 28 and was almost fully 'converted' by the Armistice.

With its strong American connections, it was logical that the USA should employ the Liberty-engined D.H.9A and at least 53 were used by the US Marine Corps Northern Bombing Group, starting in September 1918. USMC Day Squadron 9 carried out its first Ninak operations on October 13.

Further examples of Ninaks were sent to a variety of RAF naval units, including Nos. 212 and 273 (Coastal) Squadrons; while on October 24 1918, twelve D.H.9As were in transit at Turnhouse awaiting 'naval disposition'. Another

D.H.4 unit, 25 Squadron, is known to have received a few 9As late in the war, presumably on an operational evaluation basis because no confirmation has been found to indicate any official intention to re-equip the unit fully. On October 31 1918, the RAF had an overall total of 405 D.H.9As on charge, of which 149 were in France and the remainder scattered widely in units and storage in the UK.

Post-Armistice—The 'Peace' Years

With the cessation of hostilities in Europe in November 1918, the D.H.9A squadrons became part of the air complement to the Allied armies of occupation in Germany. As such during 1919, they were used primarily in a conveyance role for passengers, communications and the European end of mail services to British servicemen on the continent. As demobilization and reduction within the RAF reached its peak, the bulk of wartime squadrons were reduced to cadre and eventually disbanded. For example, of the D.H.9A units, 110 Squadron disbanded on

Winter scene—or 'The Mail must go through'. E9707 of No. 205 Squadron at Verviers, February 1919, piloted by Lieutenant Wardlaw, prepares to fly the last leg of the UK-Germany mail route to British occupation forces. (Photo: C. H. Latimer-Needham)

Excellent close-up of Ninak crew accommodation, in this case F1001, 'L' of No. 205 Sqn, Verviers, February 1919. The pilot was Lieutenant W. Esplen. Note that Vickers gun and bomb-sight were still fitted, but that the Observer's Lewis gun was removed. (Photo: C. H. Latimer-Needham)

August 27 1919, 18 Squadron in December 1919 and 205 Squadron—which handed over its aircraft in March 1919—soon followed suit and disbanded on January 22 1920.

Only 99 Squadron continued in service, based at Aulnoye, until May 1919 when it was somewhat hastily despatched to India to reinforce the meagre RAF strength there for the Third Afghan War along India's North West Frontier.

A few D.H.9As saw sporadic operational service in 1919–20 with the RAF Training Mission assisting the 'White' Russians cause in south Russia, fighting Bolshevik revolutionaries. No. 47 Squadron, reformed in June 1919, had one Flight of Ninaks—as did 221 Squadron, based at Petrovsk by mid-1919. In arctic temperatures and makeshift conditions of maintenance, the Ninaks achieved little and, by mid-1920, were withdrawn when the RAF element was taken out of the conflict. Several Ninaks, presumably abandoned, were confiscated by the 'Red' Russians who soon produced an overt carbon-copy of the D.H.9A, labelled R-1 ('Razv'edchik'—Reconnaissance). At first powered by (presumably) captured Liberty engines, these too were copied and produced as 400 h.p. M-5 engines. Further Russian development of the basic R-1 continued until 1932 and at least one claim to fame for the R-1 was that it was Russia's first 'Shturmovik' ('One who storms') when one model had additional guns fitted.

In the USA, the D.H.9A was officially adopted

D.H.9A, E752, fitted with Napier Lion, warming up for take-off during deck-landing trials aboard the aircraft carrier, HMS Eagle in 1920. (Photo: via R. C. B. Ashworth)

as a replacement for the D.H.4 although, in the contemporary mania for altering any aircraft to 'American standards', the basic design was considerably changed and even its title was changed to U.S.D-9A. In all, nine prototypes were built, the first four being delivered in October 1918; but an optimistic contract for 4,000 production aircraft was cancelled by the Armistice and no production U.S.D.-9As delivered.

India

The outbreak of the Third Afghan War in 1919 along India's northern frontier imposed a severe strain on the only two RAF units, 31 and 114

Of poor quality, but rare photo of the Russian-built R1 version of the D.H.9A. Seen here in 1920 with snow skis and fitted with nightflying landing and navigation lamps. 'Red Star' markings visible under wings.

Another Russian improvization, a metal two-float version of the Ninak with 'Red Star' markings in the mid-1920s. (Photo: via D. B. Robertson)

Squadrons, already stationed in the area. As reinforcement, three more squadrons were hurriedly sent from Germany—48 (Bristol F.2Bs), 97 (D.H. 10s) and 99 (D.H.9As), all of which arrived in India by June 1919.

Initially No. 99 Squadron moved to Ambala and later were based at Mianwali in the Punjab Province, on the east bank of the River Indus. Mianwali was a bald, rock landing strip almost totally devoid of maintenance facilities but the Ninak crews were given little time to acclimatize, being employed on anti-tribal operations almost immediately.

They soon discovered that performance figures for the Ninak applicable in more tem-perate zones bore little relation to operational conditions in India. Take-off and initial climb was painfully slow in the thin mountain air, while the usual service ceiling of 15,000–18,000 ft. (with full warload) was virtually unattainable. Even landings presented unusual problems. 'Arriving' neatly by the contemporary practice of side-slipping off a turn before touching down on 'three points' was likely to produce an even neater sideways-shearing of the undercarriage. Similarly, the violent change from the baking heat of the airfield to the bone-numbing cold of operational ceiling on each sortie did little to improve crew comfort and efficiency. In August 1920, extra tropical radiators were introduced

Key to colour

E8650 of A Flight, 84 Squadron, 1923, Shaibah.

E8723 of 27 Squadron, 1924. The Green Elephant caricature on the fin was applied to all unit aircraft—a reminder of the unit's first operational aircraft, The Martinsyde G100 'Elephant' of 1915/16.

'Racing Red Nine'— the personal transport of the AOC-in-C, RAF Middle East, 1928, AVM Sir Edward Ellington.

H3433 of 30 Squadron, Iraq, circa 1926/27.

for all aircraft in India, but even after such 'improvement' a Ninak specially flown to test warload height capability could still only reach 13,500 ft.

On April 1 1920, a change of identity for several of the units was effected; No. 48 Squadron being renumbered 5 Squadron, No. 97 becoming 60 Squadron and No. 99 assuming the reborn title of 27 Squadron. The new 'labels' scarcely affected daily routine on the squadrons which were still busily engaged in operations, although the Third Afghan War officially ended on May 7 1920. The 'peace' which followed was short-lived. In November that year, during one five-day period from the 12th to 17th, Nos. 27 and 60 Squadrons combined in support of the army's Wana Column and dropped a total of 10,814 lbs. of bombs among tribesmen attacking the column. Indeed, the term 'peace' never really applied to conditions on India's North West Frontier at any period between the two world wars of this century. If tribes were not engaged in their traditional inter-tribal feuding, they were constantly fermenting trouble with the white 'Raj' (rule). This continuing situation meant an almost constant operational footing for the British Servicemen in India.

No. 27 Squadron remained the only Ninak unit in India until March 1923 when 60 Squadron finally exchanged their D.H.10s for the more reliable 9As. Ideally, squadron establishment in each case was for 12 aircraft; though in 27's case there were seldom more than seven 9As fully serviceable at any given date. This was due mainly to the scandalous financial condition of the RAF in India in the early 1920s—a circumstance which finally resulted in Air Vice-Marshal Sir John Salmond being sent to India to investigate the whole situation in 1922. His report to the Viceroy of India included a recommendation that the existing establishment of six squadrons be raised to eight to include two extra D.H.9A units. In the event, it was to be six years later before the extra two squadrons arrived in India, by which time the Ninak was overdue for replacement by more modern designs. Thus 27 and 60 Squadrons remained the only D.H.9A units in India until their eventual re-equipment.

Apart from the near-constant operational duties, Ninaks were used to open up new communications routes across India. On January 14 1925, all six Flight Commanders of 27 and 60 Squadrons set out from Risalpur to fly to Calcutta—the first such attempted long-distance flight. Despite a series of mishaps, all accomplished the trip of 1,330 miles in four days; in a flying time of 14½ hours. But on the return leg, four of the Ninaks had to drop out and only the remaining pair completed the flight.

In March 1925, both Ninak units moved to occupy Miranshah Fort—the first RAF units to do so (although this Army post had been used in the past as an emergency landing ground on occasion). From March 9 to May 1 1925, all RAF units were engaged in operations—later titled unofficially 'Pink's War'—when, for the first time ever, the RAF was permitted to conduct a complete 'campaign' independent of the Army. In the 54 days of actual operations, a total of 2,720 hours was flown by all units. Only two casualties resulted—the crew of a 27 Squadron Ninak which was shot down by rifle-fire. This impressive demonstration of the efficacy of pure aerial power was to prove a turning point in military thinking in India.

Top
H3627, 'C II' of No. 55 Squadron displaying some of the earliest unit markings of the post-1918 era to receive official approval. Fin and fuselage checks were in Black and Flight colour: Light Blue, C Flight; Yellow, B Flight and Red, A Flight. (Photo: MOD (Air)

The beginning of the aluminium/silver-doped aircraft finishes, well depicted by this line-up of No. 27 Squadron's Ninaks in India. Individual aircraft letters A to M incl. were used by No. 27; the remainder of the alphabet by a sister unit, 60 Squadron.

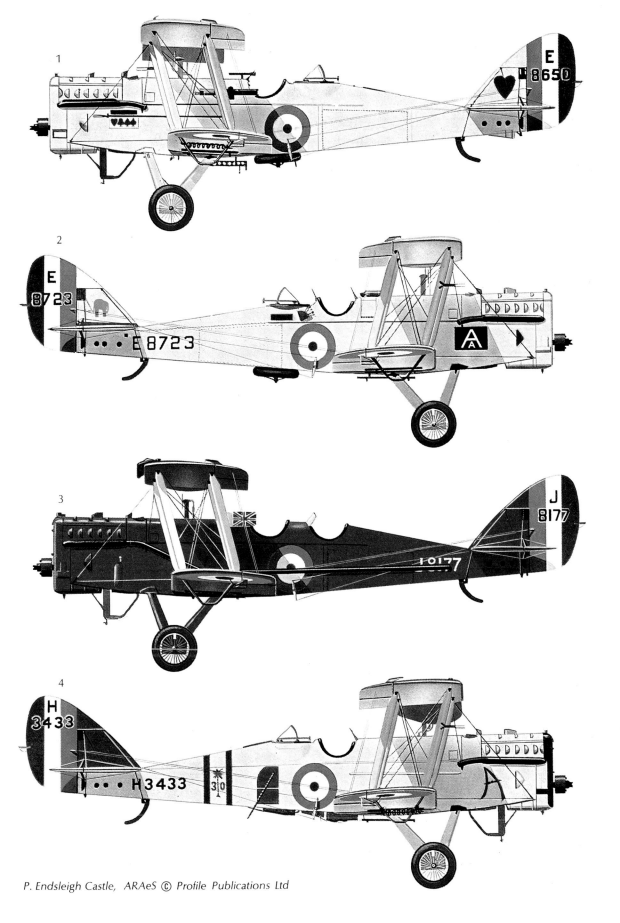

1

E
8650

2

E
8723

E 8723

3

J
8177

I 0177

4

H
3433

H 3433

P. Endsleigh Castle, ARAeS © Profile Publications Ltd

A self-explanatory view of typical terrain on India's North-West Frontier over which the Ninak crews had to operate in the 1920s, without benefit of parachutes. J7340, 'L' of No. 27 Squadron at 4,500 ft. over the region between Spin Wam and Miranshah, April 1928. (Photo: Mrs D. Cowton)

Bombed up and raring to go. D.H.9A, 'B' of A Flight, No. 27 Squadron (Flying Officers Holdway and F. G. S. Mitchell) at Miranshah, India, 1924. (Photo: AVM F. G. S. Mitchell, CB, CBE)

E828 ('A') and J7340 ('L') of No. 27 Squadron flying as aerial escort to the royal train of Amir Amanullah of Afghanistan, December 10 1927, over Chaman. On February 14 1928, Flight Lieutenant S. Graham, MC, crashed badly in E828, resulting in the Ninak being written-off and Graham being repatriated to England for hospitalization. (Photo: Author's collection)

Bottom left
E8742, 'H' of No. 27 Squadron airborne, January 14 1925, prior to setting out on the first-ever Risalpur-Calcutta long distance proving flight.

Gaudy conversion of a Ninak by No. 60 Squadron. H3626 modified as a two-seat hack communication transport. (See colour side view). (Photo: Author's collection)

Attempts to improve the useful performance of the Ninak had little success. On January 18 1926, Flight Lieutenant (later Air Chief Marshal Sir John) Baker of 60 Squadron tested the first all-metal propeller on a Ninak in India; while on October 17 1927, Baker piloted the first test (in India) of airborne oxygen equipment. These improvements were to a great extent nullified by the many extraneous impedimenta with which an operational aircraft was festooned. Apart from its nominal warload, a Ninak usually carried a spare wheel bolted on to the fuselage (in some cases, rather illogically, *under* the fuselage), while necessary equipment such as bed-roll, water bag (usually made from an animal skin), emergency rations and crews' personal kit were attached or hung on various points around the fuselage or under the lower wings. On occasion, the Ninak was called on for mercy flights, carrying wounded from forward landing grounds to base hospital facilities; the patient being strapped into a Neil Robertson stretcher on top of the fuselage immediately behind the gunner's cockpit. The Ninak bore them all stoically and continued to give sterling service; an example being the operations flown on November 15-16 1928 when Ninaks of 60 Squadron alone flew 117 hours on 59 individual sorties and dropped 146 × 112 lb. bombs, 36 × 20 lb. and four containers of incendiaries. Yet another 'encumbrance' added to the Ninak's load in December 1928 was the first issue in India of parachutes for crews—a device not so universally welcomed by pilots as might have been expected.

On December 17 1928, came an urgent request from the British Legation at Kabul for an air evacuation of all British subjects; the Legation being surrounded by an army of revolutionary tribes attempting to oust the contemporary Afghan king. The request posed a serious problem for the RAF which had no transport aircraft in its command—the nearest

such unit being 70 Squadron in Iraq. Bristol F.2Bs had insufficient range to assist any such evacuation and, on December 23, the only feasible aircraft immediately available were 24 D.H.9As, one Vickers Victoria troop-carrier and two Westland Wapitis (see *Profile* No. 32). These were immediately stripped of all war equipment and pressed into service for the airlift. In January-February 1929, the Ninaks continued to escort No. 70's Victorias through the mountains despite the worst winter conditions seen in India for many years—taking off in 17 inches of snow and suffering untold agonies in open cockpits through icy blizzards. That they succeeded in completing this first-ever historic evacuation in such desperate circumstances was a tribute to both crews and aircraft.

By the end of 1928, the long-promised extra two units for RAF India had arrived, 11 and 39 Squadrons, each equipped with Wapiti IIAs. But it was not until March 8 1930, that the first Wapiti replacement arrived on B Flight, 60 Squadron. Within eight weeks No. 60 had fully exchanged their veteran Ninaks for the more modern bombers; while in April, 27 Squadron also began re-equipment with Wapitis.

Middle/Near East

Apart from her Empire commitments, Britain's immediate post-1918 responsibilities included several mandated territories in the Middle East area; of which the largest in terms of sheer size was Mesopotamia. Beset by Turkish ambitions in the north and fierce internal dissension between the many tribal sheikhdoms, 'Mespot' (as it was familiarly known by British Servicemen) presented formidable problems of control.

The Cairo Conference in March 1921 approved in principle a scheme proposed by the Chief of Air Staff, RAF, Hugh Trenchard, whereby final control and responsibility for the area would belong to the RAF. Actual control was assumed on October 1 1921 and three weeks later Air

F2858, 'M' of B Flight, 8 Squadron, flown by Flying Officer
N. H. F. Unwin (later, Wing Commander, MBE) in Iraq, 1924.

P. Endsleigh Castle, ARAeS © Profile Publications Ltd

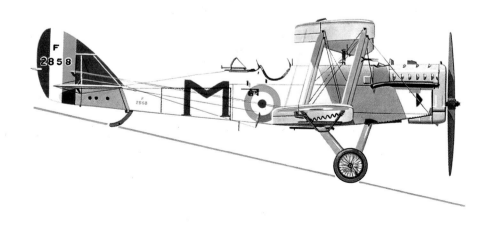

The 'Racing Red Nines'. VIP Ninaks appropriately coloured for easy distinction. All were doped overall in blood-red, with white strutting. J8177 was the personal transport of AVM Sir Robert Brooke-Popham . . .

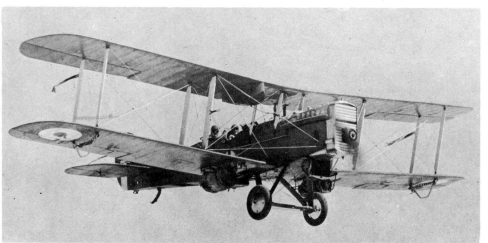

. . . E8754 of AVM Sir John Salmond (piloted here by Flight Lieutenant A. G. Jones-Williams) . . .

. . . and J6959 was the private hack of AVM Sir Edward Ellington, AOC-in-C, RAF Middle East, 1928.

A splendid view of a Ninak which epitomizes the 'Christmas Tree' capability of the type. H3510, 'L' of B Flight, No. 8 Squadron, based at Hinaidi, seen here flying over Baghdad and the Tigris River. Pilot was Flight Lieutenant A. G. Jones-Williams and gunner, Flight Sergeant Benson.

Vice-Marshal Sir John Salmond took up his appointment as the first Air Officer Commanding, Iraq[1]. Among other units, Salmond had at his disposal four squadrons of D.H.9As, Nos. 8, 30, 55 and 84. All had already been 'blooded' on operations in Mesopotamia during the previous year. No. 30 Squadron was restored from cadre to full strength on February 1 1920, at Baghdad West, equipped with a mixture of R.E.8s (see Profile No. 85) and D.H.9As, but by April was dispersed in three places—A Flight being at Baghdad, B Flight 400 miles to the north-east at Kasvin and C Flight at Mosul. Part of their operational commitment included 'disruption' of Bolshevik shipping around the port of Resht on the southern shore of the Caspian Sea. Flying dawn bombing raids each day, the 30 Squadron pilots were amazed to meet air opposition in the shape of several Avro 504s—actually, Russian-built U-1s ('Uchebnii' or 'Instructional').

No. 55 Squadron was also reformed on February 1 1920, when 142 Squadron at Suez was renumbered. Equipped initially with D.H.9s, No. 55 received Ninaks in June and, by the end of September 1920, arrived in Constantinople; flying its first operations in October. No. 84 Squadron reformed at Baghdad on August 13 1920 and soon moved to Shaibah in southern Iraq; which was to be its 'spiritual' home for the next two decades. The fourth Ninak unit, 8 Squadron, reformed at Helwan, Egypt, on October 18 1920, with D.H.9As and moved to Baghdad at the end of the year.

All four squadrons became involved in the widespread Arab revolt of 1919–20 when an estimated 200,000 Arabs attempted to throw off foreign control of their country. The British Army employed 120,000 troops during the conflict and suffered 876 killed and over 1,000 wounded. The air effort in support was pro-

digious. A total of $97\frac{1}{2}$ long tons of bombs was dropped and over 180,000 machine-gun bullets were expended during 4,000 hours of operational flying. The RAF lost 11 aircraft shot down, while a further 57 aircraft were rendered unfit to fly by accurate rifle fire from the 'rebels'.

Although these operations officially ceased by the end of 1920, the pattern of 'air policing' was to continue on an almost non-stop basis for the next 20 years. In May 1921, for example, 8 Squadron went into action against Surehi tribesmen, dropping 20 tons of bombs and flying 300 hours in an intensive ten-days period. And from June 14-16, No. 55 Squadron, in company with six Ninaks from 8 Squadron, dropped 10 tons of bombs during operations against a Turkish incursion at Rowanduz—the start of continuing anti-Turk sorties until the end of September.

In spite of the continuous operational status of the Ninaks in Iraq, they were by no means used solely on war-like pursuits. Indeed, the greater part of their efforts in the years 1920–30 in the Middle East concerned communications, air-mapping of the desert wastes and establishing new routes for the future civil air liners. On June 21 1921, Ninaks of 30 and 47 Squadrons initiated the Cairo-Baghdad mail run. No. 47 Squadron, reformed on February 1 1920—by renumbering 206 Squadron—was based at Helwan, Egypt; although one flight of their Ninaks had been almost immediately detached south to Khartoum and remained there until joined by the remainder of 47 in October 1927. The two squadrons again cooperated on opening up a permanent Cairo-Baghdad land route. Starting in May 1921, each unit supplied a Ninak escort for car convoys establishing a visible track across the Syrian desert. This primitive, but effective, route was officially 'open' on June 23 1921, and in the following year the track was literally ploughed along its 840 miles length, with emergency landing grounds being marked

[1] Mesopotamia was officially designated 'Iraq' in September 1921.—Author.

P. Endsleigh Castle, ARAeS © Profile Publications Ltd

every 20 miles as guide points for aircraft. It was the first stage of a projected 'All Red' route for mail and civil air transport to India and, eventually, Australia.

Operations soon became necessary again, however, when the self-styled 'King of Kurdistan', Sheikh Mahmoud began to assert himself by stirring anti-British rebellion in the Sulaimania district in 1922. On September 5 a force of 24 Ninaks, three Bristol F.2Bs and two Vickers Vernons evacuated a total of 67 British subjects plus a large quantity of guns and stores to Kirkuk—a little-publicized airlift which pre-dated the famous Kabul evacuation by several years. Bombing and reconnaissance sorties against Mahmoud's followers continued into 1923; although a large part of the Ninaks' duties included supply drops to army outposts and retrieving sick and wounded from positions otherwise inaccessible. One incident during bombing operations exemplified the courage

and initiative of the Ninak crews. A Ninak of 8 Squadron, piloted by Flying Officer N. Vintcent, was forced down close to the target he had just been bombing. As a vast crowd of Arabs closed in on the stranded crew, Vintcent positioned himself under the tail of the Ninak and lifted the aircraft bodily, while his passenger, Flight Lieutenant J. I. T. Jones, DSO, MC, DFC, MM—a noted wartime fighter 'ace'—made crisp use of the rear Lewis gun to ward off the vengeance-bent tribesmen. Vintcent continued to hoist the Ninak in different directions as each new threat approached for nearly an hour, before some Sopwith Snipes (see *Profile* No. 50) of 1 Squadron appeared and strafed the Arabs. Rescued by another D.H.9A, Vintcent was later awarded a Distinguished Flying Cross—the first RAF ex-Cranwell cadet to be so honoured.

In 1924, trouble erupted in Palestine when a force of 4,000 of Ibn Saud's fanatical Wahabi followers began plundering the country. On

Key to colour

J7338 of 47 Squadron, Helwan, Egypt, 1926.

J7607 of 55 Squadron, Iraq.

H3626, a two-seat local conversion of 60 Squadron, India.

J7818 of 39 Squadron, June 1926.

F2858, 'M' of B Flight, No. 8 Squadron (subject of the 5-view colour centrespread) after a forced landing in lava country, Palestine, 1924. The airman is raising the W/T aerial for communication. (Photo: Wing Commander N. H. F. Unwin, MBE)

'And on reflection . . .' Proof that the desert is not always arid. J7050, 'B' of No. 8 Squadron on Samawah advanced landing ground after a brief but torrential rainstorm. (Photo: Wing Commander N. H. F. Unwin, MBE)

Formation stuff in variety. H3529 (N), H3510 (L) and H3525 (P) of B Flight, No. 8 Squadron in broad Vic formation, 1926 . . .

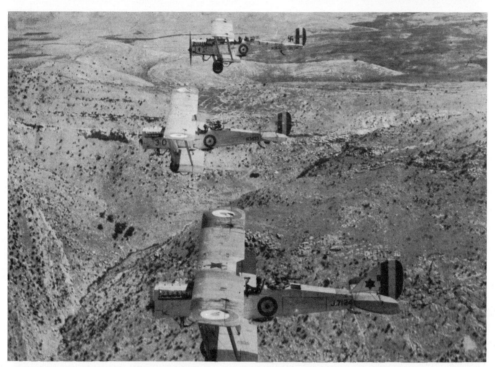

. . . Ninaks of No. 30 Squadron returning from a bombing raid on Sulamania 1924. In foreground, J7124 is piloted by Flight Lieutenant S. M. Kinkead, DSO, DSC, DFC; the leader, H3633, by 30's commander, Squadron Leader J. Robb (later ACM Sir James) while the far Ninak is H3632, piloted by Flying Officer 'Monkey' Sherlock. When the photo was snapped, Kinkead's Ninak still retained a 'hang-up' 230-lb. bomb, but he managed to unstick it before landing . . .

. . . and a neat example of line-abreast formation from No. 47 Squadron's Ninaks (B Flight) over their base station, Helwan, on December 24 1926. The fin check markings only applied to B Flight aircraft and were not (as frequently stated) a squadron marking.
(Photo: C. A. Sims)

August 14, Ninaks and Bristol F.2Bs, supporting a formation of RAF armoured cars, dispersed the Wahabis on the Ziza Plain, 12 miles south of Amman. The Ninaks were from 14 Squadron which had only recently re-equipped from their former Bristol F.2Bs. And in January 1925, No. 14 Squadron was again in action against some local dissidents; pioneering the use of a camel-mounted W/T (wireless-telegraphy) set for ground direction of their bombing sorties. In October 1925, Squadron Leader A. Coningham of 47 Squadron at Helwan, Egypt, led two other Ninaks, piloted by Flight Lieutenants Baggs and Rowley, on a long-distance formation flight to Kaduna in Nigeria. Leaving Helwan on October 27, the three Ninaks arrived in Nigeria on November 6 to a massive reception. It was the first time the residents there had ever *seen* an aeroplane! Returning to Helwan on November 19, the three Ninaks covered the round trip of 6,268 miles in 85 flying hours. One more Middle East unit employed D.H.9As; this was No. 45 Squadron which began conversion at Heliopolis on April 25 1927. In the same year, 8 Squadron was moved to Aden and began conversion to Fairey IIIFs (see *Profile* No. 44) in January 1928.

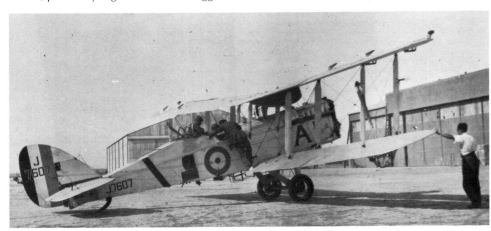

J7607, 'A' of 55 Squadron running-up, displays the mid-1920s unit marking of a red diagonal fuselage band. The squadron's unofficial badge, an uplifted arm with spear, appeared in black on the sides of the nose.
(Photo: D. I. Newman)

Before and After. A landing accident between J7321 (N) and J7102 of No. 8 Squadron on the southern frontier with Nedj territory during anti-Ibn Saud operations. Despite being deep in hostile country, both aircraft were hastily but effectively repaired by a working party airlifted in a Vickers Vernon and both Ninaks eventually flew back to base . . .

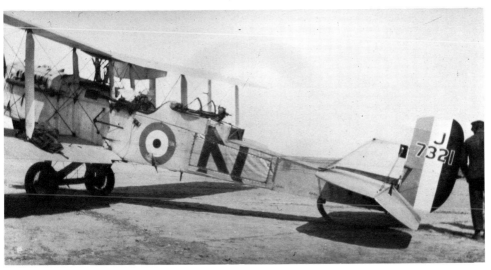

. . . The temporary repairs made to J7321 to permit air evacuation.
(Photo: Wing Commander N. H. F. Unwin, MBE)

Meanwhile in Iraq, 55 and 84 Squadrons again saw widespread action from January to June 1928, when they were detailed as part of 'Akforce' for operations against some 50,000 rebelling tribesmen in the Nedj territory. Although several Ninaks were lost to rifle-fire, all crews were rescued (usually in fraught conditions and under heavy fire) and the only RAF casualty was one pilot killed on February 20. No. 84's Ninaks performed a unique raid in May when they bombed the remote island of Gubbah, on the Hammar Lake, which had become one rebel sheikh's stronghold. Deliberately, the bombs were aimed against the bund (bank) surrounding the island, thus flooding the rebels out of their refuge—a sort of pre-'Dambusters' operation.

By 1928, however, the D.H.9A was rapidly becoming obsolete and all Ninak units soon began receiving more effective aircraft in their place. No. 47 Squadron at Khartoum exchanged their faithful 9As for Fairey IIIFs in April 1928; while No. 84 at Shaibah had two flights equipped with Wapitis by mid-September—its last Ninak leaving the unit in January 1929. No. 45 Squadron changed to IIIFs in September 1929; while 14 Squadron began re-equipment with IIIFs in December and was completely 'converted' by March 1930. No. 55 Squadron received its first Wapitis in February 1930, although it still had Ninaks on charge until the following year. Finally, 30 Squadron converted to Wapitis in 1930.

United Kingdom Service

With Trenchard's determination in the immediate postwar years to use the nucleus of his future Royal Air Force in an overseas 'police' role, the strength of the RAF in the UK was minimal. Having selected the D.H.9A as the standard light bomber, only two units were equipped with Ninaks initially. No. 207 Squadron was reformed at Bircham Newton on February 1 1920 as a day bomber formation, and in the following year, on April 1, No. 39 Squadron was also reformed as a Ninak unit at Bircham Newton. For several years these two squadrons remained the only RAF first-line Ninak units in England. In September 1922, No. 207's Ninaks were shipped to San Stefano, near Constantinople, as part of the RAF element facing Turkish incursion in Greece. After a year of non-action, and having endured a near-complete lack of reasonable maintenance facilities, No. 207 returned to England in September 1923 and took up residence at Eastchurch, on the Isle of Sheppey. Having settled into their new quarters, 207 became the vehicle for several forms of experiments, including the fitting of silencers for the Ninak engines, designed by the Royal Aircraft Establishment, Farnborough, Hampshire—although these proved virtually ineffective. In 1924, 207's Ninaks were also fitted with radio-telephony (R/T)—a refinement which proved of great help during the contemporary annual Royal Air Force Displays at Hendon.

With its sister unit, 39 Squadron, No. 207 became acknowledged as the finest exponents of bomber formation flying in the yearly 'Taxpayers' Benefit' (as the air display was referred to in Service circles). Replacements for 207's ageing Ninaks began arriving in December 1927—a mixture of Fairey IIIFs from Gosport and Hendon—and by February 1928 the squadron was fully re-equipped.

No. 39 Squadron moved base to Spittlegate in January 1928 and in November began receiving Wapitis as its new equipment. Once fully up to establishment, the squadron left the UK in February 1929 on route to India.

Several other units in the UK received Ninaks, albeit mainly for secondary duties. No. 11 Squadron which reformed at Andover on January 15 1923, was initially equipped with D.H.9As but, by April of the following year, had replaced these with Fairey Fawns. Meanwhile, at the Aeroplane and Armament Experimental Establishment, Martlesham Heath, 15 Squadron was reformed on March 20 1924 and was soon up to squadron strength with a full complement of Ninaks. For the next three years No. 15's Ninaks were employed in a wide variety of bomb ballistics trials and other experimental work and, in October 1926, the 9As were exchanged for Hawker Horsleys.

No. 3 Squadron, the RAF's senior aeroplane unit, received at least five examples of a Ninak three-seat conversion, known initially as the 'Tadpole'—possibly the ugliest version of the Ninak ever made. Specified as a Fleet Spotter, the Tadpole also served with Nos. 420 and 421 Flights, Gosport, and later became known as the Westland Walrus. Production of Walrus fleet spotters—36 in all—was made possible by utilizing the vast stocks of D.H.9 and D.H.9A components then available.

In common with most Service aircraft of the 1920s, the basic D.H.9A design was the vehicle for a vast diversity of modifications and experimental installations. These mainly concentrated on changes of engines and improvements in undercarriage designs. A reasonably small number of Ninaks was converted for use of the Napier Lion engine; one of these, E752, being used in 1920 for deck-landing trials on HMS *Eagle*, piloted by (among others) Flight Lieutenant R. E. Keys, DFC.

By the mid-1920s, the D.H.9A was rapidly approaching obsolescence, but the creation of the Auxiliary Air Force (AAF) brought a new lease of life for the doughty Ninak. The first AAF unit to be formed was 602 Squadron on September 15 1925, which took delivery of its first Ninak (H144) on October 7. Seven days later, three more Auxiliary squadrons, Nos. 600, 601 and 603, were formed; each equipped initially with D.H.9As. On October 15 1926, No. 605 Squadron came into being as a Ninak unit; while on March 17 1930, the last Auxiliary unit intended for Ninak equipment, No. 604 Squadron, formed at

Remarkable in-flight study of E8650 of A Flight, No. 84 Squadron from Shaibah, 1923. Pilot is Flying Officer F. F. Inglis (later AVM, CB, CBE). 'A' Flight used playing card symbols on fins for identification, in this case a Red Heart. Alongside nose can be seen all four Heart/Club/Spade/Diamond symbols in miniature. (Photo: C. A. Sims)

Yet another variety of unit symbolism. H3632 of No. 30 Squadron over Iraqi territory. Wing tips of 30 Sqn were painted in Flight colours (contrary to previous descriptions published). These were A Flight, Red; B Flight, Blue and C Flight, Black. Later, fins came to be doped accordingly.

Another pile-up, when Sergeant Walker of B Flight, No. 47 Squadron hit Flying Officer Coggle of A Flight during a formation landing. Of interest is the extension of B Flight's check markings under the tailplanes. The groundcrews, amazed that no one was injured, ponder on how long this mess will take to clean up . . . (Photo: C. A. Sims)

D.H.9A, E9891, factory-fresh from the production line of the Vulcan & Motoring Engineering Company.

B Flight of No. 39 Squadron at Spittlegate, Lincs, 1924, prior to a goodwill visit to France. Aircraft from left are F1611, E960 and J7073. The squadron number '39' appears in a small black circle on all fins. (Photo: AVM F. G. S. Mitchell, CB, CBE)

Practising for the public's benefit. No. 39 Squadron's immaculate Ninaks moving up into a precision line-abreast during rehearsal for an RAF Hendon Air Display. (Photo: G. S. Leslie/ J. M. Bruce)

Hendon. In the event, 604 Squadron received only two D.H.9As, being almost immediately issued with Wapitis. By the end of 1930 all of the AAF squadrons using Ninaks had exchanged them for Wapitis.

Unlike most of its wartime contemporaries, the Ninak found comparatively little application in civil use after the war. Eleven D.H.9As (E992 to E1002 inclusive) went to Canada and were used for several years, mainly in a communications role. A mere 12 found their way on to the British Civil Register. Today, the only known surviving example of a Ninak is a rather battered heap of main components of F1010, one of No. 110 Squadron's original complement of D.H.9As. Numbered '12A', this 9A was one of five shot down on September 25 1918 and captured virtually intact; its crew (Captain A. Inglis and Second Lieutenant W. G. Bodley) being uninjured and taken prisoner. The near-defunct remains of F1010 now reside in the Polish National Air Museum at Krakow.

Essentially a military aeroplane, the de Havilland D.H.9A was a rock foundation for the infant Royal Air Force. A patient, sturdy workhorse which served its crews faithfully and fulfilled its many roles, the Ninak has a secure niche in Royal Air Force history.

SPECIFICATION

Dimensions

Span (Both)	45 ft. 10¾ in.
Length	30 ft. 1½ in.
Height	11 ft. 3 in.
Chord	5 ft. 9 in.
Gap	5 ft. 10 3⁄16 in.
Track	6 ft. 0 in.
Stagger	1 ft. 4 in.
Tail Span	14 ft. 0 in.
Dihedral	3°
Incidence	3°
Propeller diameter	10 ft. (Liberty)

Weights

Empty	2,800 lb.
War Load	940 lb.
Fuel/Oil	905 lb.
Loaded	4645 lb.

Performance (Liberty 12)

Max. Speed	123 m.p.h. (sea level) 106 m.p.h. 15,000 ft.)
Climb to 10,000 ft.	15 min. 35 sec.
Climb to 15,000 ft.	33 min.
Service Ceiling	17,750 ft.
Endurance (normal)	5¼ hr.

Armament

One Vickers .303 (0.303-inch) machine-gun synchronized to fire forward.
One Lewis .303 gun on Scarff Ring in rear cockpit.
Bomb load up to max. 740 lb. carried under wings and fuselage.

A variation in No. 30 Squadron markings on H3433, showing twin fuselage bands in red with painted wing tips (for air identification if forced down in the desert). The squadron's (then) unofficial insignia of a single Palm Tree appeared between the fuselage bands. (Photo: R. C. B. Ashworth)

Above right
Clear view of the two cockpits of a D.H.9A, emphasizing the physical proximity of pilot and gunner so successful on operations.

Cockpit detail of a D.H.9A (400 h.p. Liberty) of 1918 vintage. Although this is a basic instrumentation, there are several additional instruments to norm to be seen here, eg the extra stop-watch at bottom and the added piping with turncock to left side. These were presumably fitted for a specific trial or experiment.

Hendon Air Pageant, 1924. No. 207 Squadron takes off prior to a 'bombing' attack on the 'enemy fleet' seen in background. To help tail-up, fast take-off, most gunners are standing at near-full height, leaning forward. (Photo: 'Flight International', ref. 0283)

The Ugly Sister—Westland's Walrus version, a three-seat Ninak with prone Observer's under-compartment, flotation bags (shown inflated), Napier Lion engine and forward hydrovane extended; it was not a success. (Photo: Westland Aircraft Limited)

SERVICE USE

UK
Squadrons: 3, 11, 15, 22, 24, 25, 39, 100, 207, 212, 273, 501, 600, 601, 602, 603, 604, 605.

Cranwell
Halton
Fowlmere
Waddington
Digby
Netheravon (1 FTS)
Duxford (2 FTS)
Shotwick (5 FTS)
Spittlegate (7 FTS)
Manston (6 FTS)
Eastchurch (AGS)
Leuchars (Station Flight)
Hawkinge

France/Germany
Squadrons: 18, 99, 110, 205, USMC (NB Group)

Middle/Near East
Squadrons: 8; 14; 30; 45; 47; 55; 84
Abu Sueir (4 FTS)

Russia
Squadrons: 47; 221.
RAF Training Mission

India
Squadrons: 99; 27; 60

Examples of D.H.9As used

3 Squadron	H3512, H3515, H3518, H3539, H3540 (All 3-seat conversions).
8 Squadron	E785, E954, E886, E8622, E8754, H24, H110, H175, H3510, H3525, H3628, J7050, J7102, J7321, J8194, J8195, J8200, J8201.
14 Squadron	J7035, J7067, J7116, J7254, J7829, J7839, J7831, J8098, J8101, J8197, J8203.
18 Squadron	E8415, F1018, F1042, F1051.
24 Squadron	J7310.
25 Squadron	E9705.
27 Squadron	E728, E844, E911, E993, E1098, E2772, E8389, E8468, E8573, E8636, E8660, E8674, E8722, E8761, E8799, E9683, E9948, F1098, F2772, H23, H41, H95, H3450, H3528, J7055, J7125, J7242, J7340, J7342, J7343, J7347.
30 Squadron	E773, E802, E843, E944, E961, E8512, F2815, H90, H3433, H3504, H3632, J7114, J7881, J8192.
39 Squadron	E812, E873, E948, E8491, E8631, E8673, F1611, F2851, J7037, J7067, J7613, J7792, J7812, J8105, J8133, J8143, J8152, J8170, H3552.
45 Squadron	J7832.
47 Squadron	E850, E959, E993, E8662, F1086, F1641, H3519, H3522, H3635, J7086, JR7107, J7119, J7842.
55 Squadron	E8512, E8640, E8796, E8806, E9885, E9909, F2775, F2833, F2842, F2850, H53, H77, H88, H3430, H3523, H3627, J565, J7104, J7256, J7305, J7607, J7850, J8102, J8147, J8176.
60 Squadron	E785, E878, E951, E8584, E8655, E8660, E8685, E8721, E8758, E8799, E9925, E9888, F979, F2812, H3528, H3632, J7091, J7109, J7341.
84 Squadron	E803, E849, E899, E8601, E8650, E8741, H22, H165, J6961, J7013, J7026, J7027, J7854.
99 Squadron	E720, E8560, E8561, F967, F977, F1035, F2739, H3410.
110 Squadron	E703, E8410, E8421, E8439, E8481, E8523, E9660, E9711, F977, F980, F984, F986, F992, F1000, F1005, F1010, F1021, F1029, F1065.
205 Squadron	E8413, E9029, E9707, F990, F1001, F1007, F1025, F1618.
207 Squadron	E852, E871, E8754, E8805, F1616, H138, J556, J561, J6964, J7038, J7041, J7048, J7611.
600 Squadron	J8116, J8154, J8165, J8184, J8223, J8502.
601 Squadron	E8605, J7319, J7835, J8108, J8221, J8478.
602 Squadron	H144.
603 Squadron	J8136, J8472.
604 Squadron	J7319, J8472.
605 Squadron	E8656, E8711, J7814, J8107, J8208, J8480.
Cranwell	F1636, H3488, J7317.
Fowlmere	E9664.
Old Sarum	F1635.
Halton	E9891, J8103.
Digby	18489.
4 FTS	E890, E914, E961, E8642, E8794, E9887, F2743, F2816, F2857, J7022, J8098, JR8188, J8202.
5 FTS	J7077, J7348.

No. 2 CAF Squadron—F2749, F2755.
USMC, Northern BG—E736, E8452, E8463, E8470, E8480, E8501, E8538, E8540, E8565, E8570, E8632, E9868, E9870, E9873, E9874, E9876.
RAF Training Mission, Russia—F1089, F1094.

Series Editor: CHARLES W. CAIN

Unusual photo depicting three Douglas R4D transports in formation. After 31 years of service the type is still used by the US Navy, Marine Corps and Army, but is slowly and gracefully being retired.
(Photo: National Archives, 80-G-390602)

Douglas R4D variants (USN's DC-3/C-47s)

by Arthur Pearcy Jnr, ARAeS

'The R4D has again proven herself a valuable friend and the "Grand Old Lady" of Antarctic Operations. She is economical and durable, and her versatility in short range, open field ski operations remains undisputed. It is not difficult to foresee the day, perhaps in the near future, when an equally versatile, longer-range, greater-payload, higher-flying turboprop replaces the old warrior, but until that day comes, treat her kindly, keep her warm, push the right JATO buttons, and navigate clear of all obstacles.'

**Commander M. D. Greenwell, USN
Commanding Officer VX-6 Sq, Deep Freeze 62.**

US Navy Douglas Commercials

As early as 1934, the United States Navy purchased its first example of the Douglas Commercial Two. Four more DC-2s followed and all

bore the US Navy model designation of R2D-1 and the assigned serial numbers of 9620 to 9622 and 9993 to 9994[1] (*see Table 1 for complete list of BuNos.*). The last two were allocated to the US Marine Corps at Quantico, Virginia, where—subsequently and among other applications—Marines gained airborne experience as paratroopers.

The R2D-1s provided performance advances and advantages so far removed from the ageing Curtiss R4C Condor two-motor biplane and

---

[1] As William T. Larkins points out in his book *US Navy Aircraft, 1921–1941* (Aviation History Publications, Concord, Calif, published 1961), Navy serial numbers have been traditionally the responsibility of the Bureau of Aeronautics and began in 1917 as 'Building Numbers'. Progressively they became 'Designating Numbers' until 1937, when they were termed 'Assigned Serial Numbers'. Following World War Two they have become popularly known as 'Bureau Numbers' (first as 'BuAer Nos.', then 'BuNos.').—Editor.

Douglas DC-2-125 US Navy model R2D-1 (BuNo. 9622, c/n. 1327) which was delivered to San Diego NAS on December 21 1934 and was destroyed by fire at this Naval Air Station on January 31 1941.
(Photo: Douglas Aircraft ref. 7219)

The first R4D-2 (BuNo. 4707, c/n. 4097) a DC-3-388 originally intended for Eastern Air Lines, went to Anacostia NAS and is seen at San Francisco during November 1941. It was struck-off-charge at Jacksonville NAS on May 31 1946.
(Photo: William T. Larkins)

Photo taken during late 1941 when seven horizontal red and six white stripes were added to US Navy and Marine Corps aircraft. They were removed in June 1942. Depicted is one of the two R4D-2s used by the US Navy in drab finish and carrying the new tail markings.
(Photo: National Archives, 80-G-5169)

Father J. P. Mannia, first chaplain to join the Paramarines and jump with his men, is shown leaving the open door of an R4D-1 (BuNo. 3140, c/n. 4280) which served with the Marine Corps at Cherry Point. It was struck-off-charge on August 31 1946.
(Photo: Imperial War Museum, NY8513)

Early model Douglas R4D seen over the rugged terrain of the Aleutians. Navigation aids were few and far between and the weather was not always as clear as the photo tends to illustrate. Snow remained on the high peaks throughout the year.
(Photo: National Archives, 80-G-377474)

Ford RR Tri-Motor monoplanes they were replacing that, henceforth, the Navy was to maintain a strong preference for the successive Douglas Commercials in military form for many years to come. In fact, at the time of writing, there is no sign of the 'Grand Old Lady' being pensioned-off.

Of the five R2D-1s, the first three served from Naval Air Stations Anacostia (Washington, DC), Pensacola (Florida) and San Diego (California). The remaining two R2D-1s—for the USMC at Quantico—were assigned to Utility Squadron Six (VJ-6M; from July 1937 redesignated VMJ-1) of Aircraft One, US Fleet Marine Force. All five R2D-1s were powered by 710 h.p. Wright R-1820 'Cyclone 9' single-row, 9-cylinder radials.

The R4Ds

A year after World War Two had broken out, the Navy was permitted to order more Douglas Commercials. On September 16 1940, the USN signed an initial contract for 30 R4D-1s (another 103 were purchased eventually), powered by 1,200 h.p. Pratt & Whitney R-1830 'Twin Wasp' two-row, 14-cylinder radials.

The R4D-1 was basically a commercial-standard DC-3 and the first to be delivered was not available until February 1942. This R4D-1 was built at the Douglas Long Beach plant as 4204 (constructor's number or c/n) and was assigned the Bureau Number 3131.

The only R4Ds with R2D-type Wright R-1820s the Navy ever possessed were two R4D-2s. These became available a year before the first R4D-1. NAS Anacostia was allocated one (c/n 4097; BuNo. 4707; impressed ex-Eastern Air Lines), while NAS Pensacola received the other one (c/n 4098; BuNo. 4708; also ex-Eastern). These two R4D-2s had a USAAF equivalent in the C-49D variant. Later on they were given additional suffix letters; first as R4D-2F, and then R4D-2Z, to indicate their VIP flagship interiors.

The Naval Air Transport Service (NATS) was established on December 12 1941, only five days after Pearl Harbor, under the Chief of Naval Operations to provide rapid air delivery of critical equipment and spare parts and special personnel to naval facilities and Fleet forces all over the world.

Douglas transports intended for the NATS organization were diverted from the production lines at Santa Monica and Long Beach, being designated as Douglas R4D with the appropriate 'dash number' to indicate their production block. They had certain minor aircrew and interior equipment changes. Items such as engines, propellers, instruments and other loose items of necessity to naval aircraft were supplied from US Navy stores.

These particular R4Ds were procured by the US Army Air Forces' Materiel Command for the US Navy with funds from the Navy appropriation. Various models of this period were used as personnel transports, air medical evacuation, cargo transports, and so on.

Prior to World War Two, procurement of USN aircraft from the Douglas Aircraft Company had been handled entirely by Navy procurement agencies. With the advent of World War Two, however, it was considered to be more expedient to place one large military contract, and subsequently to allocate blocks of transports for naval use—in accordance with their logistic requirements.

The basic naval R4D designation for the DC-3 aircraft configuration was simply commercial DC-3 transports fitted with an oversize loading door and were comparable to the USAAF C-53 transport. The exterior paint finish was in olive drab camouflage, spare parts were interchangeable with the USAAF C-47 Skytrain, as were the various accessory components.

Most of the 600-odd R4D transports procured for the US Navy during World War Two came from USAAF contracts. Consequently, the seven main variants in the R4D series each had a USAAF equivalent and carried the same popular names. The R4D-1 was a cargo transport counterpart of the C-47 Skytrain.

Ex-airline R4Ds used as personnel transports were the R4D-3 and the R4D-4 which, respectively, were equivalent to the USAAF's C-53 and C-53C Skytrooper.

Later major US Navy cargo transport variants were the R4D-5 (with a 24-Volt electric system, matching the C-47A Skytrain), the R4D-6 (equivalent to the C-47B) and the R4D-7, identical to the TC-47B navigation trainer.

R4Ds in the Pacific War
With the Japanese increasing their activities in the Aleutian Islands waters, the Douglas transports extended the routes to bases on Kiska, Attu, Adak and Aguttu. Where once the frozen land of the North was serviced only by the occasional 'bush pilot' operators, now the territory had become a busy aerial supply route. US Navy versions of the DC-3—the first of the R4Ds operating with NATS squadrons—were used to service Fleet units building up in the area.

The Alaska-Aleutians flying operations provided a challenge that put the aircraft to supreme tests. The extreme sub-zero weather

conditions and the salt-water atmosphere played strange tricks with engines, tyres, airframe and metal skin, hydraulic lines, brakes and other mechanical features. Oil became as thick as molasses, rubber fittings crystallized, grease froze in wheel bearings and the windshields iced-up and frosted over.

Crews learned how to winterize the rugged transports for adaption to the sometimes 40 to 50 degrees below zero temperatures. The Douglas transports came through with flying colours.

The US Navy, in an official 'well-done' statement after the Japanese gave up in the Aleutians said: 'Retaking the Aleutians would have been postponed for months if air transport had not been able to fly in men and cargo quickly and in great quantities.'

It was a similar story at Guadalcanal in the Solomons. Following the battle of Savo Island, 14 specially-equipped Marine Corps R4Ds were flown from San Diego to New Caledonia and under Southern Combat Air Transport (SCAT), they maintained a daily service into Henderson Field on Guadalcanal.

SCAT was one of the tools of the Commander Air South Pacific (COMAIRSOPAC). Their unarmed R4Ds ran regular schedules between New Zealand, Noumea, Efate, Espiritu Santo, and Guadalcanal. As the US forces built or captured

An R4D-6 (BuNo. 50821) of the Naval Air Transport Service (NATS) taken at Oakland NAS on April 1 1946. Note that the BuNo. is repeated on the nose. Also see photo of same aircraft after conversion to model R4D-8 on page 69. (Photo: William T. Larkins)

An R4D-3 Skytrooper (BuNo. 06996) of the Marine Corps seen at Alameda NAS, California on March 6 1946. This model was similar to the commercial DC-3 and the USAAF C-53. (Photo: William T. Larkins)

Only 17 Douglas R4D-4 transports were built. Photo depicts BuNo. 07003 of the Naval Air Transport Service (NATS) at Oakland NAS on April 9 1946. Two-star rear admiral insignia is carried aft of the cockpit. Model was similar to the DC-3. (Photo: William T. Larkins)

The Douglas R4D transport operated in all theatres of operation during World War Two. Photo shows an R4D over the Sugar Loaf Mountain, Rio de Janiero. (Photo: National Archives, 80-G-390598)

airfields up the Solomons chain of islands, the line was extended to them. Most flights combined passengers and cargo. When operations required, SCAT transports made all sorts of special deliveries of material and personnel.

These R4D transports and others which were added to the SCAT command flew a total of almost 1,000 sorties—aggregating 1,000,000 miles—into Guadalcanal; and, on each flight out, they carried wounded back to base hospitals.

When Japanese dive-bombers blew up a ship which had rushed in gasoline two days after the enemy had destroyed fuel dumps on the island, it meant there was no aviation spirit for the Army Air Forces' fighters based on Henderson Field. They called on the R4Ds who flew in 600 US gallons of fuel on each sortie. This was kept up for a week before surface ships arrived.

The SCAT R4Ds had two extra fuel tanks in the cabin, just aft of the cockpit bulkhead. Oval in section and about six foot long they were, supposedly, bullet-proof and rested on shaped athwartships timbers. A six-inch wide plank nailed to the timbers between the tanks was a catwalk to the cockpit. Aft of the tanks the sides were lined with bucket seats which could be folded to give more space for cargo. Even when the seats were occupied, some cargo was lashed to the floor between them.

For the retaliatory invasion of Guadalcanal in August 1942, all land-based aircraft of the USAAF, USN, US Marine Corps and Royal New Zealand Air Force—comprising about 291 aircraft—was commanded by a naval COMAIR-SOPAC and a great airfield was constructed on the island of Espiritu Santo in the New Hebrides group. A partly-built airfield was taken over by the US forces on Guadalcanal and, as Henderson Field, played a major part in the ensuing campaign.

Throughout the Pacific campaign, SCAT operated its regular schedule; which eventually extended as far as Australia. A typical SCAT unit was contained in the 3rd Marine Amphibious Corps which had an Air Delivery Unit as part of what came to be known as the 'Cactus Air Force'. These unarmed R4D-1s and early C-47s—for, like the crews, the transport models were mixed—carried a variety of loads which ranged from flying in supplies to New Zealand troops at Bougainville to dropping supplies and troops by parachute.

During 1943–44, Carrier Aircraft Service Unit 19 (CASU 19) was located at Banika Island in the Russell Islands and at Segi Point and Munda—both on New Georgia Island. Segi Point was a true backwater of the war, being a 2,200-foot strip of crushed coral with the jungle at one end and the open sea at the other. On one side was a bluff about 200 ft high and the other was bordered by a lagoon. The task of the personnel of CASU 19 was to service any Navy aircraft which flew in. Spare parts required were flown in by SCAT Douglas R4D transports.

The Marine Corps combat air transport group with its Douglas transports carried cargoes which included virtually every conceivable item used by Allied units in the Pacific Theatre of Operations. When the lift included urgent medical evacuees, jeeps, oxygen bottles, fighter aircraft belly-tanks, flame throwers, fresh meat and food, medical supplies, ammunition, mail and troops, the gross load limit was often exceeded by a ton. On occasions, the overload exceeded the gross weight limit applicable to sister transports flying with various US airlines by as much as two tons.

A Marine Corps R4D was first to land at Green Island, north-west of the Solomons and second in at Emirau Island in the Bismark Archipelago. They participated in the Munda push, transporting parapacks to be dropped to the Marines below. One of the R4Ds came overseas on August 1 1943, following a long flight from Camp Kearny, California, to Tontoula, New Caledonia, and was immediately put into service. On a flight between Guadalcanal and Espiritu Santos, New Hebrides, this transport was lost for three hours in a storm. The aircraft battery cell had blown out, leaving the instruments useless. With a cargo of stretcher patients aboard, the navigator was as bewildered as the crew but, with amazing good fortune, they completed the flight. By July 1945, this R4D was flying on its fourth complete change of engines, and its tenth complete tyre change.

Another R4D was taken straight from the Long Beach production line as SCAT was in the midst of rapid expansion. Following its commission to active duty on March 10 1943, this transport became a familiar sight as Marine Corps pilots set it down in the Carolines, Admiralties, Solomons, Russells, Hollandia, New Guinea, Auckland and Sydney. Like the other R4Ds in the group, it lifted an average gross weight of 28,500 pounds on each flight. In the beginning of the Munda campaign, when Seabees (Navy Construction Battalions) were grading out the shell- and bomb-pitted landing strip, this Douglas transport flew in from Guadalcanal with nearly two tons of badly needed supplies. Three weeks after Smar was invaded and the Seabees were grading the mud and coral landing strip, it flew in with a precious cargo of jettisonable belly tanks for USMC Chance Vought F4U Corsair fighters.

Three Japanese 'Betty' (Mitsubishi G4M) Navy bombers caught an R4D of the group on the ground at Manus Island, Bismark Archipelago. One of the bombs exploded within 30 yards of the parked transport, tearing a hole in the nose, ahead of the pilot's feet. In less than 18 months this R4D had logged a total of 1,900 hours and flown 285,000 air miles.

In a typical four weeks operations report, this SCAT group logged 2,400 combat flying hours in 948 flights, carried 1,320,848 pounds of freight, 543,629 lb. of mail, 7,034 passengers and 198 medical evacuees. The grand total of passenger, mail, cargo and medical evacuees, over the typical four-week period, equals 610,051 ton-miles. Twenty per cent. of this amazing figure involved instrument flying conditions and was accomplished by a hundred or so transport pilots averaging 24 years of age and 60 hours of transport flying within combat areas per month.

The pilots were drawn from the Navy, Marines and Army Air Force. They did a phenominal job, especially so as the majority was just out of flight school and woefully lacking in general flight experience. Most of the aircraft had external art expressions—nudes of course! —for adornment. And names to go with them; 'Vulgar Virgin', for example, was just one which survived many of the battles in the Pacific.

SCAT performed essential services in a highly commendable way. Without the R4Ds and their willing young aircrews, most certainly the Solomons campaign would have taken longer, cost more lives or, even perhaps, have failed.

When the Solomon campaign ended in 1944 the remnants of SCAT and a Marine Air Wing were located on Bougainville and were transferred to the Southwest Pacific Command. By the end of the Pacific War, one SCAT group embraced a distance of 3,360 statute miles, employing 14 landing strips and operational stations and engaging 550 pilots and 825 crew members.

Operation High Jump

The US Navy's *Operation High Jump,* with 13 ships and 4,000 men was the largest Antarctic expedition ever organised. Led by Admirals Richard E. Byrd and Richard H. Cruzen, it photographed most of the continent's coastline during 1946–47.

A total of 26 aircraft accompanied the US Navy expedition. This air armada was made up of six Douglas R4D-5 transports, six Martin PBM Mariner flying-boats, two Curtiss SOC Seagulls, two Grumman J2F-6 Ducks, two Convair OY-1 Sentinels, a Noorduyn JA-1 Norseman on skis, and a selection of seven Sikorsky helicopters— one HNS-1, two HOS-1s and four HO3S-1s— which operated from platforms on the forward deck of the ice-breakers. Most of the aircraft were painted bright orange for visibility reasons. The six Douglas R4D transports were equipped with JATO bottles for take-off from the aircraft carrier USS *Philippine Sea* (CVA-47) and were taken on board at Norfolk, Virginia during the last few days of December 1946.

In preparing for the operation the US Navy, after examining the aircraft available, decided to use the six ski-equipped Douglas R4Ds to conduct exploratory flights from the base at Little America IV. Because it was assumed—incorrectly, as later events were to show—that the distance from New Zealand to Antarctica exceeded the transports range, they would be launched from the deck of the aircraft carrier at the edge of the pack ice. This could be done with the aid of JATO—jet assisted take-off— then a comparatively new device.

A carrier take-off in any aircraft was a new experience for most *High Jump* pilots as not more than two had previous carrier experience. Pilots and crews were nominated for the expedition by Commander Air Pacific (COMAIRPAC), Commander Air Atlantic (COMAIRLANT), and Commander of the Marine Corps Aviation. The units executive officer was Major R. Weir, USMC.

Because of space limitations the Douglas transports were placed at the edge of number two elevator. On take-off they were angled slightly to starboard. Fifteen foot bamboo poles were set up on either side of the flight deck to guide the pilots on take-off. Some pilots cut their JATO in immediately the aircraft began its take-off run, others waited until the R4D was a third way down the deck. Both systems worked equally well. Each aircraft used four JATO bottles for the take-off.

Load weights had been carefully computed. Each transport carried five passengers and the varied gear was equalised to give each R4D the

The USS Philippine Sea *(CVA-47) with six Douglas R4D transports on the deck passes through the Panama Canal en route to the Antarctic. Date was January 8 1947. The aircraft were taken on board at Norfolk, Virginia. (Photo: National Archives, 80-G-615041)*

One of the six R4D-5 transports used in Operation Highjump *seen taking off from the flight deck of the USS* Philippine Sea *(CVA-47) for the flight to Little America on January 29 1947. (Photo: National Archives, 80-G-609327)*

Framed by the implements of the Antarctic, two R4D-5s from Operation Highjump *are seen parked at the Little America base. Note that the wheels have been removed completely. (Photo: National Archives, 80-G-614082)*

Douglas R4D-5 (BuNo. 17097) of the Naval Air Reserve with unusual nose markings. Tail code indicates 'F' for Oakland, 'R' for transport type. Photo taken at Oakland NAS, California on October 23 1947. (Photo: William T. Larkins)

same load. One aircraft carried a special set of camera equipment so that a good appraisal of the ice pack could be made. Other aircraft carried spare skis and fittings. Crew members were limited to 15 lb. of baggage. The landing skis were developed by the Federal Aircraft works in Minneapolis and trials were carried out on the snow fields of Montana. The ski gear consisted of an aluminium toboggan shaped runner for each wheel. A hole in the underside of the ski permitted the wheels to extend through to run on the deck. With a full load on board there was a two-inch clearance between the deck and the skis on take-off. Although the skis retracted with the undercarriage the front curved portion covered part of the engines air scoop, but the decreased capacity did not interfere in cold weather operations. The entire ski installation increased the weight of the R4D by 1,105 lb. Installation for the JATO and modifications for the skis were made by the Naval Air Station at Quonset Point, Rhode Island, later to be the home base of Air Development Squadron Six (VX-6) who were to continue using the Douglas R4D transport in Antarctica for many seasons.

The base at Little America IV was 660 miles away as the USS *Philippine Sea* turned into wind and the first Douglas R4D—BuNo. 12415 radio call-sign 'Victor 1'—roared down the deck, streaming smoke from its JATO bottles. This was another first for the ubiquitous Douglas DC-3. The first carrier take-off with an R4D was made about three hours before midnight—12:14 GMT—on January 29 1947, dusk in these latitudes with Cdr William M. (Trigger) Hawkes, USN, as pilot and with Rear Admiral Richard E. Byrd on board. It circled over the carrier for seventeen minutes until the second R4D BuNo. 17101 got airborne. In company, the two pioneers made the 600-mile flight to Little America IV, where they were sighted six hours and ten minutes later. Hawkes had no difficulty in locating the marked landing area and touched down at 05:16 local time—18:16 GMT—on January 30. Rear Admiral H. Cruzen, USN, Task Force Commander, was on hand to greet Admiral Byrd. When the two veterans of the United States Antarctic Service Expedition of 1939–41 met, Admiral Byrd reportedly said, 'Well, we're home again.'

Once the *Philippine Sea* learned of the safe arrival of the two R4D transports, the other four were launched—BuNo. 17197 at 18:33 GMT, BuNo. 17238 at 18:44 GMT, BuNo. 17237 at 19:07 GMT and BuNo. 39092 at 19:18 GMT with radio call-signs 'Victor 3' to 'Victor 6'—and made their way to Little America IV. The ski-wheel combination had accomplished its purpose, but three inches of wheel protruding through the skis was found to cause excessive drag when taxiing on snow. The wheels were therefore removed from all six aircraft and on two of them, the slots in the skis covered by an improvised

plate. This innovation, however, proved to have no significant effect on the aircraft performance.

Operations over the Antarctic continent began on February 4 and were terminated on February 21. During this brief period, 39 flights were conducted for a total of 260 hours in the air. It was found that a gross weight of 33,000 lb. could be lifted from unprepared snow. At first JATO was used, but as the temperatures dropped and the snow hardened, unassisted take-offs were made successfully with the same weight. Although the aircraft could take off from unprepared snow, it was found that dragging the strip greatly facilitated the process. Landings, however, were made preferance under open field conditions to cut down the length of slide out.

The principal mission of the six US Navy 'Gooney Birds' was to explore and photograph the interior. In all, 28 photographic flights produced 21,000 negatives covering the periphery of the Ross Sea and parts of Marie Byrd Land. An exploratory flight on February 15 in R4D-5 BuNo. 12415 with Admiral Byrd on board, crossed the South Pole and flew 60 miles beyond along the 0° meridian. The flags of the countries belonging to the newly established United Nations were ceremoniously dropped as the aircraft passed over the Pole. On four occasions, airborne magnetometers were tested by towing them aloft, and the results were determined to be useful for scientific investigation.

When flying was terminated for the season, the six Douglas R4Ds had to be left at the Little America base. They could not be landed aboard the carrier, and no other ship of the Task Force was large enough to accommodate them as cargo. They were faced into wind and their skis lowered several feet into the snow, to anchor them firmly. Oil was drained, classified instruments removed, and fabric control surfaces stored inside the fuselages. These aircraft were seen the following season, during the Second Antarctic Development Project—unofficially named 'Windmill'—when the icebreakers *Edisto* and *Burton Island* visited the Bay of Whales from January 29 to February 3 1948. Snow was cleared from one of the R4Ds and its engines started, but no attempt was made to fly them. In 1955, another icebreaker, *Atka*, was sent to Antarctica to reconnoitre base sites for the forthcoming International Geophysical Year —1957–58. On January 14 the ship vainly searched for the Bay of Whales. A gigantic calving in the Ross Ice Shelf had removed the Bay and, along with it, about two-thirds of the base of Little America IV, including the airstrip and the six Douglas R4Ds left on it, starting these pioneer 'Gooney Birds' on a drifting path to a watery grave.

Although the six ski-rigged R4Ds *Operation High Jump* left behind never flew again, they

Key to colour side views
1 *Douglas R2D-1, BuNo. 9994 of the US Marine Corps, one of two operated by VMJ-1 and based at Quantico. A model DC-2-142, c/n. 1405, acquired September 28 1935 and struck-off-charge August 5 1943.*

2 *One of the two R4D-2 transports BuNo. 4708, c/n. 4098, seen in the markings introduced in late 1941, and removed in June 1942. It was struck-off-charge with the US Navy at the end of 1946.*

3 *R4D-5, BuNo. 17243, one of eight operated by the US Coast Guard between May 1943 and July 1944 for transporting personnel, Search & Rescue, and logistics. Four were still in service in 1965, but were gradually phased out.*

4 *R4D-5, BuNo. 17197, was one of the six Douglas transports which flew to Little America in Antarctica from the USS Philippine Sea (CVA-47). The main wheels were later removed while the aircraft were in Antarctica with Operation High Jump.*

5 *One of six R4D-6 transports of the Japanese Maritime Self Defense Force (JMSDF) based at Kanoya naval air base. The aircraft depicted is ex-US Navy BuNo. 50745 and belongs to No. 205 Transport Squadron.*

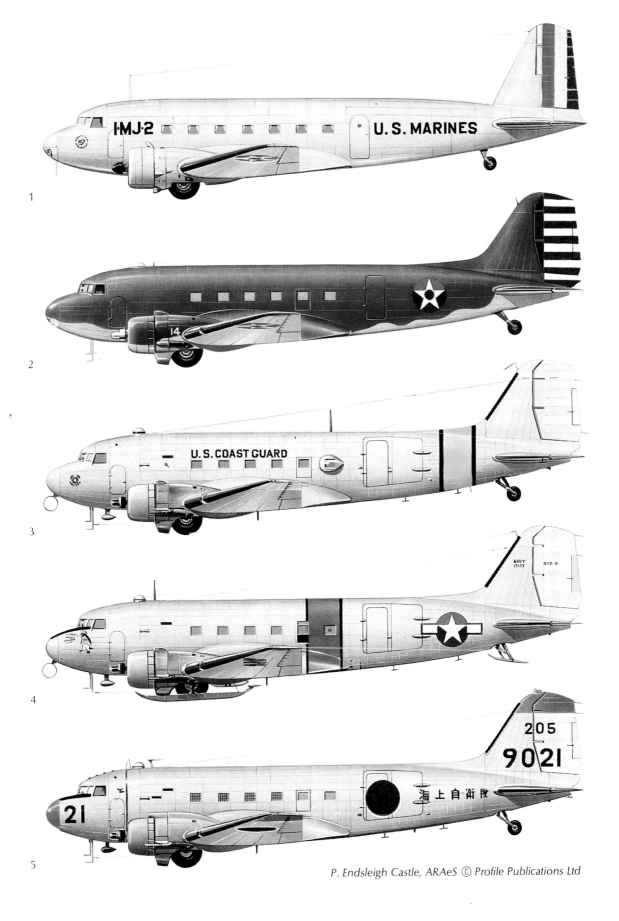

1

2

3

4

5

P. Endsleigh Castle, ARAeS © Profile Publications Ltd

wrote their share of aviation history. The story of their operations in frozen Antarctica was full of aviation firsts. In operations conducted under weather conditions that tried men and machines, the snow transports carried out their mapping missions with the minimum of difficulty. They had paved the way for the Douglas R4Ds to be operated by *Operation Deep Freeze* throughout the years until 1968 when the Douglas transport was at last retired by VX-6 from Antarctica skies.

First Landing at South Pole

Before sending construction personnel to the polar plateau, Admiral Dufek was determined that a test landing should be made, and he believed that he should go along to see for himself. So did Captain Douglas Cordiner, Commanding Officer of VX-6, whose men would be risking their lives in the aircraft. For pilot they chose Lieutenant Commander Conrad S. 'Gus' Shinn—co-pilot was 'Trigger' Hawkes, by now a captain and the US Navy's most experienced Antarctic flyer. Lieutenant John R. Swadener was navigator, and the crew consisted of Petty Officers John P. Strider and William Gumbie Jr. A US Navy R5D Skymaster and a USAF C-124 Globemaster were to accompany the flight. They were to follow the R4D-5 up the Beardmore Glacier, then fly ahead to the Pole, where they would help with the navigation and circle overhead to take photos of the historic event. They were also prepared to drop survival gear if required.

As the R4D-5 BuNo. 12418 and named 'Que Sera Sera', flew up the Beardmore Glacier, the R5D developed engine trouble and turned back. The Globemaster, piloted by Major C. J. Ellen, flew on to what its navigator calculated to be the position of the South Pole. No one knew what to expect. There was one theory that the plateau would be covered with deep, soft snow into which the skis would sink irretrievably; others had quite the opposite view, that the surface would be hard and ruffled with sastrugi. During the approach, oil pressure fell and oil streamed from the engines.

Shinn made three low-level passes to examine the surface, then made a landing. The R4D bounced a little on the sastrugi and came to a stop. It was 08:34 GMT on October 31 1956. Admiral Dufek stepped from the transport, the first man to stand at the South Pole since Amundsen and Scott. He was struck by the intense cold, 58°F below zero, that was intensified by a 10 to 15 knot wind. Followed by Captain Cordiner, carrying the American flag, he quickly settled the argument about the nature of the surface. He had to use an ice axe to plant the banner. While the pilots alternated in the cockpit to keep the engines turning over the rest of the crew set up a radar reflector to guide future flights and tried to take photographs. Only one or two were taken before all cameras froze,

Whilst on acceptance test flight at Dallas, Texas, this R4D-5 (BuNo. 17239) developed ski trouble. It landed safely, and was later delivered to Operation Deep Freeze and VX-6 Squadron. Temco Aircraft at Dallas modified the aircraft, installed the skis, extra fuel tanks and heater units. (Photo: Arthur L. Schoeni)

With the famous R4D-5 'Que Sera Sera' as a background after the first aircraft landing at the South Pole, the group includes, (l to r) John Strider, AD2; Rear Admiral George Dufek, Commander of Task Force 43; L/Cdr Conrad Shinn; Lt John Swadener; Wm. Cumbie Jr, AT2; Capt Wm. Hawkes; and Capt Douglas Cordiner. (Photo: US Navy)

Taken during January 1957 the photograph shows three R4D-5 transports of VX-6 Squadron at McMurdo. The aircraft are (l to r) R4D-5 (BuNo. 17246) 'Korara II'; the famous R4D-5 (BuNo. 12418) 'Que Sera Sera'; and R4D-5 (BuNo. 17163) 'Takahe'. (Photo: Douglas Aircraft, SM230473)

UNITED STATES NAVY

UNITED STATES NAVY

NAVY

OPERATION DEEP FREEZE
TASK FORCE 43

DEPARTMENT OF THE NAVY
★ U.S NAVAL SUPPORT FORCE, ANTARCTICA ★

XD
12418

UNITED STATES NAVY

8
QUE SERA SERA

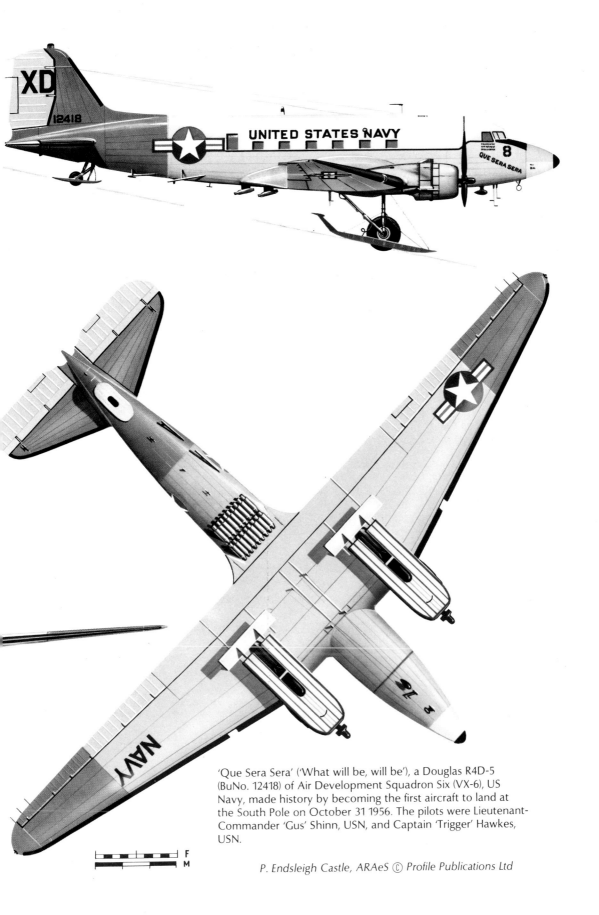

'Que Sera Sera' ('What will be, will be'), a Douglas R4D-5 (BuNo. 12418) of Air Development Squadron Six (VX-6), US Navy, made history by becoming the first aircraft to land at the South Pole on October 31 1956. The pilots were Lieutenant-Commander 'Gus' Shinn, USN, and Captain 'Trigger' Hawkes, USN.

P. Endsleigh Castle, ARAeS © *Profile Publications Ltd*

A field team of four New Zealand scientists are seen unloading their supplies from an R4D-8L (BuNo. 17188) of VX-6 Squadron at the camp site on the Nimrod Glacier where they conducted geological surveys. Date was November 30 1960. (Photo: US Navy)

Douglas R4D-8L (BuNo. 17219) is seen flying above the rugged Antarctic terrain between Byrd Station and McMurdo. The landing gear collapsed while landing in Horlicks Mountains. With the undercarriage temporarily repaired the transport was flown to McMurdo with R4D-5 (BuNo. 17246) as escort. (Photo: US Navy)

Seen at Detroit, Michigan during April 1956 this R4D-6S (BuNo. 99840) is from VX-1 (Experimental) Squadron. Note the 'thimble' radar nose and tail probe. (Photo: Bill Balogh)

making this probably the worst recorded event in recent antarctic history.

After only 49 minutes on the ground they all climbed back into the R4D. Shinn revved up the engines, but nothing happened. The skis were frozen fast. Four JATO bottles failed to shake the transport loose, so Shinn quickly fired the remaining 11 in two sets of four and one set of three. To those circling above in the Globemaster, it momentarily looked as if 'Que Sera Sera' had exploded and caught fire as it disappeared in a swirl of flame, smoke and snow. It shortly re-emerged as Shinn fought successfully to get the R4D airborne. Course was set for the Beardmore Glacier with the C-124 as company. When Major Ellen saw the R4D was safely on the ground at Beardmore-Scott Base, he flew on to McMurdo Station to spread the good news. Soon, congratulatory messages were pouring in from all parts of the world. 'Que Sera Sera' had become a marked aircraft, and when its Antarctic days were over, the US Navy retired it to the National Air Museum, in December 1958.

As a result of his chilling experience at the South Pole, Admiral Dufek decided to delay the start of construction there for two weeks, in the hope of warmer weather. His decision was also influenced by the fact, that the R4Ds of VX-6 were heavily committed elsewhere, with two being unserviceable.

Air Development Squadron Six

Two Douglas R4D-8 transports were introduced to Antarctica during *Deep Freeze III*—1957–58. Squadron VX-6 had taken these aircraft on charge during August 1957 and at the completion of the summer operating season they were returned to the US for ski modification and general rework at the Overhaul and Rework Facility at Jacksonville, Florida. Four R4D-8s flew from the US to New Zealand in September 1958, and by October 11 two had arrived at McMurdo, a third arriving on November 9. Only BuNo. 17188 failed to reach Antarctica and, as a result of considerable maintenance problems, it remained in New Zealand. In December the famous 'Que Sera Sera' BuNo. 12418 was prepared for ship transportation to the National Air Museum in Washington, DC. The R4D-6 BuNo. 17274 'Charlene' was decommissioned in January 1959 and converted into a 'wingless taxi' for use in the Williams Field area. At the completion of the summer season operations the four R4D-8s were redeployed to Quonset Point NAS, the home base of VX-6 Squadron.

The first R4D loss occurred on September 5 1959 when the starboard undercarriage folded on BuNo. 17163 during a landing at Hellett Station. In view of the age of the transport it was uneconomical to repair. The aircraft had been sent to Hallett with a doctor and hospital orderly

Douglas R4D-6Q (BuNo. 99828) from FAETULANT—Fleet Air Electronics Unit—Atlantic. Photo was taken at St Louis, Missouri, during 1957. (Photo: Gene Sommerich)

R4D-8 (BuNo. 12441) seen at Decator, Illinois on January 4 1962. The tail letters—which are very rare —stand for Bureau of Weapons, Fleet Readiness Representative, Central Region. This transport was based at Wright Field Air Force Base. (Photo: Ralph I. Brown)

aboard for emergency surgery. This was two weeks prior to the opening of the season for Deep Freeze 60 and the personnel from the previous season were still in isolation. The second loss occurred on January 6 1960 when R4D-8 BuNo. 17154 crashed near Byrd Station during a near whiteout.[1]

In May 1961 BuNo. 17246 was retired from active service with the US Navy. It had been used for five seasons in Antarctica. An R4D-5 BuNo. 17239 was accepted by VX-6 on November 20 1961 and was deployed and used in Antarctica. Eight days earlier R4D-8 BuNo. 17219 sheered a pin in the port undercarriage while making an open field landing in the Horlick Mountains. The combination of severe damage and the remote location resulted in a decision to abandon the aircraft. A second accident occurred on February 1 1962 at Byrd Station whilst R4D-8 BuNo. 99853 was attempting a JATO when the bottles failed to ignite properly. The aircraft fell back to the ski-way and made a belly landing. It was repairable but remained at Byrd Station to winter over due to the lateness of the season.

In July 1962 the Department of Defense standardized the aircraft designations throughout the US armed forces. The R4D-5/6 became the C-47H/J and the R4D-8 became the C-117D. When the aircraft was modified for cold weather operations the designation included the prefix 'L'.

Douglas R4D-5 (BuNo. 39065) drops paramedics during an exercise. Even VX-6 Squadron in the Antarctic had a pararescue team for Search & Rescue operations. This team included a jumpmaster, hospital corpsman, parachute rigger and a general specialist.
(Photo: US Navy)

When *Deep Freeze 63* summer operations commenced only two of the four R4D aircraft assigned to VX-6 Squadron were serviceable. LC-117D BuNo. 99853 was at Byrd Station in need of repairs; LC-47H BuNo. 17239 had been damaged during a late winter storm. Only LC-117D BuNo. 17188 and LC-47H BuNo. 50777 were in operation. LC-47H BuNo. 50777 had arrived at McMurdo for the first time on October 12 1962. On November 22 1962, LC-117D BuNo. 17188 crashed in the Sentinel Mountains, but the aircraft was damaged beyond repair on that location and was abandoned. Three days later on November 25 1962 LC-47H BuNo. 50777 crashed at Davis Glacier and was a write-off. The LC-117D BuNo. 99853, damaged at Byrd Station the previous season, was prepared for a one-time flight to McMurdo. It was then loaded aboard the USNS *Pvt John R. Towle* and shipped to Lyttelton, New Zealand. It was taken by road to Christchurch and repaired.

Six Douglas transports were used during *Deep Freeze 64*. BuNos. 12407 and 17221 had arrived at McMurdo on October 20 1963. This was their introduction to Deep Freeze operations. On November 30 1963 LC-117D BuNo. 99853 was flown back to McMurdo from Christchurch, repairs completed. In February 1964 LC-47H

[1] A whiteout results when light reflected back and forth between the snow surface and an overcast sky becomes so diffused that no shadows exist and the horizon cannot be seen.—Editor

6

7

8

9

10

BuNo. 17239 was shipped to the US for overhaul to be returned for *Deep Freeze 65* operations.

For *Deep Freeze 65* VX-6 gained one new LC-117D when BuNo. 12441 arrived at McMurdo on December 15 1964. Two aircraft were lost during the season. LC-47H BuNo. 12407 was lost at Lillie Glacier on October 22 1964. On January 11 1965 LC-47J BuNo. 50778 crashed at Shackleton Glacier. Both aircraft were struck-off-charge. At the conclusion of the summer season LC-47H BuNo. 17107 and LC-117D BuNo. 99853 were shipped to the US for overhaul. Both returned for *Deep Freeze 66*.

Douglas LC-47J BuNo. 50832 first arrived at at Williams Field on November 6 1965. It crashed on the Ross Ice Shelf at 78° 50' S 159° 30' W on February 2 1966. Two other transports were lost during the season. On October 6 1965 LC-47H BuNo. 17239 crashed about two miles from Williams Field. A second LC-47H BuNo. 17107 was lost in the Horlick Mountains on December 5 1965. At the end of the summer operations LC-47H BuNo. 17221 was flown to New Zealand for overhaul. It never returned to Antarctica but was used for internal flights in New Zealand.

With the three crashes during *Deep Freeze 66* it decided that the Douglas LC-47/LC-117 aircraft would be used only on prepared skiways or open field areas where the snow surface was known to be smooth. The reason for this decision was the high incident rate of undercarriage failures which resulted in the crashes.

Air Development Squadron Six (VX-6) gained one LC-117D for *Deep Freeze 67* operations— BuNo. 17092 arrived at Williams Field on November 28 1966 on completion of its deployment in the US. LC-47H BuNo. 17221 was retained in New Zealand and no Douglas transports were lost during this season. On January 10 1967, LC-117D BuNo. 99853 completed its last flight in Antarctica—BuNo. 12441 made its final flight seven days later and both aircraft, plus LC-117D BuNo. 17092 were scheduled for shipment out of Antarctica during *Deep Freeze 68*.

A historic event took place on December 2 1967 when LC-117D BuNo. 17092 made the last flight of the Douglas DC-3 type transport in Antarctica. After it returned to Williams Field from Hallett Station it was prepared for shipment to the US along with BuNo. 12411 and BuNo. 99853. In January 1968 the three aircraft were made ready for loading aboard USNS *Pvt John R. Towle* for their journey home. During loading operations BuNo. 99853 fell back onto the dock and was damaged. It was pushed off on the ice and declared a write-off. However old 99853 did not give up easily, as it was still there a year later, plainly visible from the shore station.

In Antarctica, many a geographic feature bears the name of a brave pilot or hardy crewman, frequently proposed by a scientist or other recipient of their services. The grateful news of some of the beneficiaries extended to the air-

craft itself, and on the map of the Antarctica may be found *Dakota Pass, R4D Nunatak,* and *Skytrain Ice Rise* to commemorate, as long as men go to the Antarctica to study its topography, the great contribution that the venerable 'Gooney Bird' made to the first decade of *Operation Deep Freeze*. Obviously, the ambitious programme of the International Geophysical Year could not have been successfully completed without it. Until the Lockheed C-130 Hercules was added to the inventory of VX-6, the Douglas DC-3, or by whatever name one chooses to call it, was the principal means of transport within the confines of Antarctica. During those early years, despite its limitations this Douglas transport gave to the United States programme a flexibility and scope never before achieved in the area. One can only end a review of their accomplishments by awarding them the tested US Navy accolade of 'Well done!'

The Douglas Super DC-3

After the end of World War Two, a number of DC-3 replacements appeared on the market, but were considerably faster, had a larger capacity and were naturally more expensive designs. After rebuilding some surplus C-47s and C-117s as DC-3C and DC-3D, the Douglas Company quickly decided that the only real replacement for the DC-3 would be an improved DC-3 rather than an entirely new design. Consequently, it developed the Super DC-3, which was simply a standard DC-3A airframe with extensive modifications. The fuselage was lengthened by extending the nose section 39 inches forward, and the rear compartment partition 40 inches aft giving an effective cabin increase of 79 inches. Larger vertical and horizontal tail surfaces were fitted, the R-1830 engines were replaced with 1,450 h.p. Pratt & Whitney R-2000s as used in the Douglas DC-4. The engine nacelles were enlarged to completely enclose the wheels when retracted, the tail wheel was made partially retractable and new and slightly smaller outer wing panels were swept back four degrees at the trailing edge to accommodate the rearward shift of the centre of gravity. Seating was increased from the 21–24 of the standard model to 30–38. The first flight of the Super DC-3 took place on June 23 1949. This was a Douglas DC-3S, c/n. 43158, registered N30000.

The original idea was for the customer to turn in a standard DC-3 and, for a price, get a Super DC-3 in exchange. The airlines however did not approve, since the modification price was just about what a pre-war DC-3 cost new. With no customer among the airlines Douglas turned to the USAF. The original Super DC-3 was a Long Beach-built C-47-DL, c/n. 6017, USAF serial 41-18656 which had served the 5th Air Force in Australia during World War Two. During October 1945 as a Douglas DC-3C it was in use by Western Air Lines as N56592.

Key to colour side views

6 LC-117D, BuNo. 12441, City of Invercargill, VX-6 Squadron, was retired from Deep Freeze on January 17 1966 and the airframe ex-C-47B-35-DL is basically a C-47B-35-DL with USAAF serial 42-23812, c/n. 9674.

7 Based at Yuma is the Headquarters & Maintenance Squadron 24 (H&MS-24) which is controlled by No. 24 Marine Air Group. C-47H, BuNo. 12442, shown in the markings of H&MS-24 has seen service with the Naval Air Attaches in Denmark and India and visited Blackbushe and Bovingdon, England, in the 1950s.

8 Based at El Toro, California with the 3rd Marine Air Wing (MAW-3) is C-117D, BuNo. 17182, ex-R4D-5 and originally a C-47A-10-DK, 42-92461, c/n. 12264. It is estimated that 75 per cent of the 100 C-117D transports are still flying.

9 Formed during the Golden Anniversary Year of the US Navy—1961—The Chuting Stars was a team of volunteer parachutists from the Naval Parachute Facility, El Centro, California. They used this C-117D, BuNo. 50762.

10 One of the 30 C-47s currently on the US Army inventory is 43-9095, ex-R4D-5, BuNo. 39095, of the US Army Missile Command and based at Redstone Arsenal, Alabama. It was delivered to the Army from the Naval Air Facility Litchfield Park in November 1965.

This R4D-6 (BuNo. 50753) has served with the Marine Corps, with the Commander, US Naval Forces in Germany, and was photographed at Blackbushe on a visit from Rota, Spain during the build up of US Naval forces in the 1950s. (Photo: Arthur Pearcy)

FASRON-200 had a detachment at Orly, Paris during the 1950s which operated R4D-5 (BuNo. 17226) seen at Blackbushe on July 17 1958. This transport was acquired by the US Navy on May 17 1944. (Photo: Arthur Pearcy)

Used by the staff of the US Naval Attache to Australia and New Zealand, Douglas R4D-6 (BuNo. 50797) served with FASRON-200 before transfer 'down under'. Most Naval Air Attaches used R4D transports. (Photo: AP Library)

US Marine Corps transport aircraft were only occasional visitors to the UK. Depicted is an R4D-8 (BuNo. 17194) from an unknown unit which visited Blackbushe on October 19 1956. (Photo: Arthur Pearcy)

Initially the Super DC-3 was designated YC-129 with the USAF, but in recognition of its C-47 origins it became the YC-47F with USAF serial 51-3817. The main difference from the commercial Super DC-3 were the cargo door, heavier floor, and the 1,475 h.p. Wright R-1820-80 engines instead of R-2000s. The USAF tested the YC-47F but placed no production order, deciding in favour of the Convair C-131. The aircraft was then turned over to the US Navy in 1951 and became the R4D-8X with BuNo. 138659 which was later cancelled and it became standard R4D-8 BuNo. 138820.

Accepted by the US Navy, 100 of the type were ordered which were converted from basic R4D transports flown to the Douglas factory for conversion. Still on inventory, it is estimated that 75 per cent of the R4D-8s, or C-117Ds as they were redesignated in 1962, are still in service with the US Navy and US Marine Corps, but being retired quite rapidly.

Now over 20 years old the US Navy Super DC-3s are still logging many flying hours in many parts of the globe. This includes the three currently based with the Naval Air Facility at RAF Mildenhall in Suffolk. BuNo. 17116, c/n. 43307

was accepted by the US Navy after conversion on January 11 1952, and has logged nearly 17,000 hours as an R4D-8 and has spent some it its life with the US Marine Corps with AIR FMF PAC or Aircraft, Fleet Marine Force, Pacific, BuNo. 17191, c/n. 43379 is no stranger to the UK airspace as it was logged at Blackbushe on Feb-

A familiar sight in the UK while with FASRON-200 at Blackbushe was R4D-8 (BuNo. 17150) which left for the USA during 1956. Photo depicts BuNo. 17150 in the markings of VR-22 Squadron in the USA. (Photo: National Archives, 80-G-440840)

The end of the road for the LC-117D in Antarctica. The last three Douglas transports from VX-6 Squadron await shipment to the USA during January 1968. As related, BuNo. 99853 had to be left behind. (Photo: US Navy)

Rare photo depicting a US Navy R4D-6 (BuNo. 50827) with US civil registration. This aircraft was based at Cairo with the US Embassy and was seen at Blackbushe on its return to the USA during the late 1950s. (Photo: Arthur Pearcy)

ruary 7 1960. Accepted by the US Navy on December 23 1952, it has logged over 18,000 hours since that date and survived a take-off crash in Japan during 1956. The third C-117D, BuNo. 17171, c/n. 43309 has travelled the world as it was spotted at Kai Tak, Hong Kong on April 20 1962 while serving with MAG-11. This transport was accepted during November 1951 and has flown nearly 17,000 hours since conversion. The C-117D currently in use at Rota, Spain, is BuNo. 50821, c/n. 43322, and visited London Heathrow on August 27 1954. One C-117D, BuNo. 15158, c/n. 43368, crashed at NAS Memphis, Tennessee on April 15 1963 while making a single engine approach in a rain storm.

At least one C-117D received a temporary US civil registration whilst serving with the US Navy —this was BuNo. 17119, c/n. 43378, which had once served with the Marine Corps Training and Replacement Group 20, and which was civilian registered N79966 whilst based with the American Embassy in Cairo, Egypt. The original US Navy Super DC-3 (BuNo. 138820) was last reported to be still flying at the Naval Air Station located at China Lake, California.

NATO and Europe
Apart from Korea, the US Navy had its commitments widely increased during 1952 by the American participation in the North Atlantic Treaty Organization (NATO) alliance. To the traditional Atlantic and Pacific Fleets had been added the US Sixth Fleet in the Mediterranean, where land-based patrol squadrons had started operating—from October 1951 Lockheed P2V Neptune units from Hal-Far, Malta, and later a Martin P4M-1Q Mercator unit (VQ-2) from Port Lyautey in Morocco. A Naval Air Facility was in existence at Naples, while plans were made at this time to build a US Navy airfield at Rota in Spain. For its entire existence the Mediterranean Sixth Fleet has been without a home base, and today is still maintained and replenished entirely at sea, at an extremely high level of efficiency. However the shore based units required logistic support so each facility had at least one variant of the Douglas R4D transport.

The two or three aircraft carriers in the Sixth Fleet—always at the disposal of the Supreme Allied Commander Europe (SACEUR)—regularly exercise with NATO forces in the Mediterranean. This Sixth Fleet Task Force has and does operate as part of the Allied Forces Southern Europe with its HQ at Naples.

The Commander-in-Chief US Navy Europe— (CINCUSNAVEUR)—currently Admiral William Floyd Bringle—is based in London, his main responsibilities being the operational command of both the Sixth Fleet, through the flagship of the Commander, and all shore-based aircraft in the Mediterranean, through the Commander Fleet Air Arm Mediterranean (COMFAIRMED) with HQ at Naples. He also maintains control of

all other US Navy movements both surface and air, in the European area, including the Second Fleet Atlantic when on national defence exercises in the Eastern Atlantic.

The two principal Naval Air Facilities in the Mediterranean area are Rota, Spain which serves the Western Mediterranean and Sigonella, Sicily serving the Eastern Mediterranean. These come under the operational control of COMFAIRMED and are responsible for the non-routine maintenance and repair of carrier-borne aircraft, SAR (Search and Rescue), target-towing, facilities fleet mail service and air logistic support. Detachments are located at Naples, Italy and Souda Bay, Crete and come under the control of Maritime Air Forces Mediterranean (MARAIRMED), in conjunction with British and Italian naval forces.

In World War Two Fleet Air Wing Seven with Consolidated PB4Y Liberators was based at Dunkeswell, Devon. During the early 1950s Fleet Air Service Squadron 200 (FASRON 200) appeared at RAF Hendon equipped with Douglas R4D-6 transports carrying the tail code 'JM'. These were later supplemented by the new Douglas R4D-8. During October 1955 FASRON 200 moved to the civil airport at Blackbushe as Hendon was closed as a flying station. During June 1957 the entire tail code system in the US Navy was changed and FASRON 200 was allocated the code 'FT'. While at Blackbushe the unit handled thousands of US Navy and a few USMC movements which ranged from such giants as the Lockheed WV-2 Constellation to the smaller S2F Tracker which flew direct from its parent carrier 'somewhere at sea'. With the closure of Blackbushe during 1959 FASRON 200 took its fleet of Douglas R4D transports to RAF West Malling, Kent where it remained until 1964.

The US Naval Air Facility at RAF Mildenhall, Suffolk was established on July 1 1964 upon the closure of West Malling. Currently operated at Mildenhall are three Douglas C-117D transports —BuNos. 17116, 17171 and 17191—one Convair C-131 for use by Admiral Bringle, and a Grumman C-1A Trader. As the only US Navy flying unit based in Northern Europe its mission is to support logistically all the US Navy shore installations in the United Kingdom and all US Navy ships operating in Northern European waters. The unit offers proficiency training to all US Navy pilots stationed ashore in Northern Europe.

The airports at Blackbushe, Bovingdon and Northolt have recorded numerous movements over the years of the Douglas R4D variants as the type has and still is serving in odd corners of Europe, be it with a US Naval Mission attached to a NATO ally, or in support of a US Naval Air Attache. In 1954 the Commander Naval Forces in Germany based in Berlin had a R4D-6 BuNo. 17269 which by 1957 had been replaced by BuNo. 50753. The US Naval Attache in London operated an R4D-5 BuNo. 17168 while HQs then

The Douglas R4D transport also operated in the Arctic regions, an example being R4D-5 (BuNo. 17217) which was acquired by the US Navy on May 6 1944. It carries the markings of the Arctic Research Laboratory, Barrow, Alaska. (Photo: AP Library)

Fine air to air study of R4D-8 (BuNo. 12443) of VT-29 Squadron showing the new lines introduced with the conversion to Super DC-3. Originally an R4D-5 (with c/n. 9781) this transport also had a USAF serial 42-23919. (Photo: US Navy)

First reported in Europe during 1954 this R4D-8 (BuNo. 50821) is a rebuild of the R4D-6 (BuNo. 50821) which Bill Larkins photographed at Oakland in 1946 see page 52. Carrying Mildenhall marks, it was photographed at Nice. (Photo: Aviation Photo News)

Still serving the US Navy is the first Super DC-3 to be converted and seen in the latest dayglow marks at China Lake NAS, California. It is BuNo. 138820 and now designated C-117D. (Photo: Lars Erik Lundin)

at Naples used an R4D-5R BuNo. 17147, coded 'BL'. During 1955 the US Naval Attache to France had R4D-6 BuNo. 99844 which was later transferred to FASRON 200, and the US Naval Attache to Denmark had R4D-5 BuNo. 12442.

By 1957 the new facility at Rota, Spain was taking shape and two Douglas R4Ds marked 'COMAVACTS SPAIN' were R4D-6 BuNo. 50753 and R4D-8 BuNo. 12428, the latter being known as 'Toonerville Trolley' and flown by Lieutenant Commander Albert T. Hall, had hauled everything from rocks to ribbons—typewriter variety—between bases under construction in Spain. Major maintenance had to be done at the Naval Air Facility located at Port Lyautey, whilst minor overhaul was dealt with at Getafe, Madrid.

Keflavik, Iceland, is also a Naval Air Facility which is used as a staging post on the route to and from the United States. This NAF has revealed three models of the Douglas C-47J which are out of context with the ordinary listing of BuNos.—150187, 150189 and 150190.

No Marine Corps aircraft are currently based in Europe, but occasional visits by Douglas R4D-8 transports have been made over the years in support of Fleet exercises.

Naples is the base for the Deputy Commander Naval Striking and Support Forces, Southern Europe (DEPCOMSTRIKFORSOUTH), in addition to being the base for the four star command, (CINCSOUTH), currently held by Admiral Richard Colbert, USN. Because of the situation in Malta, (NAVSOUTH), under the Italian Rear Admiral Birendelli has moved to Naples. There is a separate NATO command for the defence of the Atlantic Ocean—Allied Command Atlantic (SACLANT), with HQ at Norfolk, Virginia which was formed on April 10 1952.

Surplus to Requirements

Records show that two surplus R4D transports appeared on the British Civil Register. R4D-5 BuNo. 17126 which became G-AJIA and served with BEA as RMA Sir John Alcock, and a veteran R4D-1, BuNo. 4699, c/n. 4306 was registered as G-ATXT to Handley Page in 1966, but remained in storage in Florida. On the military side, R4D-6 transports have been supplied to the Japanese, while R4D-1, BuNo. 01985, c/n. 4441 joined the RCAF as 10912 in 1951 and in 1970 was still serving the Canadian Armed Forces.

In the United States, surplus R4Ds were retained by the Navy Department, whilst a large number were handed over to the Federal Aviation Administration who today operate nearly 50 of the type for airways and communi-

One of four USAF Douglas C-47 transports transferred to the US Navy. This is a C-47J (BuNo. 150189) which is based at Keflavik, Iceland and seen at Mildenhall. (Photo: George Pennick)

Taken especially for this Profile, this photo depicts two of the three C-117D transports currently based at the Naval Air Facility, Mildenhall, Suffolk. They are BuNo. 17116 and 17191, the former having once served with the Marine Corps. (Photo: US Navy)

cation flight checking.

Besides the Cairo-based R4Ds with US civil registrations allocated, two others were R4D-6 BuNo. 50747 as N79962 and R4D-6 BuNo. 50752 as N79963. The first was Washington, DC-based while the second was on foreign service—all mail being forwarded via 'US Naval Attache, Box E, APO 231, New York.'

The US Naval Air Facility located at Litchfield Park, Phoenix, Arizona, was a storage depot for the Douglas R4D, numbers of this transport being refurbished for the Korean conflict. During the 1960s a number of R4Ds became surplus to requirements at the depot and were sold. Today the main storage facility for US Navy aircraft, including the R4D or C-47/C-117 appears to be the huge storage complex at Davis-Monthan Air Force Base in Arizona.

It is not generally known that the 1972 US Army Aviation inventory includes 30 Douglas C-47 transports, of which all but four are ex-US Navy R4D aircraft. These perform a wide variety of tasks including paradrops, cargo and cargo parachute resupply hauls, High Altitude Low Opening (HALO) parachute jumps, training, and command and staff administration flights. 'The Golden Knights'—the US Army free-fall parachute team—is based at Fort Bragg, North Carolina, and operates the C-47 on its many demonstrations throughout the USA.

Since first joining the US Navy in the 1930s as the R2D-1, and later as the R4D, there is no doubt at all that the 600-odd transports supplied have seen the world. Despite the introduction of modern jet transports, the C-47 is still kept on inventory with the US Navy and the Marine Corps, whilst the US Army are helping to extend the already long service life this variant of the Douglas DC-3 is still giving to military aviation.

TABLE 1: DOUGLAS DC-2/DC-3 VARIANTS USED BY THE US NAVY

Variant	BuNos.	Qty (Totals)	
R2D-1	9620—9622	3	
	9993—9994	2	
			(5)
R4D-1	3131—3143	13	
	4692—4706	15	
	01648—01649	2	
	01976—01990	15	
	05051—05072	22	
	08005	1	
	12393—12404	12	
	30147	1	
	37660—37710	51	
	91104	1	
			(133)
R4D-2	4707—4708	2	
			(2)
R4D-3	05073—05084	12	
	06992—06999	8	
			(20)
R4D-4	07000—07003	4	
	33615—33621	7	
	33815—33820	6	
			(17)
R4D-5	12405—12446	42	
	17092—17248	157	
	39057—39095	39	
			(238)
R4D-6	17249—17291	43	
	39096—39098	3	
	39100	1	
	39109	1	
	50740—50752	13	
	50753—50839	87	
	99850	1	
	99852	1	
			(150)
(C-47J)	150187—150190	4	
			(4)
R4D-7	39099	1	
	39101—39108	8	
	39110—39136	27	
(DC-3A)	99099	1	
	99824—99849	26	
	99851	1	
	99853—99857	5	
	99858—99900	43	
			(112)
R4D-8	138820 (ex-138659)	1	
			(1)

Total: 682

R4D-8 (100 conversions from existing models)

NOTES

30147	R4D-1 operated by PAA—Alaskan Division
37660—37662	R4D-1 (C-47s transferred from USAF)
37681—37685	Believed cancelled
37686—37710	R4D-1 not delivered
91104	R4D-1 transfer
33615—33621	R4D-4R transfer from War Assets Admin. to PAA
150187—150190	R4D-6 (C-47J) transfer from USAF
39109	R4D-6 transfer
39110—39136	R4D-7 cancelled on VJ-Day
99099	DC-3A from PAA

Acknowledgements

The author wishes to thank the US Navy, Marines Corps, Army, Coast Guard and Operations Deep Freeze HQ for their invaluable assistance in providing material for this Profile. Also to William T. Larkins of AAHS and to the various *Air-Britain* Specialists who supplied photographs and additional material.

Additional References

Arthur Pearcy is also the author of the following *Profiles*:
No 96 (Volume 4): Douglas DC-3 (to Dec 1941 only)
No 220 (Volume 10): Douglas Dakota Mks I-IV (1941–70; RAF & Dominion/Commonwealth air forces only)

TABLE 2: US NAVY DOUGLAS R4D/C-47/C-117 DESIGNATIONS

Under a Department of Defense Directive dated July 6 1962, the R4D designations allocated to US Navy variants of the C-47 were standardized with those of the many USAF variants.

Old	New	Role
R4D-5	C-47H	Cargo Transport
R4D-5Q	EC-47H	Special Electronics
R4D-5L	LC-47H	Cold Weather
R4D-5S	SC-47H	Anti-submarine
R4D-5R	TC-47H	Trainer/Transport
R4D-5Z	VC-47H	Staff Transport
R4D-6	C-47J	Cargo Transport
R4D-6Q	EC-47J	Special Electronics
R4D-6L	LC-47J	Cold Weather
R4D-6S	SC-47J	Anti-submarine
R4D-6R	TC-47J	Trainer/Transport
R4D-6Z	VC-47J	Staff Transport
R4D-7	TC-47K	Trainer
—	C-47M[1]	Special Electronics[1]
R4D-8	C-117D	Cargo Transport
R4D-8L	LC-117D	Cold Weather
R4D-8T	TC-117D	Trainer
R4D-8Z	VC-117D	Staff Transport

[1] New type since Jan. 1963

Series Editor:
CHARLES W. CAIN.

TABLE 3: OPERATION DEEP FREEZE R4D/C-47/C-117 TRANSPORTS

Desig.	BuNo.	Name	Code	Arrived	Fate or last flight date
R4D-5	12418	Que Sera Sera	XD/8	Oct. 17 1956	Dec. 1958 to National Air Museum
R4D-6	17274	Charlene	XD	Oct. 17 1956	Jan. 1959. Wingless taxi aircraft
R4D-5	17246	Little Horrible—Korora II (1960)	XD	Oct. 17 1956	May 1961. Retired
R4D-5	17163	Takahe	XD/7	Oct. 17 1956	Sept. 15 1959. Abandoned Hallett
R4D-8	17219	Semper Shafters USMC	JD/9	Nov. 22 1957	Nov. 12 1961. Abandoned Horlicks
R4D-8	99853	Wilshie Duit	JD/7	Oct. 1 1957	Jan. 10 1967
R4D-8	17154	Negatus Perspirus	JD/8	Deep Freeze '58	Jan. 6 1960. Crashed Byrd Station
R4D-8	17188		JD/7	Deep Freeze '58	Nov. 22 1962. Cr Sentinel Mts.
R4D-5	17239		JD/8	Nov. 20 1961	Oct. 6 1965. Cr Williams Field
LC-47	50777		JD	Oct. 12 1962	Nov. 25 1962. Cr Davis Glacier
LC-47	17107		JD	Deep Freeze '63	Dec. 5 1965. Returned to USA
LC-47	50778		JD	Deep Freeze '63	Jan. 11 1965. Cr Shackleton Glacier
LC-47H	12407		JD	Oct. 20 1963	Oct. 22 1964. Lost Lillie Glacier
LC-47H	17221	Kool Kiwi	JD/14	Oct. 20 1963	Apr. 18 1969. To Ferrymead Museum
LC-117D	12441	City of Invercargill	JD/11	Dec. 15 1964	Jan. 17 1966. Retired
LC-47J	50832		JD	Nov. 6 1965	Feb. 2 1966. Cr Ross Ice Shelf
LC-117D	17092		JD	Nov. 28 1966	Dec. 2 1967. Retired

TABLE 4: SPECIFICATION

Model	R2D-1	R4D-1	R4D-2	R4D-3	R4D-4	R4D-5 C-47H	R4D-6 C-47J	R4D-7 TC-47K	R4D-8 C-117D
Wing span (ft. in.)	85 0	95 0	95 0	95 0	95 0	95 0	95 0	95 0	95 0
Length (ft. in.)	62 0	64 6	64 6	64 6	64 6	64 6	64 6	64 6	67 9
Height (ft. in.)	16 0	16 9	16 9	16 9	16 9	16 9	16 9	16 9	18 3
Powerplant	Wright R-1820-25	P&W R-1830-92	Wright R-1820-G202A	P&W R-1830-92	P&W R-1830-92	P&W R-1830-92	P&W R-1830-90B	P&W R-1830-90B	Wright R-1820-80
Take-off h.p.	710	1,200	1,200	1,200	1,200	1,200	1,200	1,200	1,475
Crew + Troops	3 + 21	3 + 28	3 + 21	3 + 28	3 + 21	4 + 28	4 + 28	3 +	3 + 35
Max. cruise (m.p.h.)	190	190	190	190	190	190	190	190	251
Height (feet)	8,000	8,000	8,000	8,000	8,000	8,000	8,000	8,000	15,400
Max. still air range (st. miles)	1,950	2,125	2,150	2,150	2,150	2,150	2,150	2,150	3,042
Weights Empty (pounds)	12,010	16,600	16,600	16,600	16,600	17,057	17,257	17,257	19,537
All-up	18,560	25,200	25,200	25,200	25,200	31,000	30,600	30,600	31,900
Fuel capacity (Imp. gallons)	467	685	685	685	685	670	670	670	1,332

Apparently damaged this C-117D (BuNo. 50780) is seen at Cam Ranh Bay in South Viet Nam. A sister aircraft, BuNo. 17124, was damaged during November 1969 when a Viet Cong rocket exploded nearby wounding some of the crew. (Photo: US Navy)

Aérospatiale/BAC Concorde

by Norman Barfield, MSc, CEng, AFRAeS, MIMechE, MAIAA

'Those projects which abridge distance have done most for the civilisation and happiness of our species.'

Macaulay (1800–1859)

Stripped of the inevitable extremes of emotion and criticism, the Anglo-French Concorde supersonic airliner is undeniably a supreme achievement by any standards. The world's first major international collaborative venture in advanced technology and the largest and most complex commercial programme ever undertaken by two nations in peacetime, Concorde has already pioneered international technological innovation and industrial collaboration on a grand scale and has restored to Europe undisputed leadership in the most advanced field of commercial aircraft development.

Conceived as the breakthrough generation of supersonic air travel, Concorde is now at the threshold of introducing the biggest step forward in the history of air transport. Twice as fast as todays jets, Concorde will halve intercontinental journey times and be faster than the sun. Significantly, it will also bring all the major popu-

lated land masses of the globe within the compass of 12 hours travel—mans natural day—and overcome the last major frontier of terrestrial travel.

· Beyond sheer technology Concorde will thus dramatically shrink the world as we know it and will stimulate whole new social and industrial developments to add a new dimension to international life—without impairing the world environment.

In gestation as a feasible technical concept since the mid-1950s, Concorde became a formal international collaborative venture by the British and French Governments through their now historic Agreement of November 1962—with the physical programme responsibility vested in British Aircraft Corporation (BAC) and Bristol Siddeley (now part of Rolls-Royce) in the UK, and Sud-Aviation (now part of Aérospatiale) and SNECMA in France.

That Concorde has survived the political viscissitudes of these two major world powers for more than a decade is high testimony to the soundness of its concept and the success of the international collaboration and programme management involved. Moreover it has prefaced

Concorde 002 (G-BSST) showing the distinctive and characteristic ogival delta wing shape.

the international industrial implications of the enlarged European Economic Community (now that Britain has joined) by a full decade.

Paradoxically, while the Anglo-French Concorde has flourished, the United States—which has traditionally dominated long-haul air transport for more than 40 years—has so far failed to launch a significantly bigger, faster and more complex SST, whereas the USSR, the only other major world 'aerospace power', has independently conceived a virtually identical slender delta solution, the Tupolev Tu-144.

Crowned by the whole-hearted support of the British and French Governments, technical and performance capability substantially demonstrated, first customer airline contracts confirmed, and all manufacturing centres working on revenue-earning series production aircraft—Concorde is now an evident asset to European political and economic union and the envied leader of commercial aerospace technology worldwide.

As with any 'high-technology' programme contesting the frontiers of man's knowledge, Concorde has also created a big and ever-growing reservoir of significant 'spin-off' benefits to sharpen the spearhead of industry and commerce at large.

Concorde's progress to date—which has been aptly labelled *entente concordiale*—is a triumphant example of what two nations can achieve by working together and is an immensely encouraging portent of the industrial strength that European nations can achieve as partners spurred by the diffusive power of high technology.

Such progress has not been achieved without very considerable financial outlay—around £1,000 million—but the realization of a basic market expectation of 200 aircraft will bring a direct return of at least £4,000 million to the exchequers of Britain and France in vital export

and foreign exchange earnings over the next decade—plus the inestimable value of the indirect benefits to society that will continue to flow from the new plateau of technology, commerce and internationalism that Concorde has established. And because any major advance on the basic Concorde concept—the hypersonic or sub-orbital transport—is clearly a '21st century science', Concorde developments can reasonably be foreseen that will go on to earn many times this sum for both nations fully to justify the investment and stabilise the progress of international air transport over the next 30 years or more.

It is inimical to the development of civilization that progress can be halted—it has to be guided. Concorde is the courageous exemplification of Britain and Frances ideas of how international air transport progress should be guided, and led, through the rest of this century and beyond.

Aside from its revolutionary and unprecedented impetus to world travel and communications, posterity will likely prove that Concorde has bequeathed an equally fundamental stimulus to mans progress through the outstanding success of the big international relationship that it has created in European industrial and political unity and future strength in the world.

The Concorde story told here is but an opening chapter because it has still only reached the end of the beginning—from conception to birth. Having successfully emerged from the most extensive and thorough development programme ever mounted for an airliner, Concorde now has to meet the challenge of the ever-toughening world of commercial air transport—which can be its only judge just as it has been its primary objective for the past decade.

The story of the maturity of Concorde will doubtless be the subject of more than one new *Profile* in the future.

Introduction

Concorde stemmed from an emerging belief in the mid-1950s—simultaneously in Britain and France—that the next major advance in international air travel could, and should, be at speeds beyond the so-called 'sound barrier'. Overcome by the imperatives of military technology in the battle for aerial combat supremacy fostered by the contemporary 'Cold War' in Europe, this barrier was now no longer considered an impassable obstacle to further significant advances in the prime asset of air transport—speed.

The relentless persuance of this imaginative ideology over the intervening years, and the massive technical and industrial pioneering that has necessarily resulted, is second only to that of the American Apollo Moon-landing programme. The progressive international co-operation is unique. Significantly, it has also

prefaced the enlargement of the European Economic Community (EEC)—to include Britain —by a full decade.

The established Anglo-French Concorde supersonic airliner programme of today is the triumphant realisation of the objectivity of the aviation expertise and ultimately the political will of the two nations.

Now poised at the threshold of introducing the most significant and dramatic advance in the history of transport, Concorde has won for Europe the leadership in international air transport development so long dominated by the United States.

The Impact of Speed and the Significance of Time

It has been said that there is only one true economy—the economy of time.

Ever since the invention of the wheel, transport has been mans principal tool in his insatiable quest to annihilate distance in minimum time.

Speed—and hence the saving of time—has always been the *raison d'être* of transport and has motivated its spectacular progress to the forefront of mans basic needs.

When the heavier-than-air craft was invented at the dawn of the 20th century, speed was the least consequence. However, the evident military significance of speed was quickly appreciated in World War One, and the initiation of commercial air service in 1919 brought a whole new dimension to transport with its ability to transcend physical terrestrial barriers and so greatly extend mans travel potential.

Spearheaded by the exigencies of military necessity in World War Two and the development of the gas-turbine engine, the speed of commercial aircraft operation had increased ten fold—to the threshold of that of sound—as air transport development entered its fifth decade in 1960.

Dramatic increases in travel, trade and economic well-being naturally resulted throughout the world in the post-war years and air journeys have long since been measured in time rather than distance.

Speed continues to be the principal commodity that commercial aviation is in business to sell and increasing speed—combined with lower fares—the main impetus to traffic growth in the 1970's and beyond.

Thesis

The core of the makers case for Concorde is the exploitation of the benefits of speed and time-saving in the supersonic regime.

After more than a decade of stagnation in speed development, supersonic Concorde will again provide this vital stimulus to air transport. Its ability to cruise at twice the speed of sound—around 1,300 m.p.h. (2,092 k.p.h.)—means that long-distance air journey times will be halved at a stroke thereby setting it in a class apart from all other airliners cruising at a subsonic 600 m.p.h. (966 km./h.).

This means, the makers assert, that supersonic Concorde will be of special appeal to the 'time priority' traveller—notably the businessman—and provide a vital complement to the proliferate high-capacity subsonic jets. Hitherto both high-yield 'First' and the low-yield 'Tourist'/'Economy' class passengers have travelled together in the same vehicle, the fare differential being accommodated by the artifice of greater space and amenities for the higher fare passenger, but with no benefit in his real requirement—minimum journey time.

Additionally, the massive growth in tourism and leisure travel all over the world in recent years has generated a whole new generation of high-capacity subsonic jets to cater for this 'cost priority' mass travel market with a wide variety of low-fare and charter promotions and concessions.

Concorde—Time-Saver

Now comes Concorde to provide a 100 per cent speed advantage for the discriminating long-distance traveller. Halved journey times, less travel fatigue and physical disorientation, less time and accommodation expense away from base, and the new ability to bring many long-distance city pairs within the compass of a 'day-return' ticket—these are among the very real benefits that will amply justify the higher fare that he has always been prepared to pay for better service. Unlike the leisure traveller, who journeys in his own time, the businessman travels in what would otherwise be highly productive and remunerated office time. Concorde will thus dramatically reduce the present major imbalance in the cost/use of his time.

Significantly, while numerically a minority of the total traffic spectrum, business and other 'full-fare' regular travellers constitute the majority source of airline revenue—around 25 per cent of the total traffic, they produce around 40 per cent of total revenue.

Consequently Concorde will enable airlines

Concorde series production at the British final assembly centre at the Filton (Bristol) factory of the BAC Commercial Aircraft Division. Foreground: second production (202); background: fourth production (204)—first for BOAC.

to achieve greater profitability and versatility of operation through being able for the first time to provide a distinct choice of service for these two basic types of traveller.

Concorde also has the ability to bring all the major populated land masses of the globe substantially within the compass of a single days travel. As transport history has consistently shown, travel, trade and commerce increase dramatically when this becomes possible.

Within this exciting new global capability Concorde will equate the long haul air travel pattern of tomorrow with the short-haul journey times of today.

This, then, is the makers commercial thesis and justification for Concorde.

Vision

The impact of speed in transport and the advent and potential of the supersonic airliner were succinctly expounded and predicted by Sir George Edwards—architect and mentor of the Concorde programme—in his Presidential Address to the Royal Aeronautical Society delivered in February 1958.

History had consistently shown, Sir George said, that 'there is a definite connection between industry, population and speed of transport'. He then went on to develop a fundamental line of reasoning which accurately forecast the advent of the practical supersonic airliner—summarised in the following extracts.

'... the demand for more and faster transport was stimulated by the world's communities becoming industrialised. In the same way ... the presence of more and faster transport enabled the world's communities to become industrialised and expand. There is a moral there somewhere.

'... increasing speed in transport has been the essential hand-maiden to increasing development all over the world and the only medium in which speed can continue to increase is in the air. There is no indication that a demand for increasing speed is going to diminish or disappear, so that the demand for faster aeroplanes is likely to go on.

'... subsonic jets will continue to do their 600 miles an hour or thereabouts right through the 1960s. There seems, however, to be no technical reason why the supersonic development of the World's Air Speed Record (and the supersonic bombers which could follow it) could not also be followed by supersonic transports, flying at speeds of over 1,000 miles an hour. If one decided that the previous gaps which had existed between the World's Air Speed Record and bomber speeds and transport speeds would be maintained, then there is no reason why civil jets should not be in existence at supersonic speeds in the 1960's. I believe, however, that the financial burden of depreciating the subsonic jets will alone make that impossible, and a

supersonic jet in operation before 1970 is of academic interest only.

'What does emerge from a general study of business travel . . . is that when a destination gets beyond the 12 hour journey circle, journey incidence falls sharply. There is much business flying inside the '12 hour circle'—in fact half of it . . .

'When we do get a supersonic jet we get with it the ability to bring practically the whole world within reach of the 12 hour journey time.

'I have tried to show that there is an increasing demand for a longer distance to be flown in 12 hours. I am certainly convinced that nothing will stop the ultimate operation of long-range supersonic civil aeroplanes.'

This classical analysis of the significance and timing of the SST by Sir George Edwards proved to be both prescient and accurate—and an outstanding landmark in aviation literature.

The Sonic Simile

Before tracing the technical, industrial and political evolution of Concorde, it is important to identify the significance of the speed of sound and the definition of the 'Mach Number'.

Man-made projectiles, such as bullets and shells, were being propelled through the atmosphere at supersonic speeds many generations before man himself had ever flown at all.

Sir Isaac Newton (1642–1727)—founder of the prime sciences of Dynamics and the Calculus—was the first to calculate the speed of propogation of pressure or sound in air—by measuring the time difference between the flash and the sound of a gun fired some distance away, on an artillery field near London. His finding, published in 1726, was that the velocity of sound in air was around 1,140 feet per second and that the square of the speed of the propogation is proportional to the ratio of the pressure change to the corresponding density change involved in the process.

The speed of sound was first attained by

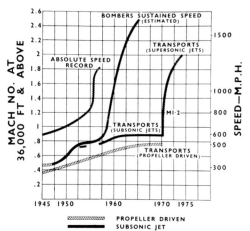

Forecast of speed trends by Sir George Edwards in his Presidential Address to the Royal Aeronautical Society in February 1958. Note his forecast of a Mach 2 SST in 1974/5. However, as he has pointed out recently, the fact that the expected large long-range supersonic bomber did not materialise has meant that the majority of the technology required for Concorde has had to be obtained within its own development programme and without the traditional prior military experience.

military aircraft during the 1940s. The physical consequence of this was a deleterious effect on performance due to the simultaneous onset of the phenomenon of compressibility of air.

The Sound Barrier

Because a disturbance in free air is propogated at the speed of sound, the disturbance which a body creates by virtue of its motion is transmitted well ahead of it when the speed of motion is much slower than that of sound. However, if the body is moving at or faster than sonic speed then the disturbance that it creates cannot be propogated ahead of it.

Consequently, as aircraft speeds approached that of sound a sharp increase in aerodynamic drag resulted—because of the inadequacy of the prevailing state of knowledge of the practical behaviour of aerodynamic wing shapes in relation to this hitherto academic phenomenon. Hence the coining of the then popular term: 'Sound Barrier'.

Overcome by the twin technical innovations of the swept wing and the turbine engine—both invented in the 1930s and greatly exploited from the mid-1940s onwards—this so-called barrier proved to be merely a transient to be avoided rather than an impassable obstacle to further speed progress.

The supersonic regime of flight was opened up in the 1950s through the prevailing imperatives of military technology—from which was to stem the essential technical stimulus for the conception of the SST and ultimately the twice-the-speed-of-sound Concorde.

The 'Mach Number'

The concept of a ratio between the speed of motion of a body and that of sound was first defined by Ernst Mach (1838–1916), an eminent Austrian Professor of Physics. This ratio was used for a long time in scientific literature before the designation 'Mach Number' was coined by Jacob Ackeret, the noted Swiss aerodynamicist.

Mach Number is now widely used in the aerospace business as a convenient means of expressing the speed of an aircraft in relation to that of sound—the datum being unity when the aircraft is travelling at exactly the ambient speed of sound i.e. the sonic speed at the prevailing altitude and temperature conditions —to which it is proportional.

In 'International Standard Atmosphere' (ISA) conditions the speed of sound is approximately 762 m.p.h. (1,226 km./h.) at sea level. With increasing altitude the temperature falls by 1.98 degrees Centigrade per thousand feet, resulting in a progressive decrease to 658 m.p.h. (1,059 km./h.) at around 36,000 ft. (10,972 m.) altitude—the beginning of the 'stratosphere'. Because the temperature remains constant above this height (at −56.5 degrees Centigrade) the speed of sound also remains constant—up to around 65,000 ft. (19,812 m.).

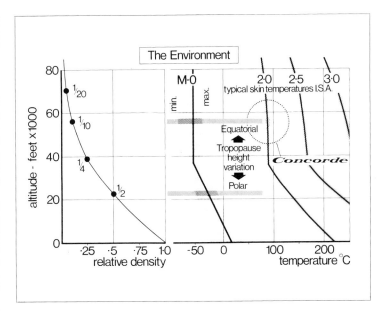

Thus Concorde's cruising speed—Mach 2—is around 1,300 m.p.h. (2,092 km./h.) at its cruising height band of 50,000 to 60,000 ft. (15,240 to 18,290 m.).

Evolution of the Bisonic Generation

The exploitation of supersonic flight in Britain dates back to a little-known British Government decision of 1943 when with commendable courage it issued Specification E.24/43 for an experimental transonic aircraft intended to reach 1,000 m.p.h. at 36,000 ft. (Mach 1.5). The outcome was the imaginative Miles M.52, a single-engine aircraft with a bullet-shaped cylindrical fuselage with a conical (jettisonable) nose section containing a pressurised cabin for the single pilot. The M.52 was 90 per cent complete in February 1946 when the project was cancelled in favour of a programme of telemetered transonic flights by air-launched models, ostensibly on the grounds of excessive risk to the human pilot.

Vickers at Weybridge (a predecessor of BAC) did much work on this subsequent approach and constructed a series of experimental pilotless transonic research models, powered by liquid fuel rocket motors, for release from de Havilland D.H.98 Mosquito aircraft at 40,000 ft.

Early Supersonic Research and Military Aircraft
Cancellation of the M.52 enabled America to take the lead in establishing supersonic flight experience—following the epic first-ever flight at supersonic speed (Mach 1.06) in level flight by Captain 'Chuck' Yeager in the Bell X-1 air-launched rocket-powered research prototype on October 14 1947. The Douglas D-558-2 Skyrocket became the first aircraft to exceed Mach 2 in February of the following year.

The physical characteristics of the International Standard Atmosphere—notably the variation of relative density, Mach Number and temperature with altitude, and (right) the added effect of kinetic heating at SST Mach Numbers. Overlaying this picture in practice are further variations due to climatic effects.

Nevertheless, the traditional inventiveness and ingenuity of the British and French continued undaunted.

The first British aircraft to exceed the speed of sound (under control) was the de Havilland D.H.108 ('Swallow') swept-wing tailless research aeroplane which reached 700 m.p.h. in a dive from 40,000 to 30,000 ft. on September 6 1948 —piloted by John Derry.

The Seeds of the Fifties

America's progressive programme of the early 1950s—spurred by the needs of the Korean War—soon disposed of the sound barrier and supersonic flight became routine, first in diving flight and eventually in level and climbing flight. By 1955 the USAF had the North American F-100 Super Sabre—the world's first combat aircraft capable of sustained supersonic speed in level flight—in squadron service.

In November 1956, Convair flew its B-58 Hustler Mach 2 delta-winged bomber—the first large supersonic aircraft—generated from its XF-92A experimental supersonic fighter (the first true delta-winged powered aircraft to fly) and its F-102 Delta Dagger and F-106 Delta Dart Mach 1.5 fighters.

Two years later the Lockheed F-104 Starfighter —the first operational Mach 2 fighter—had proved that careful matching of engine and intake design was compatible with operational service at twice the speed of sound.

Meanwhile in Britain, the P.1A of English Electric (another predecessor of BAC) exceeded Mach 1 on its third flight in August 1954. This was the prototype of what was to become the Lightning, Britain's first fighter to be designed for sustained Mach 2 performance and which became established in squadron service in 1960.

The contemporary Fairey Delta 2 experimental prototype went on to establish a World's Speed Record of 1,132 m.p.h. (1,882 km./h.) on March 10 1956 and, as noted later, was further adapted to become a key aerodynamic tool in the development of Concorde.

In France, Mach 1 was first exceeded in level flight in August 1954 by the diminutive S.F.E.C.M.A.S. 1402 Gerfaut 1A—which was France's first high-powered jet delta-winged aircraft to fly. This was followed by the Sud-Ouest Aviation S.O.9000 Trident I mixed power unit lightweight interceptor research aircraft in April 1955, and S.O. 9050 Trident II (which reached 2000 km./h. (1242 m.p.h.) in January 1957).

In 1956 the delta-winged S.E.212 'Durandal' reached Mach 1.5 on its first flight and two more French delta-winged prototypes, the Dassault Mirage III and the Nord 1500 Griffon, exceeded Mach 2 in level flight.

The Griffon has a particularly significant link with the first pilot of Concorde—on February 25 1959 André Turcat established an international speed record of 1,018 m.p.h. (1,638 km./h.) over a 100 km. closed circuit and in October that year reached Mach 2.19 (1,448 m.p.h.—2,330 km./h.) at 15,250 ft. (4,648 m.) and became the first European to exceed Mach 2.

In 1957 the Dassault Super-Mystère B-2 became the first Western European aircraft to go into service as a genuine supersonic interceptor.

By the end of the 1950s it was clear that the problems of supersonic flight for military purposes had been fully conquered technically and Mach 2 flight was routine.

Advent of the SST

The lessons and the success of these research and military achievements fostered a growing appreciation of the commercial potential that could be derived from this significant new plateau of performance capability.

The dominant physical characteristic was the delta wing shape that had its origins in the pioneering research in Germany which was

Loading a rocket-powered air-launched scale model of the Miles M.52 under the fuselage of a Mosquito parent aircraft.

The Gerfaut 1A, France's first high-powered delta-winged aircraft to exceed Mach 1.0. (Photo: S. P. Blandin)

sequestrated by the Allies at the end of World War Two.

The potential improvements in the lift/drag ratios that could be achieved with the delta wing at supersonic speeds began to indicate that the operating costs of a supersonic airliner could be brought down to a commercially realistic level.

Pioneering British Milestone

A significant if unheralded event in the evolution of the practical SST was the formation in 1956 by by the British Government of the 'Supersonic Transport Advisory Committee' (STAC)—under the most able Chairmanship of Morien (now Sir Morien) Morgan, the eminent aerodynamicist—'to initiate and monitor a co-operative programme of aimed research designed to pave the way for a possible first generation of supersonic transport aircraft'.

The 28-strong main Committee included representation from nine airframe companies—Avro, Armstrong Whitworth, Bristol, de Havilland, English Electric, Fairey, Handley Page, Shorts and Vickers; four engine companies—Armstrong-Siddeley, Bristol, de Havilland and Rolls-Royce; the national airlines—BOAC and BEA; the leading research establishments—RAE, NGTE and ARA; and the Air Registration Board (ARB), the Ministry of Transport and Civil Aviation, and the Ministry of Supply. It was supported by a 38-man technical sub-committee from these same organisations.

The first meeting of the STAC on November 5 1956 prefaced two years of quietly intensive research, costing over £700,000 and involving the production of more than 400 written contributions, to prove that the concept of a commercial supersonic aircraft was feasible. This work covered not only the primary technical disciplines of aerodynamics, structures, systems and propulsion but also operations, air traffic control, economics and the social effects of noise and the sonic boom.

Reporting its findings in March 9 1959, the STAC favoured two basic types—a medium-range (1,500 n.m.) aircraft cruising at Mach 1.2 and a long-range (3,000 n.m.) aircraft cruising at Mach 1.8.

Numerous feasibility studies were considered, employing a range of swept, compound-swept ('M' and 'W') and delta-wing planform shapes. All but the last were found suitable only for the lower speed. Theoretical and wind tunnel studies demonstrated that not only was the slender delta the best shape for Mach 1.8 but, contrary to earlier predictions, its overall suitability tended to improve up to and slightly beyond Mach 2.

The evolution of the characteristic slender ogival delta wing planform shape ultimately adopted for Concorde was probably the most significant result of the wide-ranging research and development work of the STAC.

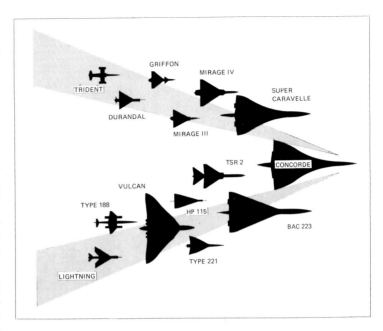

The progression of British and French research and military aircraft from which the basic technology of Concorde stemmed.

To complement and extend the highly promising theoretical and wind tunnel research, which involved over 300 test models, the Ministry of Supply subsequently sponsored two research aircraft to explore the practical characteristics of this preferred shape.

For low-speed research, Specification X.197 materialised as the Handley Page H.P.115 first flown on August 17 1961. For both high and low-speed investigation of the refined ogival delta shape of Concorde, Specification ER.193D became the Bristol (BAC) 221—a conversion of the Fairey Delta 2—which was first flown at Filton on May 1 1964.

In order to decide whether to integrate the fuselage within a fairly thick wing profile or to adopt a discrete fuselage associated with a relatively thin wing, feasibility studies of the two shapes were commissioned from Hawker Siddeley Aviation and Bristol Aircraft respectively.

In the ultimate comparison the thin wing proposal was found to have a decisive advantage and a design study contract was awarded which resulted in the Bristol Type 198, a light-alloy mid-wing slender-delta with six Bristol-Siddeley 'Olympus' turbojets (already in production for Britain's 'V' bomber force) installed under the wings. This study was submitted in August 1961—together with a Mach 3 steel and titanium aircraft (the Bristol Type 213) for comparative purposes.

The Mach 2 Decision

The cost and development time needed for the Mach 3 study were found to be much greater than those for the Mach 2 design. While much was by then known about aircraft designed for speeds of Mach 2.0 nothing at all was known about the Mach 3.0 regime.

As Sir George Edwards said later: 'This may be an old-fashioned reason for choosing Mach 2.0 but those responsible for the success of a great undertaking are always likely to be less adventurous than the enthusiastic supporter.'

Efficiency

Close study of vehicle efficiency, together with the properties of structural materials at the greatly elevated temperatures engendered by the kinetic heating phenomenon due to the friction of the air passing over the surface of the aircraft at these high flight speeds—a completely new factor in commercial airliner design and operation—amply verified this almost intuitive judgement.

Overall aircraft efficiency is essentially a function of the lift/drag (L/D) ratio of the aircraft and the propulsive efficiency of the engine.

Typically around 16 for todays jets cruising at Mach 0.8, the L/D ratio falls sharply to around 9 in the transonic region and then moves slowly to between 7.5 and 7.0 in the Mach 2.0 to Mach 3.0 speed band. Fortuitously the thermal efficiency of jet engines increases steadily from around 25 per cent at todays subsonic cruise speeds to around 40 per cent between Mach 2.0 and 3.0.

Combining these two factors to determine the overall vehicle efficiency showed that much of what was lost in the transonic region was recovered by the time Mach 2.0 was reached, indicating that between Mach 2.0 and Mach 3.0 it should be possible from aerodynamic and thermodynamic considerations to produce a vehicle with efficiency close to that of subsonic jets. Hence attention was closely focussed on this range of speeds.

Materials

On the question of airframe materials, whereas at subsonic speeds the structural temperature during cruising flight is of the order of minus 35°C, at Mach 2.0 the kinetic heating effect raises this temperature to around 120°C; at higher speeds it continues to rise rapidly—roughly as the square of the flight speed—so that at Mach 3.0 it has more than doubled again to 250°C.

While 120°C could still be tolerated by available aluminium alloys, the substantially higher temperatures at Mach 2.5 to 3.0 would have demanded exclusive use of steel and titanium.

Apart from the much higher cost and more difficult fabrication techniques required, these largely untried materials are so strong that relatively small thicknesses are required to carry the loads encountered and hence further weight has to be expended in stabilising the structure against buckling. This means that the resulting structures are even heavier and more expensive.

In addition to the choice of materials, the kinetic heating effect also influences the design of the systems.

Weight and complexity—and hence cost—increase sharply in both areas with increasing design temperature. When it is appreciated that the payload fraction of an SST is only about one-twentieth of the fully laden weight, the paramount importance of weight-saving and avoidance of complexity are obvious.

Moreover, the massive extra outlay that would have been involved in the higher speed design would still have only reduced the transatlantic journey time by around 30 minutes—from $3\frac{1}{2}$ to 3 hours—whereas the entirely feasible Mach 2 design would *halve* today's 7 hour journey time.

All these factors pointed to a cruise speed of Mach 2.0 for a practical long-range SST. Below this speed, overall vehicle efficiencies tended to be too low and above it the additional weight, cost and complexity combined completely to invalidate economic viability within the prevailing state of knowledge.

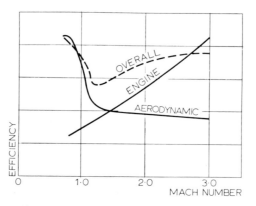

The variation of vehicle efficiency with Mach Number.

The extreme difficulties encountered with the all-steel Bristol Type 188 (built to Specification ER.134 for research into flight problems in excess of 1,500 m.p.h. and first flown on April 14 1962) were clear vindication of the ultimate decision of the British and French.

The insurmountable problems of the ill-fated North American B-70 Valkyrie Mach 3 experimental steel bomber (the first large long-range supersonic aircraft—first flown in 1964) and the stillborn American Mach 3 SST design of the late 1960s (cancelled in 1971) were yet further convincing evidence that this was the right course to follow.

Conception of the Anglo-French SST

It was a condition of the Bristol design study contract that the possibilities of co-operation should be explored with manufacturers in the USA, Germany and France. Whereas the Americans were convinced that an SST based on their experience with the B-70 should be their objective, and Germany was not willing to participate, the 'state of the supersonic art' in France was well advanced and the opportunity of collaboration was welcomed.

French experience with the Dassault Mirage III and IV fighters together with the commercial success of the pioneering Sud-Aviation Caravelle rear-engined subsonic regional jetliner, had also led (quite independently of the British work) to the choice of a cruising speed of Mach 2.0 for an SST.

Meanwhile, sonic boom studies (and the adverse economics of six engines) had shown that the Bristol 198 was too heavy to be acceptable in this respect. Consequently, in 1961 the Bristol design team, led by Dr. Archibald Russell and Dr. William Strang, submitted a new and smaller project, the Bristol Type 223 with four Olympus engines.

Significantly there was a remarkable similarity between this new design and the latest French SST study evolved by the Sud-Aviation team under Pierre Satre and Lucien Servanty—the 'Super Caravelle' which was unexpectedly revealed at the Paris Air Show in 1961.

Closer co-operation between British Aircraft Corporation (formed the previous year by a merger of the aviation interests of Bristol, English Electric and Vickers) and Sud-Aviation of France was agreed in mid-1961—to study pooling of resources and the possibility of adopting a single design.

The first joint BAC/Sud meetings were held in Paris on June 8 1961 and at Weybridge on July 10 1961. Formal agreement came 16 months later—after technical agreement had been reached on a joint design, resources in Britain and France discussed and responsibilities defined, and a full report made on all aspects of the proposals to the respective Ministers.

Historic Agreement—the Beginning of Concorde

What was to become one of the most outstanding international political and industrial treaties ever was the:

'Agreement between the government of the United Kingdom of Great Britain and Northern Ireland and the government of the French Republic regarding the development and production of a civil supersonic transport aircraft'

which was signed at Lancaster House in London on November 29 1962—by Mr. Julian Amery, the British Minister of Aviation and M. Geoffroy de Courcel, the French Ambassador to Britain.

From this impressively brief and simple agreement (with no cancellation clause) stemmed an international technical and industrial enterprise that was unprecedented in the field of commercial aviation.

Concorde thus became not only the first major international collaborative venture in advanced technology to be started in Europe but also the largest and most complex industrial

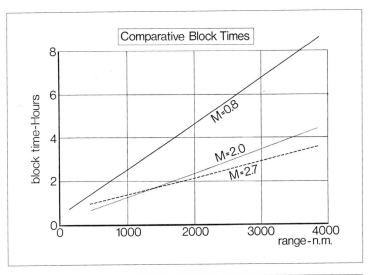

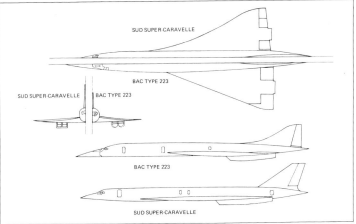

programme ever to be undertaken by two nations in peacetime.

British Aircraft Corporation in the UK and Sud-Aviation in France (that is today part of Société Nationale Industrielle Aérospatiale—SNIAS) were charged with the responsibility for the airframe and Bristol Siddeley (that is today part of Rolls-Royce) of the UK and Société Nationale d'Étude et de Construction de Moteurs d'Aviation (SNECMA) of France were to be responsible for the powerplant.

The Significance of a Name

Soon afterwards the eminently appropriate name 'Concorde' was suggested by 18-year-old Timothy Clark, son of Mr. F. G. Clark, Sales Publicity Manager of the BAC Filton Division, and officially adopted by both Governments.

However, it was to take another five years before the spelling of the name—with a final 'e' as in French or without as in English—was clarified. A gracious solution was reached on December 11 1967 when the first Concorde prototype (001) was ceremoniously rolled out at the Sud factory at Toulouse in France. Mr. Anthony Wedgwood Benn, British Minister of

Comparative journey block times with aircraft design cruising speeds.

Comparison (showing remarkable similarity) of the Sud-Aviation 'Super-Caravelle' and the BAC 223 SST designs that preceded the definitive Aérospatiale/BAC Concorde.

Technology, concluded his speech on that occasion with appropriate humour: 'Only one disagreement has occurred during the years of co-operation with France. We were never able to agree on the right way to spell 'Concorde'— with or without an "e". I consider this situation to be unbearable and I have decided to solve the problem myself. The British "Concorde" shall from now on also be written with an "e" for this letter is full of significance: it means "Excellence", "England", "Europe", and "Entente".' 'This is a symbol of the friendliness and understanding which links our two countries', he said.

Symbolic of excellence, 'Concorde' was soon adopted as a brand name for a wide range of products and business enterprises in many countries.

Anatomy of a Classic Shape

At this point it is appropriate to review the development of the characteristic shape of Concorde, the choice of engine and powerplant installation, and of airframe materials.

Wing Design

The primary objective in the design of the Concorde wing was the achievement of maximum aerodynamic efficiency consistent with the conflicting requirements of high and low speed flight. Hence the ultimate configuration had to be a compromise, but largely determined by the design Mach number. The higher the Mach number, the higher the angle of sweepback required, and because of the spanwise drift of the boundary layer, the aspect ratio had to be kept small to prevent a large build-up at the wing tip.

In considering the ideal planform for supersonic flight the point is reached where it is possible to lengthen the root chord of a highly swept wing and straighten the trailing edge for lateral and pitch control placement and thus eliminate the need for a horizontal stabiliser The result is the 'delta' planform.

A major advantage of this shape is that the greatly lengthened root chord means that the enclosed volume of the wing and hence the fuel capacity are considerably increased for a given thickness/chord ratio. The large root chord also means that the delta wing can overcome all the disadvantages of lack of structural stiffness and lack of wing volume associated with thin, highly swept wings, and yet remain aerodynamically thin.

The sudden drop in lift/drag (L/D) ratio that occurred at around Mach 1.0, as mentioned earlier, was associated with a rearward shift of centre of lift. Experience at speeds beyond Mach 1.2 showed that the fore and aft control problem could be solved by provision of adequate trimming and that the rapid fall in L/D in the transonic regime is checked at around

Sir Archibald Russell.

Dr. William Strang.

M. Pierre Satre.

M. Lucien Servanty.

Mach 1.15 and thereafter decreases quite gradually if a suitable delta shape was chosen. The optimum theoretical shape for cruise performance for Mach 2.0 was found to be a slender delta about three times as long as its semi-span with slenderness increasing for higher speeds—more slender shapes having completely unacceptable handling characteristics at low speed.

For the Concorde mission the simple 'triangle' had unsatisfactory characteristics at low speed and also required further development to meet a number of conflicting requirements implicit in that mission which can be broadly summarised in four main respects: supersonic wave drag— due to lift and volume—minimised by the use of large wing chord; vortex drag—at all speeds —minimised by the use of large wingspan; skin friction drag and wing structure weight— each minimised by scrupulous adherence to close tolerance engineering and assembly standards; and kinetic heating which, as already explained, is a direct function of the design cruising speed.

Satisfying these conflicting requirements led to the development of the now familiar 'Ogee', (or 'Wine Glass') wing planform shape for Concorde and it was found possible to achieve the required L/D, with a moderately long fuselage nose.

At the same time a position for the centre of gravity could be obtained with realistic location of payload and fuel—which had to be forward of the subsonic aerodynamic centre in low speed flight and coincident with the centre of lift in supersonic cruise. It was found that the distance between these centres could be substantially reduced by suitably shaping the triangle to a curved ogival shape, with increased sweepback at the root and tip. By using curved 'streamwise' tips and extending the root fillets forward it was found possible to ensure attachment of the leading edge vortex sheet—which is formed naturally on this type of wing—right down to and below the 'stall'.

The resulting wing has a very important additional aerodynamic characteristic in that it does not have a stall in the generally accepted sense; the development of these vortices means that the stall angle is so large that it is impossible to reach a stalled condition in any reasonable condition of flight. At minimum control speed the attached vortex increases lift by as much as 30 per cent in free air and twice as much in the ground cushion. It thus acts as a 'variable area wing' without the attendant problems of a mechanical system—other than the need for an automatic throttle control to cope with speed instability.

The flow development is smooth with increase in incidence and so is the lift and pitching moment. The flow also changes smoothly with Mach number. There are therefore no abrupt changes in aerodynamic characteristics through the operating range of incidence and Mach number.

Because of the considerable rearward shift of aerodynamic centre of pressure as the aircraft passes through the transonic acceleration phase, substantial retrimming of the aircraft becomes necessary.

This is achieved on Concorde by the unique feature of transferring fuel from a group of tanks forward of the centre of gravity (CG) to a tank in the rear fuselage. After supersonic cruise, the fuel is transferred forward again to restore the subsonic CG position. By using fuel transfer to maintain the trim of the aircraft there is no penalty in extra drag which would be involved if aerodynamic means had been used. All the trim fuel is usable, being part of the total fuel load.

In the necessity to optimise the fuel load—taking into account both supersonic and subsonic performance—the low speed regime is especially significant in the Concorde mission. Fortuitously the final shape of the aircraft has also resulted in a pattern of holding and approach performance that is comparable to current subsonic jets. Hence, as its now extensive route flying has shown, Concorde can be readily integrated with existing air traffic control and airport procedures.

In summary, the ultimate design of the Concorde wing has resulted in an excellent compromise between good low-speed controllability, high supersonic cruise efficiency and optimum overall efficiency, since, as predicted, the increase in drag from around Mach 1.5 up to Mach 2.0 has been more than balanced by the steady increase in propulsive efficiency of the Olympus engine.

Fuselage

The technical demands of the operating domain of Concorde have also resulted in a slim and sleek payload carrier. Since frontal area is very expensive in terms of supersonic drag, the fuselage cross-section is a minimum consistent with an optimum standard of four-abreast seating.

Sized to provide a natural growth in productivity compared to first generation intercontinental jets, Concorde will carry between 108 and 144 passengers.

The external temperature of the fuselage skin at cruise of around 120°C has to be reduced to around 20°C inside the passenger cabin within the space of only 5 in. (12.7 cm.). This is a completely new problem in commercial airliner design.

Because Concorde cruises $1\frac{1}{2}$ times as high as today's intercontinental jets, a maximum cabin working differential pressure of 10.7 lb./sq. in. (0.75 kg./sq. cm.) is necessary.

While these factors accentuate the physical problems of the design of the interior, as stated earlier, the drastically reduced journey times effectively equate Concorde operation to that of a short-haul jet. However, this has not resulted in any relaxation in comfort or environmental standards.

Despite the severe technical and operational restraints and the inability fully to exploit 'sculpturing' techniques, the experienced BAC/ Charles Butler partnership has evolved a most attractive and space-efficient interior concept to match the imaginative new marketing concepts discussed later.

All delta wing aircraft have a relatively high angle of incidence at slow speeds, including approach and landing. Improvement of pilot visibility for Concorde is achieved by moving the nose downwards and by lowering the transparent visor—another completely new requirement for a commercial aircraft. For landing, the nose is in the fully drooped position (−15°) and for taxi-ing and take-off it is in the intermediate (−5°) drooped position. The visor is fully raised for high speed flight to give a clean aerodynamic shape by covering and hence fairing off the windshields. It also protects the windshield from the effects of kinetic heating.

The Propulsion System

The choice of engines for Concorde was also the end-product of many conflicting requirements. Essentially these were that it should have a high specific thrust for take-off, transonic acceleration and supersonic cruise, together with low fuel consumption in both supersonic and subsonic conditions. A very high pressure-ratio turbojet would have given a low power-plant weight but would have resulted in an excessive turbine entry temperature. A high by-pass ratio engine could have shown improved fuel consumption but with its lower specific thrust would have required a heavier overall powerplant installation and its large diameter would also have meant a high momentum drag; the weight penalty more than offset the weight of fuel saved.

Consequently a moderate pressure-ratio turbojet with a cooled turbine was chosen because at supersonic speeds a substantial compression occurs in the nacelle intake and therefore the pressure ratio required from the engine itself is much lower.

Such an engine could be made available in the required size by development of the Bristol 'Olympus' military turbojet that was already in production for the BAC TSR.2 supersonic bomber.

The commercial version of this engine—the Olympus 593—with a compressor pressure ratio of 11.3:1 at the design cruise condition of Mach 2 at 60,000 ft. ISA + 5°C, combined with a small frontal area and low overall powerplant weight, has proved to be an excellent choice for Concorde. Nevertheless it has been a major development. Its thrust was increased partly by modifying the compressors and partly by using the high turbine entry temperature permitted by the cooled turbine essential for sustained cruising at supersonic speeds.

The location of Concorde's powerplant under the wing ensured that the intakes were in a region of minimum-thickness boundary layer and favourable pressure fields, and changes in intake flow direction during take-off and final approach were minimised. Additionally, it made for ready accessibility for servicing.

Due to the wide speed range the intake/exhaust systems have to be carefully matched to the engine. To meet the engine air demands, variable area intakes are required to enable the engine compressor inlet to be presented with a subsonic airflow and to ensure maximum pressure recovery at all flight speeds. Thus the engines are arranged in pairs in rectangular cross-section nacelles giving substantially two-dimensional flow in the intake ducts, and to simplify mechanical control of the variable geometry intake.

The convergent/divergent intake duct is formed by means of moveable ramps in the roof of the intake and a spill door, incorporating intake flaps, in the floor of the intake. The front ramp causes the formation of a shock-system to reduce the speed of the inlet air to just below the speed of sound. The air is further decelerated in the divergent duct formed by the rear ramp. During take-off the ramps are fully raised and the flaps in the spill door automatically open inwards to provide maximum air flow to the engine. At speeds above Mach 1.3 the ramps start to lower automatically to control the position of the shock waves and achieve the required reduction of air velocity at the engine face. During Mach 2.0 cruise, conditions at the compressor inlet are Mach 0.45 and pressure equivalent to about seven times ambient.

A variable convergent/divergent exhaust system is also essential for thrust and performance optimisation at all conditions, and a reheat system is used to provide thrust boost at take-off and during transonic acceleration.

The exhaust assembly—incorporating the latest system known as the TRA (Thrust Reverser Aft) or Type 28 nozzle—comprises a variable area primary nozzle, the TRA feature which is a combined secondary nozzle with reverser buckets, and retractable 'spade' type silencers. This assembly forms a monobloc structure for each pair of engines. The two 'clamshell buckets' at the rear of the unit perform the dual function of variable secondary nozzle and thrust reverser. Apertures in the upper and lower surfaces allow exit of the deflected exhaust gas during reverse operation and inward passage of tertiary air to control exhaust gas expansion during flight.

The TRA is also used to reduce airport noise by the action of the secondary nozzle on the exhaust jet stream. 'Fish Tailing', or squashing, the jet at take-off reduces significantly the side-line noise level. This system also incorporates eight equi-spaced retractable spade silencers, housed in the main body of the secondary exhaust assembly, which are deployed to reduce community noise during the fly-over phase.

The Olympus 593 Mk.602—the production standard engine—is a substantial improvement over earlier variants, with greater thrust and lower fuel consumption. Its new-design pre-vaporisation type annular combustor virtually eliminates all smoke emission by ensuring more complete combustion of the fuel/oxidant mixture.

By the time the Olympus 593 is introduced into airline service it will have undergone one of the most extensive development programmes ever and will have logged more than 35,000 bench and flight hours—including an initial programme of airborne testing in a complete nacelle unit mounted under a Vulcan bomber testbed aircraft.

The Thermal Problem and Materials

For reasons already discussed, the primary airframe constructional material for Concorde is aluminium alloy.

The under-wing variable-geometry engine air intake section monobloc for two of Concorde's Olympus engines on one side of the aircraft.

However, the thermal problem is a complex one. Because the creep-resistance of this material falls rapidly with increasing temperature the strongest types were not suitable. Hence it was decided to adopt the more conservative aluminium/copper alloys of a type long used for engine components—since become known as 'Hiduminium RR 58' in Britain and 'AU2GN' in France.

Hitherto these alloys had been employed mainly as forgings but they have since been made available as sheet and plate in the sizes required for Concorde. Very substantial fatigue and sustained-load tests on these materials at elevated temperatures have been in progress since 1962 and Concordes makers are satisfied that they are completely safe and satisfactory within the aircraft flight envelope.

In addition to these considerations of basic material choice, exceptional care has been taken in the structural design process to take account of thermal stresses.

While the external skin temperature of Concorde's wing is raised to around 120°C at supersonic cruise, the internal structure only picks up heat by conduction, thus putting the skin into compression and the internal structure into tension. Special provisions, such as pin-jointed attachments and fluted webs, are used to relieve the resultant strains.

All these problems of thermal fatigue are being studied by carefully simulated tests in which a complete Concorde airframe, located in a major new thermal test facility at the RAE Farnborough, is being subjected to alternate heating and cooling cycles to represent flight conditions. This complements the static loading test airframe at the CEAT facility at Toulouse.

Analogous considerations and provisions have also been made in the design of the systems, all of which are also being subjected to rigorous full-scale facsimile testing.

The Concorde Formula

In summary, the principal ingredients of a practical and efficient long-range supersonic airliner were found to be a cruising speed of Mach 2.0; a slender ogival delta wing, with controlled separation aerodynamics; a slim 100-140 seat fuselage, with drooping nose section for adequate pilot visibility in low speed flight and on the ground; four moderate pressure ratio Olympus turbojet engines; and a substantially aluminium-alloy structure.

Close-up of a pair of the TRA (Thrust Reverser Aft) variable-area engine exhaust nozzle and thrust reverser/silencer 'clamshell bucket' units.

The Rolls-Royce-SNECMA Olympus 593 axial-flow two-spool turbojet engine of Concorde.

From Concept to Reality

As stated earlier, the independent SST studies in Britain and France during the late-1950s exhibited a remarkable degree of agreement on how to design an SST.

Significantly, both BAC and Sud had decided on the same design cruising speed for the same reasons and both had chosen a low aspect ratio slender delta wing planform, a slim (four-abreast passenger seating) fuselage with a large nose overhang, and a single fin but no tailplane —and hence 'elevons' on the wing trailing edges to combine the lateral and pitching control functions. Another common feature was the location of the underwing nacelles housing pairs of engines fed by rectangular intakes. So too was the side-folding landing gear inboard of these nacelles.

However, Sud believed that a conventional pilots windscreen could be designed with adequate visibility without generating excessive supersonic drag, whereas BAC proposed a more radical downward-hinging nose for this purpose. BAC initially believed that the wing needed to be in the mid-position with the rear spar box passing right across the fuselage—which meant restricting the available passenger space ahead of it—while Sud favoured a low-set wing.

It is perhaps rough justice to say that each company misjudged one major design feature. On the other hand, it is particularly impressive to note just how little the eventual joint design has had to be changed and hence how evidently sound it was.

Nevertheless, a substantial difference did exist in the definition of the operational mission. Based on its most successful experience with the

Part of the Concorde airframe thermal fatigue cycling test facility at the Royal Aircraft Establishment (RAE), Farnborough, England—showing sections of the electrical heat cycling 'glove' being lowered over the rear fuselage.

Underside view of the Olympus-Vulcan flying engine test bed aircraft incorporating a full-scale facsimile of one of Concorde's power-plant units (but with the earlier-type exhaust system)

The complete airframe thermal test rig facility at Farnborough.

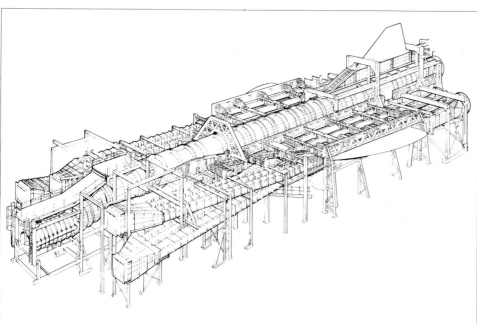

Caravelle, Sud proposed a 70-80 seat medium-range 'Super Caravelle', whereas BAC, influenced by its Britannia and VC10 experience, was convinced that a 125-seat aircraft with transatlantic capability was the right course to follow.

The Problems of Compromise

To achieve the joint agreement of 1962 a compromise was made whereby the technical proposals comprised both versions—a medium range one with a ventral entry (à la Caravelle) and a long-range one with the necessary extra fuel in cells in the rear fuselage.

Failure of the two sides to unify their thoughts in a single design at this stage has since proved to be very expensive.

However, working together, the short-haul requirement was slowly eroded away, but a vestige of that early period is to be found in the fact that by the time Concorde enters service three quite distinct versions will have been built —the prototypes (001 and 002), the pre-production aircraft (01 and 02), and the production-standard (201 onwards)—assembled alternately in Britain and France.

From Prototype to Production

When it was ultimately decided to concentrate on the long-range mission, the initial two-version compromise design required considerable revision.

The provision of more fuel disposed around the aircraft centre of gravity demanded more underfloor fuel tanks. In turn, this used up existing baggage space for which an alternative had to be found in the tail cone. This led to the demise of the ventral stairway and hence a second access door was needed on the port side.

Experience gained in the incorporation of these features in the initial prototypes, together with emerging airline influences, led to the need to build two more development vehicles—the so-called 'pre-production' aircraft. Increased passenger capacity was provided by extending the fuselage ahead of the wing and moving the rear bulkhead further back. Four important aerodynamic refinements were also incorporated at this stage: a new fully transparent nose visor to provide greater pilot visibility; new outer wings—to improve airflow by increasing tip chord and revising the camber and twist—thereby reducing the supersonic trim drag; new wing leading edges to improve performance; and improved nacelles to incorporate the higher thrust smoke-free production standard engines and the new TRA thrust reverser/silencer nozzles—providing improved thrust, reduced noise and a substantial weight reduction.

In the second pre-production aircraft (02) a new-design lengthened low-drag rear fuselage shape was also incorporated to reduce supersonic afterbody drag and increase fuel capacity,

and further changes were made to the wing leading edge shape to improve low incidence interference with the engine intakes at cruise Mach number.

Construction of the two prototypes began in April 1965. The first of these—Concorde 001 (F-WTSS) assembled by Aérospatiale at Toulouse—was first flown on March 2 1969 by André Turcat, the company's Director of Flight Test. Concorde 002 (G-BSST)—assembled by BAC at Filton—was flown six weeks later on April 9 1969 by Brian Trubshaw, Director of Flight Test of the BAC Commercial Aircraft Division.

The first pre-production Concorde 01 (G-AXDN) was first flown by Trubshaw from BAC Filton on December 17 1971 and the second, Concorde 02 (F-WTSA) which is fully representative of the production aircraft, by Jean Franchi at Toulouse on January 10 1973.

British Government Declares Support

The growing acceptance of Concorde by Government and Airline VIPs from many parts of the world was eventually crowned by the whole-hearted public declaration of support by the British Government which was announced by Mr. John Davies, Secretary of State for Trade and Industry, on December 10 1971. After his Concorde flight he said: 'Concorde is now an aircraft which, having passed through periods of great controversy and debate and argument and discussion, is in a new phase of its life—a new phase because we are now going to see this aircraft become a great commercial proposition, and I think every one of us in the Government feels that there is no effort to be spared to see that the Concorde gets the commercial success that this great project is due.'

This support has since been keenly sustained by Mr. Michael Heseltine, Minister for Aerospace —notably during the big demonstration tour of Concorde 002 in mid-1972 detailed later.

Flight Development

By the time Concorde enters airline service, it will have been more thoroughly researched, tested and proven than any previous commercial aircraft. More than a decade of ground testing and around 3,890 hours of flight testing will ensure safety and reliability.

Seven aircraft are being used in the flight development programme: the two prototypes, 001 and 002, the two pre-production aircraft, 01 and 02, and the first three series production aircraft. The bulk of this flying is being done by the four test aircraft and the three production aircraft will be used mainly for route proving and endurance flying, after which they will be refurbished for airline service.

An indication of the scope and thoroughness of prototype testing, 001 and 002 each carry around 12 tons (12.2 tonnes) of specially developed equipment which is capable of simultaneously measuring and recording 3,000 separate data points.

Progress to date has been highly satisfactory with both the British and French flight test teams, with remarkably few problems encountered, and performance and handling have been progressively ratified by many airline pilots throughout the operational speed range.

Production Standard Concorde

The series production standard Concorde will be 203 ft. 9 in. long (61.66 m.); 37 ft. 1 in. high (11.32 m.); and 83 ft. 10 in. (25.56 m.) wingspan; carry 108-144 passengers; be powered by four Rolls-Royce Olympus 593 Mk602 turbojets of 38,050 lb. (17,260 kg.) static thrust each; cruise at a speed of Mach 2.0 (about 1,300 m.p.h. or 2,092 k.p.h.) at altitudes of 50,000 to 60,000 ft. (15,240 to 18,290 m.); have a range capability of 3,853 miles (6,196 km.); and a maximum take-off weight of 389,000 lb. (176,450 kg.).

The design payload of 20,000 lb. (9,072 kg.) on entry into service is equivalent to 100 passengers and baggage matched to the Paris-New York sector. This payload capability is to be increased to 24,000 lb. (10,886 kg.) two years after entry into service. The volumetric capacity is 28,000 lb. (12,701 kg.).

Series Production

From the prototypes onwards, Concorde manufacture has been progressively organised on a series production basis with fully developed tooling.

The British share of Concorde manufacture is the responsibility of the BAC Commercial Aircraft Division, the Filton (Bristol) factory of which is the 'control' and final assembly centre. The Weybridge (Surrey) factory is the largest single contributor to the entire Concorde programme and builds and equips virtually all British-made components—the nose and forward fuselage, the rear and tail fuselage, and the fin and rudders. The droop-nose is built at the BAC Hurn (Bournemouth) factory and the engine nacelles at Filton and BAC Preston. Flight testing of British-assembled Concordes is at Fairford (Gloucestershire).

The French share—which comprises the wing and centre fuselage is handled by the Aérospatiale factories at Toulouse, Marignane, St. Nazaire, Bourges and Bouguenais. Flight development is conducted at Toulouse.

The Olympus engine is made at the Rolls-Royce factory at Patchway (Bristol) and the thrust reverser/silencer unit by SNECMA at Melun-Villaroche, near Paris.

Because there are two final assembly centres in the overall Concorde production programme —at Filton and Toulouse—it became essential to organise the dispersed component manufacturing programme in Britain and France in such a way that as much equipment as possible be installed at each component manufacturing centre in order to eliminate the 'double learning factor' that would be entailed if all the equipment was installed at the final assembly stage. Additionally, this enabled considerable benefit to be derived from the greater working access available at the component build stage.

Typifying this process is the nose and forward fuselage built and equipped at BAC Weybridge. This 50 ft. long component comprises the flight deck and engineer's station, the forward part of the passenger cabin and the nose landing gear bay. It is equipped to a very high standard with electrical, hydraulic, flying control and air-conditioning systems and cabin insulation and incorporates 25,000 parts and 90 miles of wiring.

The completion of these major airframe components to such a high standard away from the final assembly centres, is unique. It is the first programme in which major components for such a sophisticated aircraft have been pre-equipped to such an advanced standard and high quality of completion prior to final assembly of the complete aircraft.

The complexity and compact nature of Concorde engineering has demanded a high level of co-ordination within the many BAC and Aérospatiale factories and subcontractors and suppliers involved in Britain and France.

Quality control has also had to be of a high order, especially in respect of the complex interfaces between components which clearly must mate precisely in final assembly.

Odd-numbered aircraft (201, 203, 205 etc.) are being assembled in France and the even-numbered ones (202, 204, 206 etc.) in Britain and capacity has already been established for a combined output of three aircraft per month.

Full authorisation for the first 16 series production Concordes has already been given by the two Governments, plus the procurement of long-dated parts and materials for a further six aircraft. This means that the total programme—including prototype, pre-production and test aircraft—now embraces 28 Concorde airframes.

Concorde—The Great Collaboration

The task of organisation and management that stemmed from the Anglo-French agreement of 1962 was unprecedented in the aerospace business, not only because the aircraft was to be developed on a collaborative basis but also because of its sheer size and complexity.

Grappling with the problems of working with two frequently changing national governments and policies, two languages, monetary and measurement systems; two design, assembly and flight test centres separated by physical and national barriers 600 miles apart; and the co-ordination of around 800 subcontractors and suppliers—have been the principal challenges of collaboration and programme management.

Component manufacturing breakdown and responsibilities.

Nose and forward fuselage (Component 30) assembly line at BAC Weybridge. These (and all other major airframe components) are equipped to a high standard at this stage prior to transfer to the Filton and Toulouse final assembly centres.

Part of the 12 tons (12.2 tonnes) of flight test measuring and recording equipment carried by the Concorde prototypes 001 and 002.

PRODUCTION MANUFACTURE BREAKDOWN — MAJOR ITEMS

	COMPONENT	DESIGN	MANUFACTURE
07	Air Intakes	BAC	BAC — Preston
08	Engine Bay	BAC	BAC — Filton
09	Droop Nose	BAC	BAC — Hurn
10	Nose Fuselage	BAC	BAC — Weybridge
11	Forward Fuselage	BAC	BAC — Weybridge
12	Intermediate Fuselage	BAC	A-S — Marignane
24	Rear Fuselage	BAC	BAC — Weybridge
26	Fin	BAC	BAC — Weybridge
27	Rudder	BAC	BAC — Weybridge
13	Forward Wing	Aerospatiale	A-S — Bouguenais
14	Centre Wing	Aerospatiale	A-S — Marignane
15	Centre Wing	Aerospatiale	A-S — Bouguenais
16	Centre Wing	Aerospatiale	A-S — Toulouse
18	Centre Wing	Aerospatiale	A-S — Toulouse
20	Centre Wing	Aerospatiale	A-S — St Nazaire
21	Outer Wing	Aerospatiale	A-S — Bourges
23	Elevons	Aerospatiale	A-S — Bouguenais
51	Main Landing Gear		Hispano/Messier
51	Nose Landing Gear		Hispano/Messier
06	TRA Nozzles		SNECMA
	Engines		Rolls-Royce (1971) Ltd.

SYSTEMS RESPONSIBILITIES

BRITISH AIRCRAFT CORPORATION	AEROSPATIALE
Electrics	Hydraulics
Oxygen	Flying Controls
Fuel	Navigation
Engine instrumentation	Radio
Engine controls	Air conditioning supply
Fire	
Air conditioning distribution	
De-icing	

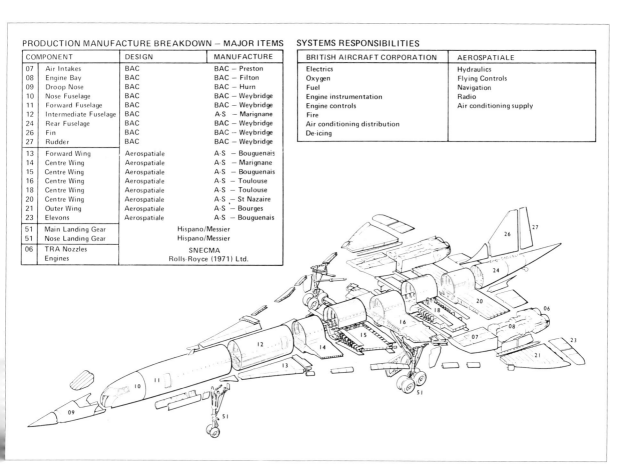

A few basic statistics give dimension to the current scope and magnitude of the Concorde task.

Around 24 thousand people are now engaged directly on the programme in Britain and a similar number in France. Several times that number are involved indirectly. Expenditure is currently running at a level equivalent to £1½ million a week in each country. These numbers will increase substantially when full series production is established. The co-ordination of activity on this scale is clearly a very formidable management task.

Task Distribution

The industrial task distribution was based on the principle of an equal sharing of work, expenses and the proceeds of sales.

Because the Olympus 593 engine constituted 60 per cent of the powerplant package the overall 50/50 split between the two countries was maintained by BAC being given approximately 40 per cent of the airframe and systems i.e. the forward and aft sections of the fuselage, the fin and rudder, engine nacelles, and the electrical, oxygen, fuel supply, engine controls and instrumentation, fire warning and extinguishing systems, air-conditioning distribution and de-icing systems. On the French side, Sud was thus given the other 60 per cent of the airframe i.e. the wings and the centre fuselage plus the hydraulic, air conditioning supply, flying controls, and radio and navigation systems —and SNECMA became responsible for the remaining 40 per cent of the powerplant i.e. the re-heat, exhaust and thrust reverser/silencer nozzle assembly.

In practice, work contracts on BAC and Rolls-Royce are placed by the British Government and those with Aérospatiale and SNECMA by the French Government. Each Government and company is then responsible for the control of expenditure within its own area.

Financing the Concorde development and production programmes is being wholly undertaken by the two Governments. This means that they are intimately involved in all aspects of the programme, including its commercial exploitation, with a mandate to scrutinise and control the deployment of funds provided by their taxpayers.

Programme Management Directorate

In addition to specifying the allocation of development and manufacture, the 1962 Treaty also laid down the principles of the basic organisational structure for the programme. While there have been changes in the meantime to reflect the evolving maturity of the programme, these fundamental principles have stood the test of time extremely well and continue to be the basis of the programme supervision and administration.

Whereas the day-to-day management is

necessarily the responsibility of the manufacturers, officials of the two Governments play a fully complementary supervisory role. Hence Boards of management were established at both Government and industrial levels.

The overall management policy instrument at Government level is the Concorde Directing Committee (CDC) with members drawn from the two countries 'to supervise the progress of the work, report to the Governments and propose the necessary measures to ensure the carrying out of the programme.'

The Chairmanship of the CDC rotates periodically between Britain and France. Representation on the British side is drawn from the Department of Trade and Industry (which is currently responsible for the overall policy of the Concorde programme in UK), the Procurement Executive of the Ministry of Defence (whose headquarters, branches and R. & D. establishments—in particular the RAE and the NGTE—provide considerable assistance to the Concorde programme), and the Treasury. The French members of the CDC cover a similar span of responsibilities.

The CDC is supported by the Concorde Management Board (CMB) which is composed of senior civil servants. Under the general direction of the CDC, this Board is responsible for the day-to-day oversight and co-ordination of the programme. Chairmanship of the CMB rotates annually between the British and French, alternating between the Director-General, Concorde—DoTI and the Directeur General Projects de le Secretariat Général a l'Aviation Civile respectively.

Reporting to the CMB are the 'Aircraft Committee of Directors' and the 'Engine Committee of Directors' which together comprise the senior industrial executives.

Two governments and four major industrial companies are thus inter-linked in the Concorde programme by means of four committees of management, each of which consists of officials from each nation, duplicating responsibility, chairman and deputy, functional directors and deputy, with seniorities alternating but always with equal representation.

This arrangement has now worked for more than a decade because, as Sir George Edwards puts it: 'Success has revolved around personalities, the great desire for each to understand the other, to respect his point of view, and to get on with him as a man.'

While the two Governments and their Ministers have undergone frequent and fundamental changes, and there has been a succession of leaders on this side of the Concorde team, industrial chiefs have been subject to very few changes.

The progress of Concorde from conception to hardware has been strongly characterised by the interplay of personal characteristics of its industrial leaders.

Geographical location of Concorde manufacturing centres.

Concorde Governmental and Industrial Programme Management Directorate.

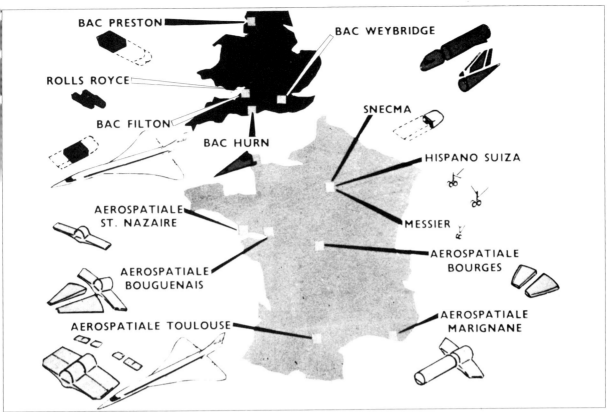

BAC PRESTON
BAC WEYBRIDGE
ROLLS ROYCE
SNECMA
BAC FILTON
HISPANO SUIZA
BAC HURN
AEROSPATIALE
ST. NAZAIRE
MESSIER
AEROSPATIALE
BOURGES
AEROSPATIALE
BOUGUENAIS
AEROSPATIALE
MARIGNANE
AEROSPATIALE TOULOUSE

Sir George Edwards, who has lead the British Concorde team with outstanding acumen since its inception, accredits 'the great breakthrough' to the late General André Puget—President of Sud Aviation 1962–66—who was first given the job of managing the Concorde programme in France. 'These were critical times, when the Concorde project was going to be made or broken', says Sir George. 'It was Puget, more than anyone else, who saw to it that Concorde would be made.'

Significantly the two current industrial leaders —Sir George Edwards of BAC and General Henri Ziegler of Aérospatiale—have a long working relationship. They first worked together in 1952 when Sir George was head of Vickers-Armstrongs (Aircraft) and selling Viscount prop-jets to Air France which General Ziegler headed at that time. Later they worked closely together again on the BAC-Breguet Jaguar military strike/trainer aircraft programme when General Ziegler was in charge of Breguet Aviation. General Ziegler has been President of Aérospatiale since 1968 and has made a major impact during the critical period from prototype first flight to the initiation of first customer contracts.

Collaboration in Practice

The first practical link in Anglo-French collaboration was forged by Sir George in 1958 when he arranged for the fin and tailplane components of the Super VC10, then in production by Vickers-Armstrongs at Weybridge, to be built by Sud-Aviation at its St. Nazaire factory—

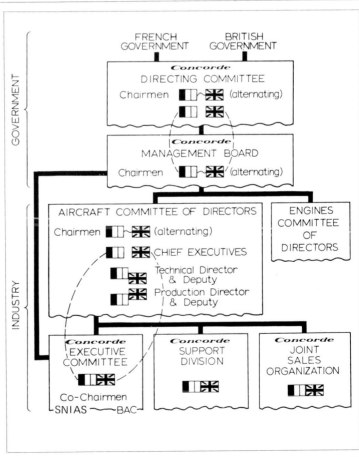

GOVERNMENT

FRENCH GOVERNMENT   BRITISH GOVERNMENT

Concorde
DIRECTING COMMITTEE
Chairmen (alternating)

Concorde
MANAGEMENT BOARD
Chairmen (alternating)

INDUSTRY

AIRCRAFT COMMITTEE OF DIRECTORS
Chairmen (alternating)
CHIEF EXECUTIVES
Technical Director & Deputy
Production Director & Deputy

ENGINES COMMITTEE OF DIRECTORS

Concorde
EXECUTIVE COMMITTEE
Co-Chairmen
SNIAS — BAC

Concorde
SUPPORT DIVISION

Concorde
JOINT SALES ORGANIZATION

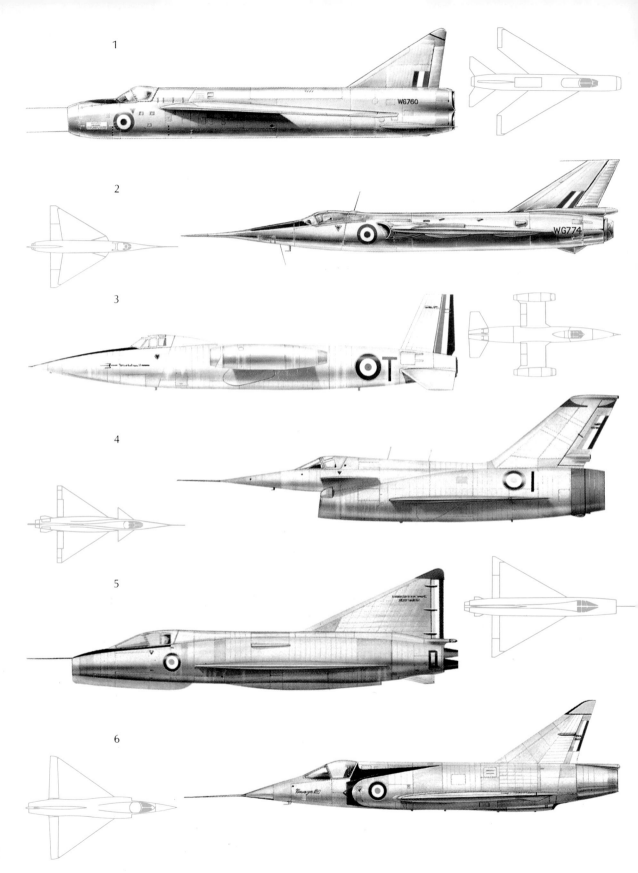

1

2

3

4

5

6

fundamentally to establish the plain human job of working together. This initiated the essential experience of interchange of personnel, working drawings and manufacturing techniques, and, of course, of language and measurement conversions. The result was a complete success and a vital preface to the large scale production dispersal on Concorde that has since been organised in Britain and France.

Language and measurement have not, in fact, resulted in any insurmountable problems. Manufacturing drawings carry both English and Metric units. Each side designs in its own units and then the corresponding equivalent is added as a routine. Thus it is fair to say that, despite the current topicality of 'Metrication', Concordes designers overcame this problem long ago.

A much more formidable task has been the mutual agreement of standards for materials— normally a routine. A special organisation was set up for this purpose and to date more than 2,500 joint standards have been established.

The inevitability of different approaches to the solution of technical problems has at times proved to be most arduous and frustrating. However, the value of the ensuing cross-fertilisation of ideas and practices has been amply vindicated by the substantially trouble-free flight development of Concorde so far, especially in view of the radical advances in so many areas compared with the previous levels of technology of which the partners had experience.

Communications

As in all successful businesses, good communications have been essential. This has been especially evident in the complexities of the joint design engineering organisation which totals over 2,000 people.

There are teams of each nationality resident in each other's camps to hammer out the day-to-day problems associated with their particular responsibility because each aeroplane, whether it be assembled in Filton or in Toulouse, is assembled from components and equipments produced from many sources in both countries.

International communications consist of tie-line telephone and telex links and land-line facsimile reproducing facilities, while for physical transportation there is a fleet of communications aircraft.

BAC currently uses an eight-seat Hawker-Siddeley H.S.125 jet (G-AVPE) which operates a thrice weekly schedule between Filton and Toulouse and numerous VIP flights as required. Rolls-Royce also uses an eight-seat H.S.125 (G-ATPB) for personnel and an H.S. Argosy (G-APRM) freighter for engines and parts transport between the UK and France.

Aérospatiale uses a 12-seat Nord 262 propjet (F-BLKE) for personnel transport. The Aero-Spacelines G-201 'Guppy' freighter (F-BTGV), operated by Aéromaritime of France, is now used for the international transport of the majority of large Concorde airframe components.

Marketing the Twelve-hour World

Concorde's ability to halve journey times and to enable the longest journey on earth to be completed in a single day will open up an entirely new vista in international air transport marketing.

First practical evidence of this came in September 1971 when Concorde 001 made an exacting and impressive demonstration tour to South America.

This was confirmed on a wide-ranging geographical basis by the 45,000 mile sales demonstration tour of the Middle and Far East, and Australia by Concorde 002 between June 2 and July 1 1972. Flying substantially faster and higher (Mach 2.05 at 57,000 ft., 17,373 m.) than any previous commercial aircraft, Concorde established its huge speed advantage while fitting effortlessly into the traffic patterns of thirteen international airports.

The most arduous and ambitious sales demonstration mission ever undertaken by a prototype aircraft, this tour was successfully completed exactly on time with only minor and insignificant faults and delays—of the kind that a fully-established current jetliner experiences in service—and with a significant improvement in predicted fuel consumption.

Concorde flew in 62 hours what scheduled subsonic airliner flights would have taken a total of $24\frac{1}{2}$ hours longer.

On the ground, Concorde's serviceability was quite outstanding and in four weeks of almost constant flying only six hours were lost through purely technical reasons. This was achieved by a small support team travelling in RAF VC10 and Belfast aircraft and without the normal in-service benefits of service support and spare part supplies at most major international airports.

Contributing to Concorde technology (see also page 109)

1 English Electric (now BAC) P.1 (serial WG760); August 1954.

2 Fairey Delta 2 (WG774); October 1954.

3 Sud-Ouest S.O. 9050 Trident II ('T'); July 1955.

4 Nord-SFECMAS 1502 Griffon ('I'); September 1955.

5 Sud-Est S.E.212 Durandal ('D'); April 1956.

6 Dassault Mirage IIIC; October 1960.

Concorde's industrial programme leaders: (left) Sir George Edwards, Chairman of British Aircraft Corporation and (right) General Henri Ziegler, President of Aéro-spatiale of France.

The late General André Puget —first French industrial leader of the Concorde programme.

93

Airline chiefs, VIPs and over 300,000 people in 12 countries saw Concorde for the first time during this tour.

Commenting on this exceptional performance Sir George Edwards pointed out: 'We satisfied ourselves that we could meet the original design objective of operating in and out of existing airports and using existing traffic control procedures. When one remembers that the advent of the big American subsonic jets had to be almost universally accompanied by major extensions to airport runways and facilities, this is quite an achievement.'

New Marketing Concept—The Mixed Fleet Philosophy

The situation that will arise when Concorde and the wide-bodied subsonic jets are in service together has no precedent in aviation history. There will for the first time be two new, entirely different but complementary, types of air transport available, one offering advantages of high speed and the other offering advantages of high capacity.

To explore the economic potential of both types to full advantage, the manufacturers have evolved an imaginative new marketing concept for Concorde customers. The core of this is the advocation of a 'mixed fleet philosophy' of both supersonic and subsonic services. Both types of aircraft could be operated as single-class units and there are cogent economic and operational arguments to support this.

Supersonic services would cater at peak times for the businessman, and others to whom time means money, and subsonic services would be operated at fares and frequencies calculated to preserve a profitably high payload factor.

Although the business clientele represents a minority of the total traffic, it is an important and stable element which by its very nature is normally not eligible for promotional fares; one major intercontinental airline has recently established that its business traffic, amounting to about 25 per cent of the total, produces more than 40 per cent of its total revenue. Business travel is, therefore, subsidising the much less remunerative leisure traffic.

A great deal of interest has thus been generated in what has come to be known as the 'single class' philosophy as the most expeditious means of integrating Concorde into their fleet operations. This visualises the use of Concorde as a single class premium-fare vehicle catering for the business traffic, leaving the high capacity subsonic jets to be used as single-class vehicles catering for the mass travel market. In this way both types of airliner would be used in a role for which they are specifically suited, and it can be demonstrated that a correct mix of Concordes and subsonic airliners produces a higher level of profitability than an all-subsonic

Concorde centre fuselage and wing section (Component 15) being unloaded from the Aéromaritime 'Super Guppy' freighter at Filton.

fleet of similar capacity.

Because Concorde will be offering a clearly superior product—halved journey times—it is argued that it is only reasonable that this should command a higher fare and it has therefore been proposed that the interior should be configured to a 'Superior Class' offering superior standards of comfort and cabin service, but at a fare level of around 15 per cent below the current first class fare.

At present, for a surcharge of about 50 per cent over the standard economy fare level the first class passenger enjoys a somewhat higher standard of cabin amenity than the economy class passenger, but does not receive the advantage of speed.

Using the full-scale mock-up at Filton, the standard of cabin comfort and service facilities for this new concept, comparable with those of present-day first class cabins, has been demonstrated to Concorde customer airlines. The overall result is that these standards can be offered, in conjunction with enormous passenger-appeal of halved journey times, at a fare level of 15 per cent below first class (or at a premium of about 35 per cent above the economy fare level) and a healthy economic return on investment is predicted.

In this way, Concorde is confidently expected to attract all the existing first class traffic from the subsonic jets, where the two types are operated together, and to attract a significant proportion of the business traffic which currently takes advantage of promotional fares on subsonic aircraft. There are numerous business and other passengers who can afford to pay the first class fare but who do not consider the increased cost to be justified. However, it is a reasonable assumption that if these travellers can have the benefit of halved journey times, many of them will be prepared to pay the premium fare.

Configured to this new concept Concorde will be operated in a 108-seat layout with four-abreast seats at 38 inches pitch between seat rows with generous passenger amenities.

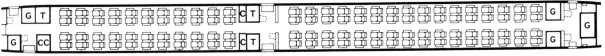

Operating Economics

According to the manufacturers, Concorde can be as profitable in operation as the Boeing 747. Recent detailed analysis of four key routes (Paris-New York; Paris-Tokyo; London-Johannesburg; and London-Sydney)—has shown that the break-even payload factors of the Concorde can be expected to be below 50 per cent and better than or equal to those of the 747.

Despite its substantially higher unit operating costs it is held that the Concorde can therefore be used on suitable routes at a level of profitability as high as or higher than that achieved by the 747.

In this respect, it is relevant to note—the makers say—that, whereas the Jumbo has to win around 165 passengers on every flight in the extremely intensive and diverse competition from the charter companies at the cheaper end of the market in order to break even, Concorde needs only 50 or less high-fare (regular) travellers to cover its costs.

First Customer Orders

Initiation of the first firm orders for Concorde was greatly facilitated when the initial pricing formula was announced in December 1971—a base price of around £13 million per aircraft.

This led to the most important event in the entire Concorde programme which occurred on July 28 1972—BOAC and Air France signed the first firm commercial contracts for five and four Concordes respectively. The Peoples Republic of China had signed a preliminary purchase agreement for two Concordes four days early and added a third a month later. Following an initial declaration of intent by the Shah of Persia at the time of the visit of Concorde 002 to Tehran in June, Iranair also signed a preliminary purchase agreement for two Concordes in October 1972.

However, the much hoped-for conversion of options into firm contracts by the key American operators Pan American and TWA at the end of January 1973 did not materialise. Though obviously a setback, the confidence of the manufacturers and the British and French governments was undiminished and firm resolve was expressed to maintain the planned date of January 1975 for the achievement of the Certificate of Airworthiness to enable BOAC and Air France to inaugurate service during that year.

30 Year Programme

Of the long-term future of Concorde Sir George Edwards said: 'The thing that lays before us is to get this programme on a proper and sensible even keel so that at the end of it there is a lot of Concordes. We must keep going until the airlines who are currently turning their backs on Concorde realise they can't afford to do so any longer. In this way we can build up to the big 30 year programme I have always envisaged the Concorde as having.

Concorde will show that the combination of standards of comfort and saving in time will make it attractive to customers. I think the operating costs are getting firmer and firmer every day and are costs which will enable the aircraft to be operated on the North Atlantic and other world routes on a profitable basis' Sir George said.

Intensive market negotiations continue throughout the world.

Inauguration of the Supersonic Age of Air Travel

Concorde will thus begin service during 1975 on the key international routes of BOAC and Air France.

BOAC's initial Concorde schedules are expected to be: twice daily between London and New York, three times a week between London and Sydney and between London and Johannesburg, and twice a week between London and Japan.

At the same time, Air France plans to begin Concorde services on the Paris-New York route twice weekly, Paris-Buenos Aires six times weekly, and the Trans-Siberian Paris-Tokyo route twice weekly.

The Civil Aviation Administration of China says that Concorde could cut the present journey time between Peking and Paris from around 20 hours to only 8 hours.

Product Support

To match the needs of these global operations,

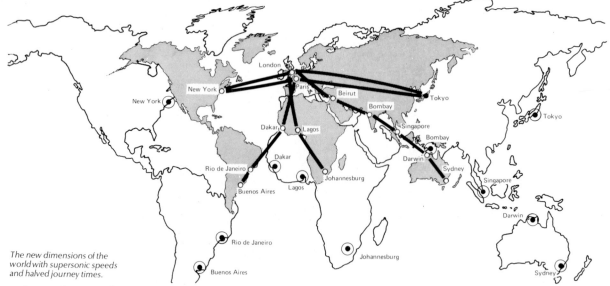

The new dimensions of the world with supersonic speeds and halved journey times.

a big and comprehensive product support organisation is already well advanced in the planning stage—through the joint BAC/Aérospatiale Concorde Support Division (CSD) and the Rolls-Royce/SNECMA Concorde Engine Support Organisation (CESO).

Environmental Factors

Concorde's manufacturers are convinced that the benefits of supersonic transport can be achieved without excessive pollution of the environment or disadvantage to society in general.

Concern about the possible impact of SSTs on the environment has been expressed in three main areas: High Altitude Effects, Pollution and Noise.

High Altitude

It has been suggested that supersonic operations in the stratosphere could cause serious disturbance to the natural balance and structure of the atmosphere and so produce considerable changes in the earth's climate. Some scientists have made pessimistic forecasts, based on extreme assumptions, about the possible effects of SST operations on the ozone layer which protects the earth against ultraviolet light. These forecasts have been refuted by scientists of equally eminent standing, and the fact that there is already a great volume of aircraft operation, both supersonic and subsonic, in the stratosphere which has produced no discernible adverse effects on the climate. The manufacturers' conviction is (and this is shared by many responsible scientists) that, analysed scientifically and mathematically rather than emotionally, there is little evidence to support the forecasts of adverse effects in the stratosphere and that monitoring will, in any event, they claim, provide an absolute safeguard.

Pollution

It has also been suggested that the ozone layer would be destroyed by the oxides of nitrogen from jet engine exhaust of high flying supersonic aircraft. To this charge the manufacturers say that it will be impossible to detect the variation of the ozone amount so caused within the naturally occurring variation which can be of the order of 10 per cent over a period as short as a few days.

They also point out that despite periodic injections of oxides of nitrogen by nuclear weapon tests and the increasing volume of stratospheric operation by commercial subsonics and military supersonics, the amount of ozone in the stratosphere as measured at several stations around the world had been steadily increasing, in some cases, by more than $\frac{1}{2}$ per cent per year.

Radiobiological risks associated with exposure to cosmic radiation at high altitudes are believed to be extremely remote, but Concorde will still carry special warning equipment—although the total risk both in supersonic and subsonic aircraft is said to be only one-thirtieth the risk of death by aircraft accident.

Noise and the Sonic Boom

Concorde's airfield noise on entry into service will be of the same order as that of current subsonic jets—such as the Boeing 707 and the McDonnell Douglas DC-8—large numbers of which will continue in front-line service for many years after Concorde's introduction.

Concorde has already demonstrated that it can operate into and out of existing airports without special attention. The manufacturers have a major long-term research programme in hand to effect further reductions of Concorde noise levels.

The 'sonic boom' phenomenon is the principal new problem associated with supersonic

Concorde 001 (F-WTSS) the French-assembled first prototype on its first flight from Aérospatiale's Toulouse factory on March 2 1969. The chase plane is a British-built Meteor NF.11.

Ceremonial roll-out of Concorde 002 (G-BSST) the British-assembled second prototype at the BAC Filton (Bristol) factory on September 12 1968. This aircraft was first flown from Filton on April 9 1969.

Concorde 01 (G-AXDN)—the first pre-production aircraft—seen at Filton outside the famous 'Brabazon' assembly hall shortly before its first flight to Fairford on December 17 1971. Notable new features were the revised flightdeck glazing and visor and longer forward fuselage.

Concorde 02 (F-WTSA)—the second pre-production aircraft—and the first to be representative of the series production standard—seen at Toulouse, France, where it was assembled, and first flown on January 10 1973. The two significant new features seen here are the extended low-drag rear fuselage and the engine thrust reverser/silencer (TRA) units.

Concorde's sophisticated wing leading-edge shape—twice revised from the original during flight development.

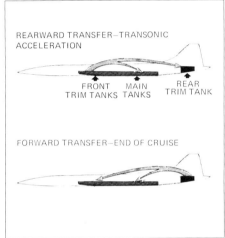

REARWARD TRANSFER—TRANSONIC ACCELERATION

FRONT TRIM TANKS   MAIN TANKS   REAR TRIM TANK

FORWARD TRANSFER—END OF CRUISE

Main inward-retracting four-wheel bogie landing gear unit.

Concorde's special fuel transfer system used to control the aerodynamic trim change that occurs during transonic acceleration and deceleration.

Main landing gear units being test-retracted on the ground.

The first Concorde to fly incorporating the refinements of the series-production aircraft—low-drag extended rear fuselage, cleaner, quieter Olympus 593 Mk.602s and thrust-reverser/silencer-nozzles—was Number 02, registered F-WTSA, the second production aircraft and fourth Concorde built. F-WTSA was flown from the Aerospatiale factory airfield at Toulouse, France, on January 10, 1973. The pilot was Jean Franchi.

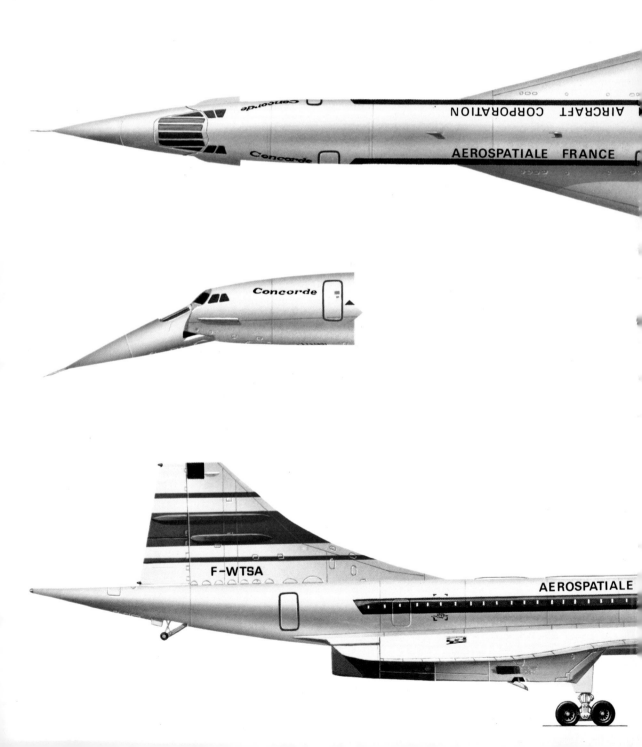

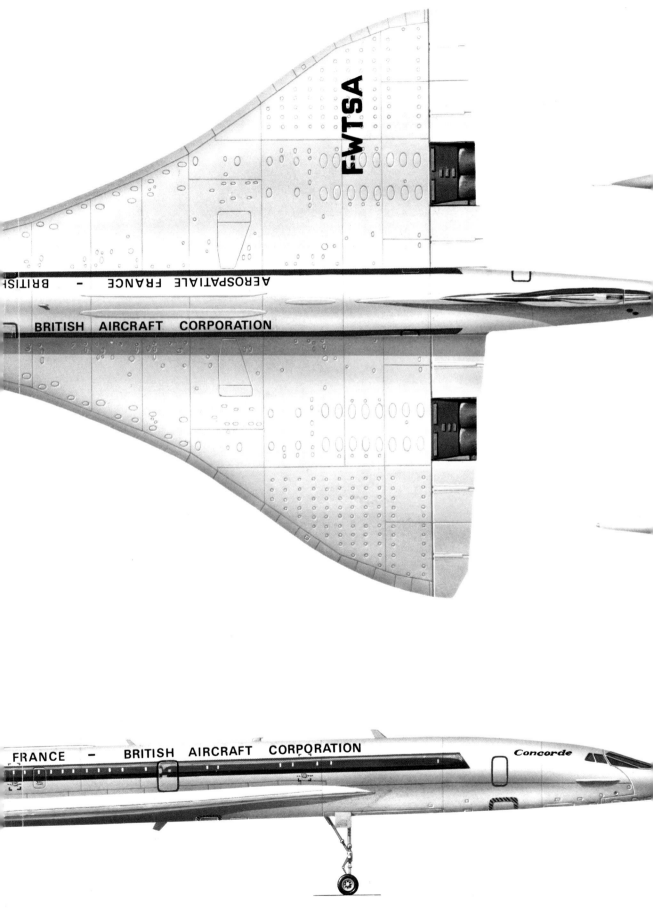

The ogival curve of the delta wing leading edge of Concorde.

Sequence of operation of variable geometry powerplant air intake and exhaust systems.

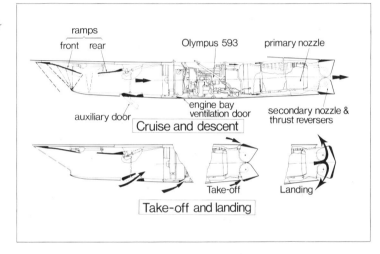

The long forward-retracting twin-wheel nose landing gear required to accommodate the characteristic high incidence approach and landing attitude of delta-winged Concorde.

Close-up of the extended low-drag rear fuselage of Concorde 02.

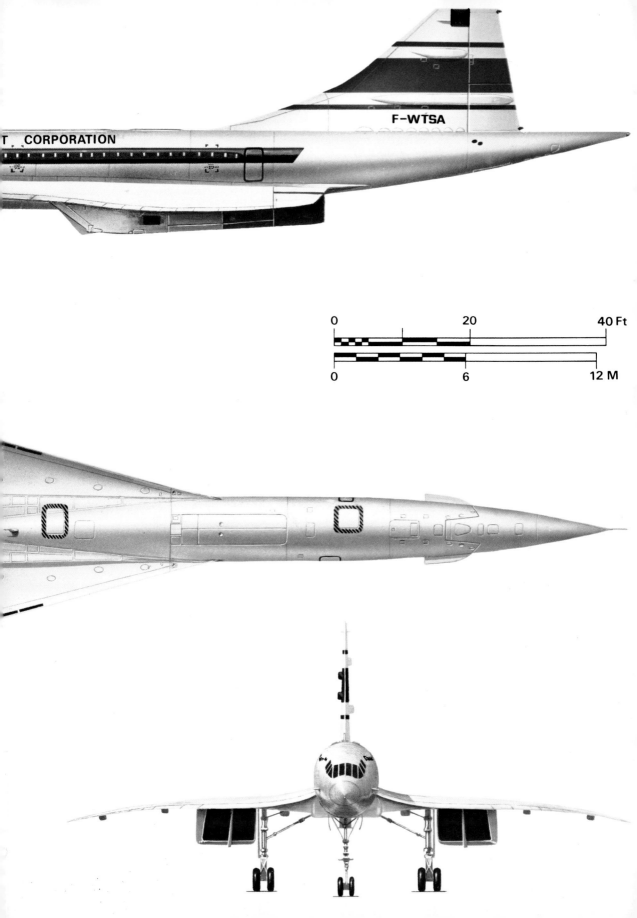

T CORPORATION

F-WTSA

0	20	40 Ft

0	6	12 M

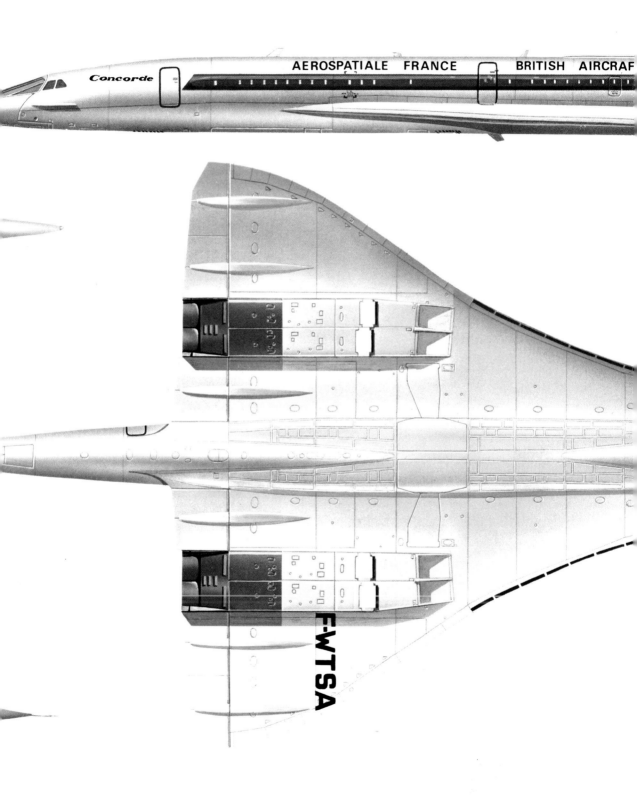

AEROSPATIALE FRANCE BRITISH AIRCRAF

Concorde

F-WTSA

transport operation. The intensity of the boom depends mainly on two factors: the weight at which the aircraft is flying and its altitude. The heavier the aircraft, the greater the intensity of the boom that it is capable of generating. The higher it is flying, the more the boom will be attenuated by the time the sound pressure wave reaches the ground.

Evidence so far is that Concorde's sonic boom is unlikely to cause physical damage, nor will it cause material damage to any reasonably well-maintained structure. Whether or not the boom is socially acceptable will be a decision by Governments, taken in the light of public opinion. Concorde's manufacturers have always assumed, in their market research, that supersonic flight would only be permitted over the oceans and overland by national governments over areas of sparse population and the large and uninhabited deserts which form a' considerable element of the earths surface. In this context it is significant that between 74 and 80 per cent of todays intercontinental seat-miles are, in fact, flown over the sea.

The Cost/Benefit Equation

The R. & D. Bill

The main area in which Concorde continues to be called into question is that of launching costs—how what was estimated to be £150-£170 million in 1962 has grown to £970 million in 1972 (shared equally by Britain and France).

The notional research and development (R. & D.) cost estimate of 1962 was made in complete absence of knowledge of the very demanding technology that has since become necessary, with no relevant datum for cost prediction, and was in the *prevailing monetary values and took no account of inevitable escalation.*

Although this figure has apparently escalated by £800 million, more than half of this growth—around £430 million—is due to progressive monetary inflation, which has averaged $7\frac{1}{2}$ per cent per annum over the intervening 10 years—together with two devaluations of the British Pound and one of the French Franc—all completely beyond the control of the manufacturers.

Additionally, substantial extra work has become necessary as the programme has been progressively defined in the light of evolving airline requirements—none of which could have been foreseen in 1962. This accounts for around £180 million in 1972 terms. It has been due to several major factors—notably post-certification development (£80 million), general contingencies (£50 million) and, of course, the incorporation of substantial technical development (both airframe and engine) through three successive build standards—the initial prototypes, the pre-production and series production models—that have been made necessary by the

developing requirements of the airlines and airworthiness authorities and the greater length of time needed to achieve the Certificate of Airworthiness, none of which were anticipated in the original estimate.

To set the ultimate figure of £970 million in perspective it is worth noting that a recent US Government paper has disclosed that development of the Boeing 747 airframe cost the equivalent of £500 million and the McDonnell Douglas DC-10 £450 million, to which in both cases has to be added something between £150-200 million for development of the engines. Both these programmes were straightforward extensions of existing technology and both were completed in correspondingly shorter time scales and under a single design authority. Concorde programme costs for research and development are thus not as excessive as may at first be supposed.

The USA is reported as having spent £365 million on its abortive supersonic airliner project (and a further £280 million in cancellation penalties and the various human resources costs resulting therefrom).

What it Buys

The £970 million R. and D. funds for Concorde cover:
- Design and construction of two prototypes 001 and 002;
- Design and construction of two pre-production aircraft 01 and 02;
- Construction of two airframe specimens and other major components for static and fatigue testing;
- The static and fatigue test programmes;
- The flight development programmes, shared by the two prototypes, two pre-production and the first three production aircraft and leading to award of a certificate of airworthiness;

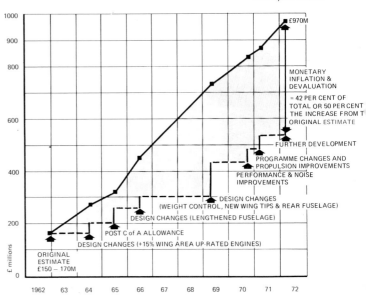

Concorde programme development costs.

- Initial production tooling;
- Continued development after C. of A.;
- Design and development of a new engine through successively more powerful marks, and of a new rear nozzle for commercial supersonic operation.
- The build of 63 Rolls-Royce Olympus engines for ground and flight testing;
- Design, development and tooling of a new range of aircraft equipment for commercial supersonic operation;
- A complete range of ground handling and test equipment.

(While use of the first three production aircraft for flight development is an R. and D. cost their actual construction is a production charge.)

Production Loans

Financing of Concorde production work-in-progress is quite separate from the basic 'non-recurring' R. and D. charges and is being covered by interest-bearing bridging loans from the two Governments to cover the period when outgoings in wages and materials are high before income, in the form of progress payments from customers, begins.

To meet this need the British Government authorised in February 1968 a sum of £125 million to launch production of aircraft and engines which was made up of loans from public funds, plus bank loans guaranteed by the Government. This was increased to £250 million in March 1973—with the provision for a further £100 million later as required. Similar arrangements are being made by the French Government. These loans will be wholly repaid from the proceeds of sales.

In summary, the £970 million R. and D. finance is for the creation of a fully tested and certificated aircraft, an element of which is to be repaid by sales levies. The production finance is a straight loan transaction bearing the going rate of interest to be repaid as the manufacturers deliver the completed aircraft and get paid for them.

There is also provision for the supply via HMG of certain special tools and plant to a value of about £30 million to BAC and Rolls-Royce and for which an appropriate rental is charged.

The Benefits

The Concorde R. and D. expenditure is regarded by Britain and France as an investment for the future.

The purely financial benefit readily estimated is Concorde's contribution to the balance of payments: BAC and Aérospatiale's expectation of sales of up to 200 Concordes by the beginning of the 1980s will result in a contribution to the trade balance over the operational life of these aircraft of the order of £4,000 million of the exchequer of Britain and France. When, in addition to this, account is taken of the sales and operation of potential Concorde derivatives up to at least the end of the present century, the size of the investment and the immense resulting benefits can be seen in true perspective.

Concordes effect on the British and French national economies is to create substantial and sustained employment, and hence tax repayments, to provide an immense modernising force across a wide range of industries and geographical areas. At the same time input-output studies of these economies have demonstrated clearly that such an outlay in high technology industry has a greater overall growth effect than does investment in less sophisticated areas. This arises principally because of the dominating element of payment for brainpower and skills rather than imported raw materials—in a 90/10 ratio.

This stimulation has already spread to many new products and processes. A survey shows that around 70 per cent of the 600 odd British firms contributing to Concorde have admitted to material benefits from the programme. These range from improved management procedures through to new products and capabilities, all of which mean that they are better able to produce, market and export their goods—another item which should be entered in the Concorde 'credit ledger'.

The scope of the returns in terms of new manufacturing techniques and processes and technological advance throughout industry are claimed to be inestimable.

In this respect there is clear evidence that the great advances in the use of numerically controlled machine tools and in electro-chemical machining has been largely stimulated by work on Concorde. There are also comparable advances in manufacturing techniques, such as electron-beam welding and the use of laser beams in the working of titanium.

Again, the materials and precision and medical equipment industries have benefited substantially from research and development initiated specifically for Concorde—such as titanium, plastics, glass, lubricants, paints, seals and plumbing techniques, miniaturisation, electric motors and actuators, brakes and anti-skid devices, and thermal controls.

Scientific and data processing computer techniques which have accrued from Concorde design and production are acknowledged as industry-leading in Europe.

Finally, it is pointed out that expensive as the Concorde programme obviously is, there is no other basis for true comparison—nothing is known of the development costs of the Russian Tu-144—and the ultimate aircraft is substantially better all round than its original conception.

The Way Ahead

Concorde is Europe's proudest airliner achievement and the world's fastest. Its ability to halve international journey times at a stroke, coupled with its uniquely distinctive visual appeal, will enable it to introduce a completely new concept of air travel and the greatest advance in the history of air transport.

The spearheading concept of Concorde has lifted transport aircraft technology to a new plateau—and has crossed the sonic and heat barriers in one leap. In turn, it will stimulate exciting new horizons in future generations of air transport development throughout the world.

Todays aircraft represents only the first of the inevitable development stages in size and range which will be achieved as Concorde matures to fulfill its enormous potential in a wide range of roles and its concept is unlikely to be outmoded in this century.

As Sir George Edwards points out:

'We read much of a second-generation supersonic transport, often in the context of a super-giant Mach 3 plus aeroplane which would sweep the Concordes out of the sky.

'The expense and long development time which would be needed to replace the now defunct US SST suggests that the right course to follow is that of steady development based on what we already have and know about. As with all successful designs, I see Concorde following the standard procedure of stretch—range and capacity—which will result from improvements already more than a twinkle in the eye.

'The second generation SST will almost cer-tainly look and fly like a Concorde although geometrically it may be scaled up here and there.

'In Concorde we have found an elegant solution to the problem of efficient supersonic flight and any immediate successor which might appear within the century will, I feel certain, bear the same family relationship to Concorde as the Boeing 747 bears to the 707—the same format, but not much faster.

'The ultimate replacement of the Concorde on the very long-haul routes may well arrive as a spin-off from the Space Shuttle programme rather than as an extension of any aircraft family tree.

'Certainly the plan for the years ahead must be to sell what we have to offer—a first class product with built-in stretch.'

Concorde—Worldshrinker

While Concorde continues to have its dissenters, conjecture is steadily being supplanted by fact and demonstration as it faces up to its real judges—the worlds airlines and their ever-discerning passengers, the sole arbiters of air transport progress.

The thoroughbred consolidation of un-matched experience, research and development, Concorde should well justify its significance and its newest accolade 'The Worldshrinker' through into the hypersonic era. Soon pass-engers will have the opportunity to prove it.

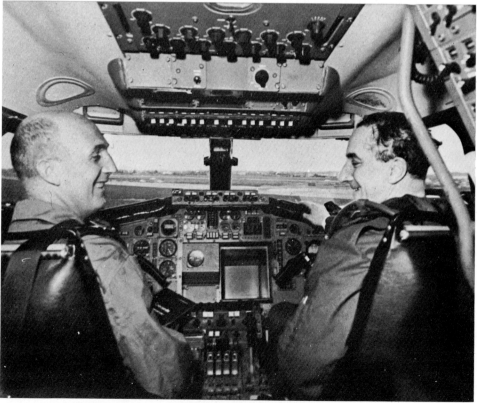

Concorde's famous pilots: (left) André Turcat, Director of Flight Test of Aérospatiale, and (right) Brian Trubshaw, Director of Flight Test of the BAC Commercial Aircraft Division—seen together on the flightdeck of Concorde 002 at Toulouse.

Agreement between the Government of the United Kingdom of Great Britain and Northern Ireland and the Government of the French Republic regarding the development and production of a civil supersonic transport aircraft
London, November 29 1962

The Government of the United Kingdom of Great Britain and Northern Ireland and the Government of the French Republic;

Having decided to develop and produce jointly a civil supersonic transport aircraft;

Have agreed as follows:

Article 1
(1) The principle of this collaboration shall be the equal sharing between the two countries, on the basis of equal responsibility for the project as a whole, of the work, of the expenditure incurred by the two Governments, and of the proceeds of sales.

(2) This principle, which shall be observed as strictly as possible, shall apply, as regards both development and production (including spares), to the project considered as a whole (airframe, engine, systems and equipments).

(3) The sharing shall be based upon the expenditure corresponding to the work carried out in each country, excluding taxes to be specified by agreement between the two Governments. Such expenditure shall be calculated from the date of the present Agreement.

Article 2
The two Governments, having taken note of the agreement dated 25th October, 1962 between Sud Aviation and the British Aircraft Corporation (BAC) and of the agreement dated 28th November, 1961 between Bristol Siddeley and the Société Nationale d'Etudes et de Construction de Moteurs d'Aviation (SNECMA) have approved them, except in so far as they may be in conflict with provisions which are the subject of agreement between the Governments.

Article 3
(1) The technical proposals, which shall form the basis for the joint undertaking by Sud Aviation and BAC comprise a medium range and a long range version of the aircraft.

(2) The Bristol Siddeley-SNECMA BS593/3 turbojet engine shall be developed jointly for the aircraft by Bristol Siddeley on the British side and by SNECMA on the French side.

Article 4
In order to carry out the project, integrated organisations of the airframe and engine firms shall be set up.

Article 5
A Standing Committee of officials from the two countries shall supervise the progress of the work, report to the Governments and propose the necessary measures to ensure the carrying out of the programme.

Article 6
Every effort shall be made to ensure that the programme is carried out, both for the airframe and for the engine, with equal attention to the medium range and the long range versions. It shall be for the two integrated organisations of the British and French firms to make detailed proposals for the carrying out of the programme.

Article 7
The present Agreement shall enter into force on the date of its signature.

In witness whereof the under-signed, being duly authorised thereto by their respective Governments, have signed the present Agreement.

Done in duplicate at London this 29th day of November 1962 in the English and French languages, both texts being equally authoritative.

For the Government of the United Kingdom of Great Britain and Northern Ireland:
JULIAN AMERY
PETER THOMAS

For the Government of the French Republic:
G. de COURCEL

LEADING PARTICULARS AND TECHNICAL DESCRIPTION

The following data and description applies to the intial production Concorde:

Aircraft Type: Supersonic transport airliner.

External Dimensions: Wing span 83 ft. 10 in. (25.56 m.); Overall length 203 ft. 9 in. (61.66 m.); Overall height—at Operating Empty Weight 37 ft. 1 in. (11.32 m.); Main wheel track 25 ft. 4 in. (7.72 m.); Wheelbase 59 ft. 8 in. (18.19 m.).

Areas: Wings, gross 3,856 sq. ft. (358.25 m.^{2}); Aspect ratio 1.7; Elevons (total) 344.44 sq. ft. (32.00 m.^{2}); Fin (less dorsal) 365 sq. ft. (33.91 m.^{2}); Rudder 112 sq. ft. (10.4 m.^{2}).

Weights and Loadings: Maximum Taxi Weight 393,000 lb. (178,260 kg.); Maximum Take-off Weight 389,000 lb. (176,450 kg.); Maximum Landing Weight 245,000 lb. (111,130 kg.); Maximum Zero Fuel Weight 203,000 lb. (92,080 kg.); Typical Payload 25,000 lb. (11,340 kg.); Basic Operating Weight 172,500 lb. (78,245 kg.); Fuel Capacity 206,000 lb. (93,440 kg.); Max. wing loading approx. 100 lb./sq. ft. (488 kg./m.^{2}); Max. power loading approx. 2.5 lb./lb. st (2.5 kg./kg. st).

Performance: Estimated at Max T-O Weight: Minimum airborne speed 200 knots (230 m.p.h.; 370 km./h.); Cruise altitudes 50,000-60,000 ft. (15,240-18,290 m.); Max. cruising speed at 51,300 ft. (15,640 m.) Mach 2 or 530 knots CAS, whichever is the lesser—equivalent to TAS of 1,130 knots (1,300 m.p.h.; 2,032 km./h.); Max. range speed approx. Mach 2.05; Rate of climb at SL 5,000 ft. (1,525 m.)/min.; Service ceiling approx. 60,000 ft. (18.290 m.); T-O to 35 ft. (10.7 m.) 10,050 ft. (3,063 m.); Landing from 35 ft. (10.7 m.) 7,980 ft. (2,432 m.); Range with max. fuel, FAR reserves, and 12,500 lb. (5,670 kg.) payload: 3,750 n.m. (4,313 miles; 6,936 km.); Range with max. payload, FAR reserves: at Mach 0.93 at 30,000 ft. (9,100 m.) 2,650 n.m. (3,050 miles; 4,900 km.); at Mach 2.05 cruise/climb 3,350 n.m. (3,853 miles; 6,196 km.); Min. ground turning radius 63 ft. 6 in. (19.35 m.); LCN at max. T-O weight 89.

Operational Noise Characteristics: Take-off: (flyover) 3.5 n.m. (4 miles; 6.5 km.) from start of T-O roll 114 EPNdB; Approach: at 1 n.m. (1.15 miles; 1.85 km.) from landing threshold on 3° glideslope 115 EPNdB; Sideline: 0.35 n.m. (0.40 miles; 0.65 km.) from runway c/l 111 EPNdB.

Powerplants: Four Rolls-Royce/SNECMA Olympus 593 Mk.602 axial flow two-spool turbojets plus partial reheat—with thrust reversers and silencers.

Performance Rating: Nominal take-off thrust, S.L. static, reheat 'On' 38,050 lb. (17,260 kg.); Cruise thrust (60,000', ISA+5°C M=2.0) 6,791 lb. (3,080 kg.); Cruise fuel consumption (lb./lb. thrust/hour) 1,189; Cruise engine pressure ratio 11.6:1.

Dimensions: Max. diameter at intake 47.75 in. (121.3 cm.); Length, flange-to-flange nozzle 154 in. (391 cm.); Intake flange to final nozzle 273 in. (693 cm.).

Weight: Basic, dry, 'undressed' 6,090 lb. (2,762 kg.).

Air Intake: Each Olympus engine installed downstream of intake duct incorporating auxiliary intake and exit door systems and a throat of variable profile and cross-section.

Compressors: Seven-stage axial-flow LP and HP compressors.

Turbines: Single-stage air-cooled co-axial HP and LP turbines.

Exhaust System: New design thrust reverser and secondary nozzle known as TRA (thrust-reverser aft) based on use of reverser buckets as both reverser and secondary nozzle for noise attenuation.

Accessory Drives: Two gearboxes beneath compressor intermediate casing, both mechanically driven off HP shaft. LH gearbox drives main engine oil pressure/scavenge pumps and the first-stage fuel pump. RH gearbox drives aircraft hydraulic pumps and CSD/alternator.

Fuel System: Mechanically driven first-stage pump with second-stage pump driven by air turbine shut down at cruise when fuel requirements can be met by first-stage pump alone. The first-stage pump also supplies reheat fuel. Fuel cooled air-cooler incorporated. Electronic system, with integrated-circuit amplifier, provides combined control of fuel flow and primary nozzle-area. Electrically controlled reheat fuel system.

Lubrication System: Closed-type using oil to specification DERD 2497, MIL-L-9230B. Pressure pump, multiple scavenge pumps, and return through fuel/oil heat exchanger.

Starting System: Air-turbine driving HP spool. Dual high-energy ignition system serves igniters in annular chamber.

Mounting: Main expansion type trunnions on horizontal centreline of delivery casing. Front stay from nacelle roof locates on top of intake casing.

Accommodation: Flight Crew: Pilot and co-pilot side-by-side on flight deck, with third crew member behind on starboard side at systems management panel. Provision for supernumerary seat behind pilots Cabin Layout: Wide variety of four-abreast seating layouts to suit individual airline requirements: Typically: Superior Class—108 at 38 in. (96.5 cm.) pitch. Standard Class—128 at 34 in. (86 cm.) pitch (with full galley and toilet facilities). Maximum—144 at 32 in. (81 cm.) pitch. Two gallery areas. Toilets at centre and/or rear. Baggage space under forward cabin and aft of passenger cabin. Passenger doors forward and amidships on port side, with service doors opposite. Baggage door aft on starboard side. Emergency exits in rear half of cabin on each side.

Internal Dimensions: Cabin: Length (flight deck door to rear pressure bulkhead, including galley and toilets) 115 ft. (35.04 m.); Width—external 9 ft. 5 in. (2.9 m.); Width—internal 8 ft. 7½ in. (2.63 cm.); Aisle Width 17 in. (0.43 m.); Height 6 ft. 5 in. (1.96 m.); Volume 8,440 cu. ft. (238.5 m.²); Window size 6.3 in. × 4 in. (16 cm. × 10 cm.); Window spacing approx. 20 in. (50.8 m.); *Passenger doors (each): Height 5 ft. 6 in. (1.68 m`; Width 2 ft. 6 in. (0.76 m.); Sill height: fwd. 16 ft. 3 in. (4.96 m.), amidships 15 ft. 7 in. (4.74 m.), *All doors 'Type 1' Emergency Exits; Baggage/freight compartments: Underfloor 227 cu. ft. (6.43 m³.); Rear fuselage 470 cu. ft. (13.3 m³.) Total 697 cu. ft. (19.74 m³.); Baggage hold door (underfloor): Length 3 ft. 3 in. (0.99 m.); Width 2 ft. 9 in. (0.84 m.); Sill Height 11 ft. 7 in. (3.33 m.); Baggage hold door (rear, stbd.): Height 5 ft. 0 in. (1.52 m.); Width 2 ft. 6 in. (0.76 m.); Sill Height 12 ft. 11 in. (3.94 m.).

Airframe:

Wings: Cantilever low wing of ogival delta planform. Thickness/chord ratio 3 per cent at root, 2.15 per cent from nacelle outboard: Slight anhedral. Continuous camber. Multi-spar torsion-box structure, manufactured mainly from RR58 (AU2GN) aluminium alloy. Integral machining used for highly loaded members and skin panels.

Three elevons on trailing-edge of each wing, of aluminium alloy honeycomb construction each independently operated by a tandem jack, each half elevon being supplied from an independent hydraulic source and controlled by a separate electrical system and auto-stabilisation provided. Autopilot control by signals fed into normal control circuit. No high-lift devices. (Air-brakes on prototypes only). Leading-edges ahead of air intakes electrically de-iced.

Fuselage: Pressurised aluminium alloy semi-monocoque structure of oval cross-section, with unpressurised nose and tail cones. Hoop frames at approx. 21.5 in. (0.55 m.) pitch support mainly integrally-machined panels having closely-pitched longitudinal stringers. Nose section droops hydraulically to improve forward view during take-off, initial climb, approach and landing. Retractable visor raised hydraulically to fair in pilots windows in cruising flight.

Empennage: Vertical fin and rudder—no tailplane. Fin—multi-spar torsion box of similar construction to wing. Aerodynamic reference chord at base 84 ft. 9 in. (10.59 m.). Two-section honeycomb rudder controlled as elevons. No de-icing.

Landing Gear: Hydraulically-retractable tricycle type. Retractable tail wheel. Four-wheel bogie main units retract inward. Twin-wheel steerable nose unit retracts forward. Oleo-pneumatic shock absorbers. Main wheel tyres (eight) 47 × 15.75–22, pressure 184 lb./sq. in. (12.9 kg./cm².). Segmented disc brakes and anti-skid units. Nosewheel tyres two 31 × 10.75–14, pressure 174 lb./sq. in. (12.25 kg./cm².).

Engine Nacelles: Each consists of hydraulically-controlled ramp variable-area air intake, engine bay and nozzle support structure. Intakes of aluminium alloy with steel leading-edges. Engine bay has 'Inconel' centre wall with aluminium alloy forward doors and titanium rear doors. Nozzle bay, aft of rear spar, of welded 'Stresskin' sandwich panels and heat-resistant nickel alloys. Thrust reverser buckets—also used as secondary nozzle. Eight equi-spaced retractable spade silencers actuated by pneumatically-operated ball-screws driven through flexible shafts. Leading-edges of intake walls, rear ramp sections and intake auxiliary doors de-iced by engine bleed air.

Systems:

Fuel: Also used as heat sink and as a means of maintaining aircraft trim.

All tanks of integral construction and arranged in two groups. Main tank group comprises five compartments in each wing and four in the fuselage and is arranged to maintain aircraft centre of gravity automatically in cruising flight. Trim tank group—three—comprises two tanks in the wings and one of 2,800 Imp. gallons (12,730 litres) capacity in fuselage beneath fin. This group maintains correct relationship between CG and aerodynamic centre of pressure by transferring fuel rearward during transonic acceleration and forward during return to subsonic flight. Four pressure refuelling points in underwing fairing—two forward of each main landing gear unit.

Engine Oil: Capacity 3.0 Imp. gallons (13.6 litres) per engine. Oil for CSD in separate tank-capacity 0.75 IG (3.4 litres).

Pressurisation/Air Conditioning: Comprises four independent sub-systems with heat exchangers. Cabin working pressure differential 10.7 lb./sq. in. (0.75 kg./cm².). In each sub-system the air passes through primary ram-air heat exchanger to air cycle cold-air unit, and then through secondary air/air and air/fuel heat exchangers. Air then mixed with hot air and fed to passenger cabin, flightdeck, baggage holds, landing gear, equipment and radar bays.

Hydraulic: Two primary and one standby system Pressure 4,000 lb./sq. in. (280 kg./cm².) each actuated by two engine-driven pumps. Oronite M2V fluid temperature limited by heat exchangers. Main systems actuates flying control surfaces, artificial feel units, landing gear, wheel brakes, nosewheel steering, pilots visor, droop nose engine intake ramps, and fuel pumps in rear transfer tank.

Electrical: System powered by four 60 kVA engine-driven constant-speed brushless alternators giving 200/115V AC at 400 Hz. Four 150 A transformer-rectifiers and two 25 Ah. batteries provide 28V DC supply.

Electronics: Primary navigation system comprises three identical inertial platforms (each coupled to digital computer to form three self-contained units), two VOR/ILS systems, one ADF, two DME, one marker, two weather radars and two radio altimeters. Provision for supplementary system including long-distance radio fixing system of the Loran 'C' type. Optional equipment includes second ADF. Basic communications equipment consists of two VHF and two HF transmitter/receivers, one Selcal decoder and two ATC transponders. Provision for third VHF transmitter/receiver and data link equipment.

All-Weather Operation: Duplicated autopilots, autothrottles and the above navigation systems will enable certification to Category II all-weather landing minima at entry into service and Category IIIA automatic landing when sufficient flight experience accumulated. Provision also made to accommodate automatic chart display and area navigation when standards for this type of equipment finalised.

CONCORDE 002 SALES TOUR—1972

Middle, Far East and Australian Sales Demonstration Tour, 2 June to 1 July 1972.

Distance flown: 45,000 miles (72,500 Km.)
Twelve countries visited: Twenty sectors flown through Greece; Iran; Bahrain; India; Burma; Singapore; Philippines; Japan; Australia; Saudi Arabia; Lebanon and France.

Flights:	32—25 supersonic;
	13 demonstration
Total Flying time	62 hrs.
Block time	70 hrs. 20 mins.
Supersonic time	23 hrs. 10 mins.
Supersonic time at Mach 2	13 hrs. 40 mins.
En-route time	43 hrs.
Demonstrations	19 hrs.
Concorde 002 total journey time	40 hrs. 45 mins.
Scheduled subsonic time	65 hrs.
Engine flight time:	252 hrs.
	92 hrs. supersonic
VIP passengers included:	One Head of State
	14 Ministers
	12 Airline Chiefs
Seen by airport crowds:	Over 300,000 (estimated)

London—Heathrow static display 1–5 July witnessed by an estimated 50,000 people.

Contributing to Concorde technology (see also page 92)

7 Dassault Mirage IV-01; June 1959.

8 Handley Page H.P.115 (XP841); August 1961.

9 BAC (Bristol) Type 188 (XF926, 2nd. prototype, c/n. 13519); April 1963.

10 BAC Type 221 (WG774, ex-F.D.2); May 1964.

11 BAC TSR.2 (XR219); September 1964.

12 Hawker Siddeley (Avro) Vulcan (XA903, Olympus engine test bed); September 1966.

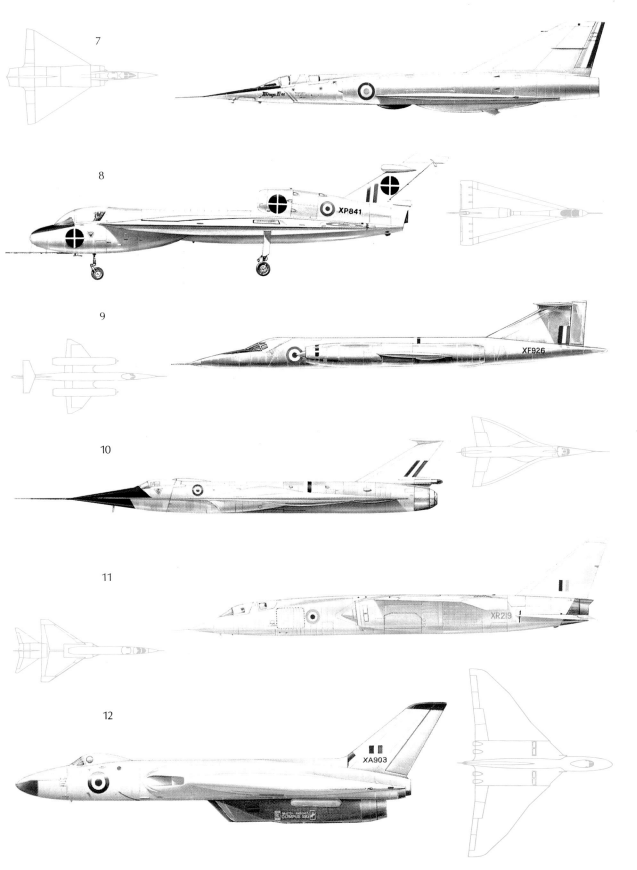

7

8

XP841

9

XF926

10

11

XR219

12

XA903

Terry Hadler/David Palmer © Profile Publications Limited

Concorde Chronology

1956	Basic supersonic airliner research starts in Britain and France.
November 5 1956	British Supersonic Transport Aircraft Committee (STAC) first meets.
1959–1961	SST feasibility and design studies in Britain and France.
1961–1962	Preliminary Anglo-French discussions on commonality of SST requirements and design studies, leading on to investigation of possible collaboration.
1961	First discussions between BAC and Sud Aviation—Paris.
June 8 1961	
July 10 1961	—Weybridge.
November 29 1962	British and French Governments sign Agreement for joint design, development and manufacture of a supersonic airliner.
1963	Preliminary design for 100-seat SST discussed with key airlines.
May 1963	First metal cut for test specimens.
June 3 1963	First Concorde sales option signed by Pan American.
June 1963	BOAC and Air France sign Concorde sales options.
May 1964	Announcement of developed aircraft (at IATA Technical Committee Meeting in Beirut) with increased wing area and lengthened fuselage providing accommodation for up to 118 passengers—the design subsequently 'frozen' for prototype manufacture.
July 1964	Olympus 593 'D' (Derivative) engine first run at Bristol, England.
April 1965	First metal cut for Concorde prototypes.
May 1965	Pre-production Concorde design (130 seats) announced.
October 1965	Prototype Concorde sub-assemblies started.
November 1965	Olympus 593 'B' (Big) engine first run at Bristol.
March 1966	Sixteen-ton centre fuselage/wing section for static and thermal testing delivered to CEAT, Toulouse, France.
April 1966	Final assembly of Concorde prototype 001 begins at Toulouse.
June 1966	Concorde main flight simulator commissioned at Toulouse.
June 1966	Complete Olympus 593 engine and variable geometry exhaust assembly first testbed run at Melun-Villaroche, France.
August 1966	Final assembly of Concorde prototype 002 begins at Filton (Bristol), England.
September 1966	Vulcan flying testbed with Olympus 593 makes first flight.
September 1966	Olympus 593 first run in Cell 3 high altitude facility, NGTE Pyestock, England.
October 1966	Olympus 593 achieves 35,190 lbs. (dry) thrust on test at Bristol, exceeding 'Stage 1' brochure requirement.
December 1966	Seventy-foot long fuselage and nose section delivered to RAE Farnborough for fatigue testing.

1966	Detailed and continuing discussions begin on all aspects of Concorde development between manufacturers and specialist engineering committees representing all customer airlines.
February 1967	Full-scale Concorde interior mock-up at Filton first presented to customer airlines.
April 1967	Complete Olympus 593 engine first test-run in the high-altitude chamber at Saclay, France.
May 1967	Concorde options reach a total of 74 from 16 airlines.
August 1967	Concorde 001 undergoes resonance testing at Toulouse.
December 11 1967	First prototype Concorde 001 rolled out at Toulouse.
January 1968	Vulcan flying testbed logs first 100 hours in the air.
January 1968	SNECMA variable-geometry exhaust assembly for Olympus 593 engine cleared at Melun-Villaroche for flight in the Concorde prototypes.
February 1968	British Government announces provision of £125 million loan to launch production aircraft and engines.
March 1968	Preliminary engine testing in Concorde 001 at Toulouse.
August 1968	First taxi trials by Concorde 001 at Toulouse.
September 1968	Second prototype Concorde 002 rolled out at Filton.
December 1968	Olympus 593 ground testing reaches 5,000 hours.
March 2 1969	Maiden flight of French-assembled Concorde prototype 001 at Toulouse.
March 1969	Governmental authority given for a total of nine Concorde airframes—two prototypes, two pre-production, two ground test airframes and three series production aircraft.
April 9 1969	Maiden flight of British-assembled Concorde prototype 002 from Filton to Fairford (Gloucestershire).
June 1969	Both Concorde prototypes make first public appearance at Paris Air Show.
July 1969	Annular combustion system design specified for all subsequent Concordes to remove exhaust smoke.
October 1 1969	Concorde 001 first achieves Mach 1.
November 8 1969	First airline pilots fly Concorde 001.
December 1969	Governmental authority given for three more series production Concordes—numbers 4, 5 and 6.
February 1970	Longest single engine test on Olympus 593. Engine ran for 300 hours—a time equivalent to nearly 100 transatlantic Concorde flights.
March 25 1970	Concorde 002 first achieves Mach 1.
April 10 1970	Mr. Wedgwood Benn, British Minister of Technology, makes first VIP flight in Concorde (002).
May 1970	New-design TRA (Thrust Reverser Aft) engine nozzle specified for improved

	weight, aerodynamic and noise qualities on production Concordes.
August 1970	Flights resumed with Olympus 593-3B engines and auto-controlled air intakes.
September 1 1970	Concorde 002 makes first flight on British West Coast test corridor.
September 13 1970	Concorde 002 appears at SBAC Farnborough Air Show and then makes first landing at an international airport—London Heathrow.
November 4 1970	Concorde 001 first achieves Mach 2.
November 12 1970	Concorde 002 first achieves Mach 2.

January 1971	First 100 supersonic flights logged.
April 1971	Four more production Concordes (numbers 6-10) are authorised together with approval for purchase of long-dated materials for the next six production aircraft (numbers 11-16).
May 7 1971	President Pompidou of France becomes the first Head of State to fly supersonic—in Concorde 001.
May 13 1971	Concorde 001 makes first automatic landing.
May 25 1971	Concorde 001 appears at Paris Air Show and then flies to Dakar in West Africa (2,500 miles) in 2 hours 7 minutes—first intercontinental flight.
June 1971	Total Concorde flight test time reaches 500 hours. Bench and flight development engine testing totals 10,000 hours.
July 1971	Airline pilots fly at Mach 2.
July 16 1971	Mr. Frederick Corfield—British Minister for Aerospace flies in Concorde 002.
August 1971	Flight clearance obtained for Olympus 593-4 engine standard. First 100 bisonic flights logged.
September 20 1971	Concorde 01—the first pre-production aircraft—rolled-out at Filton.
September 4-18 1971	Concorde 001 makes trouble-free 15 day tour of South America.
September 1971	Concorde design team awarded special diploma by the Federation Aéronautique Internationale on joint recommendation by Royal Aero Club of Britain and Aero Club de France.
November 12 1971	HRH Princess Anne visits Concorde assembly hall at BAC, Filton.
December 10 1971	Mr. John Davies—British Secretary of State for Trade and Industry—and Lord Carrington—Minister of Defence—fly in Concorde 002. Assurance of continued British Government support for Concorde publicly announced.

December 13 1971	President Pompidou of France flies to the Azores in Concorde 001 to meet President Nixon of the USA.
December 14 1971	US Federal Aviation Agency announces that Concorde will be within American airport noise limits.
December 17 1971	Concorde 01—first pre-production—makes maiden flight from Filton to Fairford.
December 21 1971	All three flying Concordes—001, 002 and 01—on test flights simultaneously.
December 22 1971	Pricing formula for initial Concorde customer airlines announced in British Parliament.

January 6 1972	Three Concordes—001, 002 and 01—together at Fairford.
January 12 1972	HRH Prince Philip The Duke of Edinburgh pilots Concorde 002 during a two-hour supersonic mission.
January 13 1972	BOAC Board of Directors flies in Concorde 002.
February 7 1972	Concorde 002 flies with production undercarriage.
February 12 1972	Concorde 01 flies supersonic.
February 1972	Concorde 02—the second pre-production aircraft—structurally complete at Toulouse.
March 1972	First and second series production Concordes near structural completion at Toulouse and Filton. Work well advanced on major components for Concordes 3-10.
April 13 1972	British and French Governments authorize production of further six series production Concordes (11-16) and announce Concorde 002's mission to Far East and Australia in June. Prince Bernhard of the Netherlands, accompanied by Prince Philip, inspects Concordes 002 and 01 at Fairford.
April 22-23 1972	Concorde 002 makes first appearance in Germany—at Hanover Air Show with Mr. Michael Heseltine the new Minister for Aerospace.
April 1972	Delivery of first Olympus 593 Mk.602 to Toulouse for Concorde 02. Total Olympus 593 engine running experience exceeds 20,000 hours.
May 3 1972	Concorde 001 flies from Toulouse to Tangier.
May 8 1972	HRH Princess Margaret, the Duke of Kent, Prince William of Gloucester, and Lord Snowdon fly in Concorde 002.
May 18 1972	One thousand Concorde flying hours now logged by 001, 002 and 01.
May 19 1972	British Prime Minister Edward Heath flies in Concorde 002.
May 25 1972	BOAC announces that it is to order a fleet of five Concordes.

Concordes 001 (left) and 02 (right) at Toulouse, France. These two aircraft, together with Concordes 002 and 01 in Britain, had flown 2,000 hours by mid-1973.

June 2 1972	Concorde 002 leaves Fairford to begin 45,000 mile sales demonstration tour of 12 countries in the Middle and Far East and Australia.
July 1 1972	Concorde 002 returns on time to London-Heathrow on completion of tour.
July 3 1972	HM The Queen (with Princess Anne) inspects Concorde 002 at Heathrow.
July 24 1972	Representatives of The People's Republic of China sign preliminary purchase agreement with Aérospatiale in Paris for two Concordes.
July 28 1972	BOAC signs contract with BAC in London for five Concordes and Air France with Aérospatiale in Paris for four Concordes. Both airlines to take delivery in 1975.
August 10 1972	Concorde 01 returns to Filton for ground programme to bring it up to near full production standard—notably the installation of Olympus 593 Mk.602 powerplants.
August 28 1972	China signs preliminary purchase contract with BAC in Peking for a third Concorde.
September 4-10 1972	Concorde 002 appears daily at the flying display at the SBAC Show at Farnborough and also makes 'show-the-people' flights to several areas of the UK.
September 14 1972	Governmental approval given for the procurement of advance materials for six more series production Concordes (numbers 17 to 22).
September 28 1972	Concorde 02—the second pre-production aircraft—rolled-out at Toulouse.
October 5 1972	Iranair signs preliminary purchase agreement for two Concordes together with an option on a third.
December 11 1972	British Government approves Bill to raise production financial loan from £125 million (see February 1968) to £350 million.
January 10 1973	Concorde 02—second pre-production aircraft—makes maiden flight at Toulouse.
January 22 1973	Concorde 002 leaves Fairford for a 2½-week period of 'hot and high' airfield performance trials at Jan Smuts airport at Johannesburg, South Africa.
January 31 1973	Pan American and TWA decide not to take up their Concorde options—but to 'leave the door open' for further proposals.
February 20 1973	Concorde 002 successfully completes performance trials at Johannesburg and demonstrations at Cape Town.

February 23 1973	Concorde 02 makes 3,728-mile (6,000-km.) non-stop flight from Toulouse to Iceland and return—equivalent to Paris-New York —in 3 hours 27 minutes of which 2 hours 9 minutes at Mach 2.
February 24 1973	Concorde 002 returns to Fairford from South Africa trials.
March 1973	Complex sales option system abolished.
March 3 1973	Concorde 02 makes 3,900-mile (6,280-km.) flight from Toulouse to West Africa and return in 3 hours 38 minutes—equivalent to Frankfurt-New York.
March 14 1973	Arab ambassadors and charges d'affaires make a 2 hour 25 minutes (one hour at Mach 2) flight over the Mediterranean in Concorde 02 from its base at Toulouse.
March 15 1973	Concorde 01 returns from Filton to Fairford after major modification programme, notably the installation of production standard engine air intakes and the smoke-free Olympus 593 Mk.602 engines as in 02.

ABBREVIATIONS

Numerous major organisations and establishments involved in the Concorde programme are commonly known in abbreviated form and those referred to in this *Profile* are listed below:

ARA	Aircraft Research Association
ARB	Air Registration Board
BAC	British Aircraft Corporation
CDC	Concorde Directing Committee
CMB	Concorde Management Board
CEAT	Centre d'Essais Aéronautiques de Toulouse
CEP	Centre d'Essais Propulseur
DoTI	British Department of Trade and Industry
NGTE	National Gas Turbine Establishment
RAE	Royal Aircraft Establishment
SNECMA	Société Nationale d'Etude et de Construction de Moteurs de Aviation
SNIAS	Société Nationale Industrielle Aérospatiale
STAC	Supersonic Transport Advisory Committee

ACKNOWLEDGEMENTS

The Publishers wish to thank Aérospatiale-France and the British Aircraft Corporation for their help in compiling this *Profile*.

Also, the author especially thanks Miss Wendy Parkes for her patience and meticulous care in typing the manuscript.

Concorde—the dramatic new airliner shape now dubbed 'Worldshrinker' and poised at the threshold of halving the world in size.

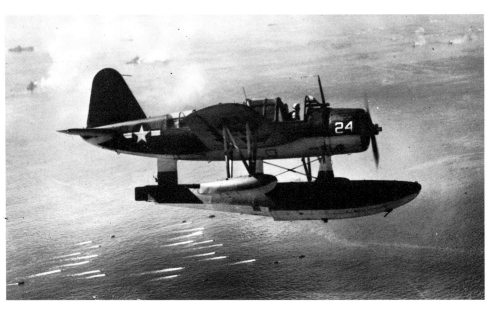

Vought-Sikorsky OS2U Kingfisher

by T. E. Doll and B. R. Jackson

OF the Kingfisher it can be said that in its time of war it performed well enough that men are alive today because of its rugged versatility and the dedication of the virtually unsung airmen who plied their trade from the fantail of a battleship, the mid-section of a cruiser or destroyer and from shore bases.

Kingfisher Design and Production

The OS2U was designed by Rex B. Beisel of the Chance Vought Aircraft Division, one of four divisions of the United Aircraft Corporation which included Pratt & Whitney, Hamilton Standard and the other aircraft division—the Sikorsky Aircraft Corporation. In 1939 the aircraft manufacturing operations of the United Aircraft Corporation were merged into the Vought-Sikorsky Aircraft Division at Stratford, Connecticut, and this situation remained in existence until January 1943 when the two companies reverted to their earlier status of separate firms.

The two companies were then able to concentrate on the development and production of widely differing types of aircraft—Vought on combat aircraft and Sikorsky on helicopters for military and commercial application. The greater part of Kingfisher production was under the Vought-Sikorsky banner.

The OS2U was unique in design for two reasons. First it was the first US Navy scout observation two-seater to incorporate the monoplane wing design specifically for catapult launching from battleships and cruisers. Secondly, from its conception in the late 1930s, the designer tackled the problem of sturdy construction capable of withstanding the constant stress of countless catapult launchings. Rex Beisel was the first designer to exploit spot-welding in order to create a non-buckling fuselage structure. This method he introduced into the Kingfisher design. With the new method of spot-welding, not only was conventional maintenance time (on the OS2U) lowered but also the new technique helped extend the Kingfisher's service life. Additionally, the OS2U-1 was to be the first Vought production aircraft with full-span flaps and spoiler lateral control.

XOS2U-1—On March 1 1938, the prototype Kingfisher—XOS2U-1, Bureau of Aeronautics serial 0951—was flown for the first time at East Hartford, Connecticut. The pilot was Paul S. Baker who, on May 19 1938 undertook the first seaplane flight. The prototype was powered by a Pratt & Whitney R-985-4 which was rated at 450 h.p. The XOS2U-1 had its own distinctive paint scheme; dark blue fuselage, wings and horizontal tail surfaces; aluminium floats and yellow rudder.

OS2U-1—In April 1940, the first production OS2U was airborne and, four months later, August 16, the first OS2U joined the US Fleet.

The Aviation Unit of the battleship USS *Colorado* (BB45), began operational trials with the

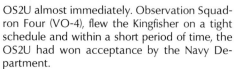

All 'first-offs'. (Top left, bottom right) Prototype XOS2U-1 (Bureau Number or serial BuNo. 0951) in 'dry' and 'wet' forms and subsequent all-silver finish in 1938. This July 1938 view of the landplane shows Aldis-type telescopic gun-sight has been incorporated; similarly, floatplane now has the additional rear pylon strut to float which became wider on production models. Transparency curve amidships only applied to BuNo. 0951. (Bottom left) May 1940 view of first production OS2U-1 (BuNo. 1681) showing only one 100-lb. bomb in position on the two Mark XII Mod. 1 racks. (Top right) First production OS2U-2 (BuNo. 2189) also in 1940. Aluminium varnish finish provides clear outlines to the Beisel lateral-control spoilers visible immediately aft of national insignia. (Photos: United Aircraft Corp. via Harry S. Gann and Lloyd S. Jones)

OS2U almost immediately. Observation Squadron Four (VO-4), flew the Kingfisher on a tight schedule and within a short period of time, the OS2U had won acceptance by the Navy Department.

By the end of 1940, no fewer than 54 Kingfishers had been completed by the Vought-Sikorsky Division. Fifteen of these were sent to Naval Air Station Pensacola, Florida, six to the Pearl Harbor Battle Force and 12 to NAS Alameda, California.

OS2U-2—Following closely behind the OS2U-1, the -2 Kingfisher began to take shape and, before the end of 1940, the first two OS2U-2 examples had been delivered to the Navy. These were the first of 158 OS2U-2s that would see operational service with the Fleet. They were basically the same as the -1 but incorporated the later Pratt & Whitney R-985-50 radial.

Forty-six of these aircraft went to NAS Pensacola and 53 to NAS Jacksonville, Florida, to be used in the formation of the new Inshore Patrol Squadrons; for example, VS-1D1 and VS-2D1.

OS2U-3—The last production model of the Kingfisher was the -3 version. More of this type were built than any other model of the OS2U.

First deliveries of the -3 began in 1941 following the first flight by Boone Guyton at Stratford on May 17 1941. The major improvements over the -1 and -2 were more fuel capacity and additional armour protection for the pilot and aircrewman.

The total production run of the OS2U Kingfisher amounted to 1,219 aircraft. Of this total, 55 were OS2U-1s (including the XOS2U-1), 158 were OS2U-2s and 1,006 were OS2U-3s.

OS2N-1—An additional 300 Kingfishers were built by the Naval Aircraft Factory in Philadelphia, Pennsylvania. These carried the designation OS2N-1. Although the NAF built 300 Kingfishers there is documented evidence that they

actually assembled a total of 31 extra of the type. The extra aircraft were apparently sent to the NAF for construction as they still maintained the Vought designation—OS2U (see Bureau Number list at end of this *Profile*).

Kingfisher Operation

Shipboard operation of the OS2U differed a great deal from the shipboard operation of other aircraft in the US Fleet, excluding the Curtiss SOC Seagull biplane. Battleship and cruiser operations with the OS2U were not unconventional for the times but they were something a little bit different from that which most pilots would experience during their Navy careers.

Float-equipped Kingfishers serving on battleships, cruisers and some destroyers were, of necessity, catapult-launched. On most battleships and cruisers these stern catapults were located on the port and starboard sides.

Light cruisers of the *Omaha*-class (CL4 to CL13) had two catapults located side-by-side abaft the rear funnel. Each catapult was 68 ft. in length and held a tracked cradle in which the Kingfisher's float rested. With the floatplane's engine at maximum revolutions, a power charge—similar to that of a 5-inch shell—was fired putting the cradle into motion and the aircraft would be catapulted at about 70 m.p.h. to become airborne.

Launching procedure—In charge of the overall catapult operation was the Launching Officer. The personnel under his command were divided into four groups: (1) the floatplane crew; (2) the deck crew; (3) the catapult crew; and (4) the signal and communications crew.

The floatplane crew consisted of the skilled mechanics and riggers attached to the aviation unit on board the ship. Assuming the aircraft was ready to fly, this crew was responsible for securing the aircraft to the launching car. They

The 34th production OS2U-1 (BuNo. 1714) in early 1941 before the change to drabber non-specular (non-reflecting) 'warpaint' greys (from March '41) and blues. Markings reveal that this OS2U-1 was allocated to Observation Squadron Three (VO-3) aboard USS Mississippi (BB41) of Battleship Division Three, United States Fleet. VO-3's Disney-like emblem ('Oswald the Lucky Rabbit' riding a 16-inch shell) is located between the cockpits. Colour scheme: aluminium-varnished fuselage, white bands encircling motor cowling and rear fuselage and 'True Blue' tail surfaces. Top surfaces to wings were orange-yellow and under-surfaces silver. Hamilton Standard 2-blade propeller silver but anti-dazzle rear faces; normal tri-colour tips (see photo above) with outer red, centre yellow and inner blue. This colourful display was of practical origin providing both ship-to-air identification and facilitating air-search recovery in the event of an out-of-sight emergency alighting. (Photo: Vought Aeronautics via authors)

were also in charge of fuelling oiling, equipping and testing the aircraft in accordance with the latest check-off list. They also manned the steadying lines and fending poles whenever the OS2U was being handled.

The deck crew consisted of about 10 men. They assisted the floatplane crew if needed and available. Their duties were to break down the rails on both sides of the deck far enough forward to be well clear of the catapult when it was trained and the aircraft was ready for launching. Also, they ensured that all booms, davits and so on were clear. As if the deck crew did not already have enough to keep them busy, they had also to rig the floatplane boom-and-snatch blocks and to assist in training the catapult.

The catapult crew consisted of five men and they were trained specifically to prepare and fire the catapult. The 'cat crew' prepared the catapult for firing 30 minutes before the set launch time. Under the direction of the catapult officer, these men performed a multitude of duties. There was a catapult operator, brake operator, valve operator, pin operator and a crewman who trained the catapult into firing position.

Lastly, the signal and communication crew consisted of men responsible for all communications between the bridge and catapult, keeping the launching officer informed by both hand

Still colourful. (Top) OS2U-1 (BuNo. 1685) of Observation Squadron Four (VO-4) assigned to USS Colorado in August 1940—the first battleship aviation unit to receive OS2Us. White bands and black tail assembly. (Bottom) Second production OS2U-2 (BuNo. 2190) of VS-5D4 (Fourth Naval District), one of the then-new Inshore Patrol Squadrons which were formed in 1941–42. Naval Air Station Cape May, New Jersey, is recorded on the red fuselage band; cowling also red. Compare with side-view colour illustration No. 3. Later, for easier recall, these squadrons dropped the Naval Districts' coding to become, for example, simply VS-5. (Photos: Vought Aeronautics via authors)

flags and telephone. They also kept in voice contact with the Kingfisher pilot.

The actual firing procedure of the aircraft was accomplished through a series of signals between the pilot and the men in charge of firing the catapult.

The pilot, waving his right arm in a circular motion, would declare 'My engine is OK, and I am standing by to be launched'. Upon receiving this signal, the catapult operator would move the control valve lever to the 45° position, equalizing the pressure on the piston valve. The crewman on the piston valve station would then open the handwheel to the 'full' out position.

The catapult officer would then wave his left arm in a circular motion signifying 'I am ready to fire on your signal'. The pin operator would then remove the securing pin from the release mechanism and hold it aloft for the pilot to see.

The pilot would then extend his arm horizontally and withdraw it; informing the catapult operator, 'I am ready to be launched. You may fire when ready.' The Kingfisher would then be launched into the air from the catapult.

During the catapulting operations a series of flag signals were being carried out between the catapult crew on the quarter-deck and the ship's bridge. A red flag or disc displayed on the bridge and acknowledged by a similar signal on the quarter-deck meant 'Stand by to catapult plane(s) but do not catapult until further notice.'

A green flag or disc signal from the bridge meant, 'Catapult as soon as ready.'

If a green flag or disc was shifted to red on the bridge, the quarter-deck would acknowledge by waving a green flag. As soon as the pilot and the valve control-man understood the order, the green flag would be shifted to red. This meant 'Hold all catapulting.'

A red flag waved vigorously from the bridge similarly answered by the quarter-deck meant, 'Do not catapult any more planes.'

Red and green flags waved together between the bridge and the quarter-deck was the signal to 'Secure, no more catapulting.'

Recovering the OS2U, at sea, presented another lesson in teamwork and skill. The word given this exercise was 'cast pick-up'. A tow pawl about six inches long was fitted on the keel of the forward end of the main float just at the waterline. A sled device was fitted to the recovery crane and hung in a position that enabled it to be towed by the ship. At the end of this 6-ft. wide sled was a 6-ft. length of cargo netting.

The recovery ship would turn sidewise and 45° into the wind, towing the sled. When the order to 'execute' was initiated the ship turned with full rudder through the wind to a course 45° off the wind. This created a 'slick' or relatively smooth surface on the sea for the OS2U to alight on. The pilot would then attempt to land his OS2U in this slick at a point close enough to the ship so that with full power he could then taxi up astern and place the nose of the Kingfisher's float on the sled as the ship completed its turn. As the Kingfisher hooked the cargo net attached to the sled, the pilot cut his engine and the rear-seat man—usually an Aviation Radioman—made ready to attach the hoisting sling

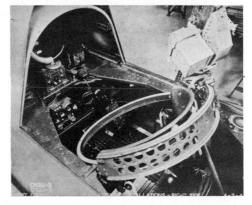

from the crane to the lift point on the OS2U as the sled and aircraft were being towed alongside the ship.

In the recovery procedure, as in launching, a series of flag signals between the OS2U and the bridge were used to coordinate operations.

The Baker flag (all red in colour), hoisted at flagstaff or on the aircraft boom, was to notify all aircraft to return to the vicinity of the ship in formation and wait for the signal to land. The numeral 6 on the search-light signified recall and was used in addition to the Baker flag. The number 6 was also transmitted by radio to the aircraft and used in addition to the other two signals.

Baker two-blocked at flagstaff or on the

Layout of pilot's cockpit and aircrewman's rear 'office' were more or less standard for all models of US Navy OS2U/OS2Ns. The Aldis-type Telescopic Gun Sight Mark III Mod. 4 is set in the windshield, the pilot firing his single, engine-mounted 30-calibre (0.300-inch) Browning M-2 through the propeller arc. The aviation radioman's flexible rotating and tilting gun-ring shows the single Browning M-2 mounted. Fixed m.g. had 500 rounds and the flexible m.g. 600 rounds. Radio direction-finding D/F loop just visible top left of lower picture.
(Photos: Vought Aeronautics via authors)

aircraft boom and landing 'tee' laid out on the quarter-deck told the pilot that manoeuvres were being made or were about to be made for the purpose of taking aircraft aboard. 'Land in slick as soon as possible after formation is broken and prepare for hoisting.'

After the Kingfishers were pulled alongside, a red flag was placed on the bridge and then answered by the quarter-deck. This signal meant to stand by to be hoisted aboard but keep clear until the green flag is displayed.

As the green flag appeared on the bridge it was again answered by the quarter-deck. The pilot then manoeuvred his OS2U alongside and was hoisted aboard. When the quarter-deck waved a green flag back to the bridge, the last OS2U had been cleared from the water and the aft was now clear for using engines. The float-planes were then secured as the ship proceeded to its next location.

An additional set of signals between the ship and scout plane were used for various situations. If the Kingfisher came close to the ship and zoomed; then cut the engine off-and-on rapidly and flew away at low altitude on a steady course, this would be a signal to the ship that an aircraft was down and in need of assistance, 'Follow me.'

A white strip of canvas stretched across the OS2U on the catapult told the pilot already in the air that this floatplane was delayed and he should not wait for it.

If the rear-seat man held his hand over his head it meant that he was trying to contact his visual sighting by radio. If he held his arm in a vertical position this meant 'Radio out of commission.' Finally, if he waved his arm over his head, this would be the signal to the ship that his receiver was not working and the ship should hoist the ADV flags if his voice transmission was coming through and the NDV flags if it were not.

Unit unidentified OS2U-3 post May 1942 when the horizontal red and white tail stripes and the red disc from the national insignia were deleted.
(Photo: via Harry S. Gann)

Rare trio of OS2U-1s from Observation Squadron One (VO-1). Less than two months after these photographs were taken in October 1941, the host USS Arizona (BB39), Flagship of Battleship Division One, Battle Force, US Fleet, met its end by Japanese bombs and torpedoes at Pearl Harbor. Demonstrating (see big photo) 'Dog' method of under-way, 10-knot, into wind sea recovery by engaging the 6-sq. ft. cargo-netting sled is '1-0-2' (BuNo. 1696, delivered August 23 1940). The aviation radioman is about to make the hazardous clamber forward to retrieve the hoist-sling stowed behind the pilot. For this tricky recovery manoeuvre, the pilot angled the radio mast to port. The second picture ('1-0-1', BuNo. 1695, del. Aug. 22 '40) shows BB39's portside recovery hook. The third photograph ('1-0-3', BuNo. 1697, del. Aug. 25 '40) reveals the crewman in the act of hoist-sling retrieving. Colour scheme: top surfaces non-specular blue-grey and similar non-reflecting light grey undersurfaces.
(Photos: Navy Dept., National Archives, refs. 80-G-66115, -66111 and -66108 respectively)

The OS2U and the US Navy

Before America's entry into World War Two, the United States Navy had 17 battleships in commission plus the USS *Wyoming* (ex-BB32 which had been converted to a gunnery training ship, AG17) which carried no aircraft. The 17 battleships in the Fleet had been completely re-equipped with the OS2U by December 1941. All light cruisers of the *Omaha*-class (CL4 to CL13), also had the OS2U by that time.

Prior to the adoption of the Kingfisher, all US Fleet battleships (BBs) and heavy (CAs) and light (CLs) cruisers were using the Curtiss SOC Seagull. The coming of the Kingfisher did not mark the end of the SOCs career in the US Navy. For example, many Fleet heavy cruisers kept the SOC because limited storage facilities aboard were better suited to the wing-folding Seagull biplanes.

Battleships normally carried three OS2Us, while all cruisers carried four Kingfishers—an exception being the *Omaha*-class cruisers which carried only two floatplanes.

The aviation units aboard the battleships were comprised of units from VO-1 through VO-5 (Observation Squadrons), while those aboard the cruisers consisted of units from VCS-3 through VCS-9 (Cruiser Scouting Squadrons). The only two battleships that did not have a numbered VO unit aboard were USS *North Carolina* (BB55) and USS *Washington* (BB56).

Shortly after Pearl Harbor, the long time VO and VCS squadrons became a thing of the past. The aircraft and men became part of the ship's company with replacements being assigned to the ships as needed. The VO and VCS aviators and crews became the 'lost men of naval aviation'. When their ships put into a port where there happened to be a Naval Air Station, they often found that the station did not have an organization plan for their respective unit. More often than not, they were on their own. When spare parts were needed no-one seemed to know where they were. In consequence, the VO/VCS units had to resort to the well-known navy supply system of 'midnight stores'. If an item to keep 'your' OS2U in the air was required, you 'liberated' it after Lights Out.

OS2U Destroyer Operations

A little-known episode in catapult-aircraft history relates to the US Navy's use of OS2Us aboard a few destroyers (DDs).

On May 27 1940, the Secretary of the Navy approved an order for six destroyers of the *Fletcher*-class to be modified and equipped with catapults, floatplanes and other related equipment. The following destroyers were selected for the experiment: USS *Pringle, Stanley, Hutchins, Stevens, Halford* and *Leutze* (DD476 to DD481).

Earlier in 1940, the destroyer USS *Noa* (DD343) had conducted experiments with the Curtiss XSOC-1 floatplane. These operations were successful and eventually led to the May 27 order for the six *Fletcher*-class destroyers to have aircraft handling equipment installed.

The rotating catapult was placed where the number three main battery and after torpedo tubes were normally situated. A tank for aviation fuel was built on the main deck, aft of the superstructure. It held 1,780 gallons of aviation fuel and was surrounded by a cofferdam filled with CO_2 for safety purposes. The DD carried an aviation mechanic, an aviation ordnance-man and a pilot in addition to her regular crew.

Trouble which developed in the floatplane hoisting gear eventually led to the removal of the aircraft handling equipment from USS *Pringle, Hutchins* and *Stanley* between late-1942 and early-1943. USS *Stevens* and *Halford* actually had good success with their OS2Us. These two ships participated in the Marcus Islands actions. USS *Halford* took part in the Wake Island raids and *Stevens* helped in the Tarawa actions of late-1943.

Operating OS2Us on destroyers, though not unsuccessful, nevertheless did prove troublesome in the area of recovery. Destroyers could not effect the 'Charlie' method of recovering aircraft because, unlike the battleships, could not form a slick big enough for the OS2Us to

USS Halford *(DD480) with OS2U on catapult: one of six destroyers of the Fletcher-class planned for aviation unit conversion in 1940. This rare photograph was taken on July 14 1943 and is featured in the companion* Warship Profile *series—No. 9: USS Charles Ausburne (DD570).*
(Photo: US Navy)

alight on. Consequently the destroyers had to use the 'Baker' method of recovery which meant that the ship had to come to almost a complete standstill in order for the Kingfisher to be hoisted aboard. This might have been acceptable in peacetime but in a combat zone it could cause its share of problems.

Heavy seas also put a damper on DD aircraft recovery operations and in heavy swells damage to the aircraft almost always resulted when the floatplane was being hoisted. For example, the OS2U would be 'bounced' against the after funnel.

Launching was always to the starboard side of the ship, 360° training of the catapult could not be accomplished. Recovery was always to port. The stowage of the aviation fuel onboard was another headache involved in operating OS2Us from destroyers. In December 1943, both USS *Stevens* and *Halford* had their aircraft handling equipment removed and the short era of floatplanes on destroyers came to an end.

USS *Leutze* never received aircraft handling gear.

OS2Us Other Duties

The Kingfishers that were assigned to the battle-ships and cruisers provided much-needed service during the early stages of US involvement in World War Two. With an extreme shortage of aircraft carriers, protection still had to be maintained for the numerous Atlantic and Pacific convoys. Battleships and cruisers assigned to convoy duty also provided the tactically and psychologically important 'air umbrella'. A constant patrol was kept throughout the day-light hours and each OS2U was equipped with either two 350-lb. depth bombs or general-purpose bombs.

In the event that an enemy submarine was spotted, the Kingfisher would engage it until the convoy's escorting destroyers could close-in and hopefully, make the 'kill'.

The Kingfisher also became the 'eyes' of the

*Pearl Harbor—I. Within Honolulu's Pearl Harbor lies Ford Island. This was the scene on the morning of December 8 1941. US Navy OS2Us did not escape the fate meted out during the surprise attacks by aircraft of the Imperial Japanese Navy Air Force on Sunday, December 7. To the left of the wrecked OS2U and behind a truck is a possibly undamaged OS2U of Observation Squadron Two (VO-2) marked '2-0-3'.
(Photo: Navy Dept., National Archives, ref. 80-G-32477)*

*Pearl Harbor—II. Same period as above, a seemingly and amazingly undamaged OS2U on the single catapult aboard the sunken battleship USS California (BB44). Ship's gun crews are manning the anti-aircraft 5-inch-38s (i.e. size-calibre). The battleship was raised and rebuilt, 1942–43.
(Photo: Navy Dept., National Archives, ref. 80-G-32423)*

(Left) OS2U-3s aboard a US Navy battleship, part of a task force serving with the British Home Fleet. Period, December 1943.

Wearing the uniform of an Admiral of the Fleet, HM King George VI toured USS Washington (BB56, commissioned May 15 1941) when it was attached to the British Home Fleet in Atlantic waters in 1942. The 'at rest' securing struts on the OS2U-3s are noteworthy. (Photos: Imperial War Museum, ref. A.17647/XF)

battleship's and cruiser's big guns during the bombardment of shore installations. Many times they provided the location of the enemy fleet while being used as a search aircraft.

Perhaps the most important rôle the Kingfisher performed during the war was that of rescuer of downed airmen. The OS2U was second only to the reliable old Consolidated PBY Catalina in this function.

Kingfisher pilots flew in all types of weather. Often they would be launched on a relatively clear and calm day, only to return to find the weather conditions foul and the sea rough and choppy. They also faced the possibility of returning to the ship's plotted position only to find it nowhere in sight. The OS2U pilots would then have to fly a square-search pattern. It was almost always impossible for the ship to send out a radio signal for the pilot to home in on because radio silence had to be observed. Good navigation plus luck were all the OS2U pilots had going for them in this kind of situation.

US Navy Kingfishers were also assigned to

several Fleet Auxiliary Seaplane Tenders and, by December 1941, no fewer than 14 OS2Us were in service with eight such ships. For example, the large seaplane tender USS Tangier (AV8) had been assigned a trio of Kingfishers and was part of Patrol Wing Two at Pearl Harbor.

In September 1940, the first of the new Inshore Patrol Squadrons, VS-5D4, was commissioned and allocated OS2Us. Before the end of 1942 a total of 30 Inshore Patrol Squadrons was to be in operation with Kingfishers. The majority of these squadrons flew the Naval Aircraft Factory OS2N-1 duplicate of the OS2U-3. The Kingfisher also served with the US Coast Guard Inshore Patrol Squadrons. The first of 53 Coast Guard Kingfishers were received in early 1942; but all remaining USCG Kingfishers were relinquished by 1944.

On January 23 1942, the Kingfishers of VS-1D14 became the first US Navy aircraft to operate from the Samoan Islands.

One of the first recorded uses of the OS2U as a glide or low-level bomber—carrying 350-lb.

Key to colour illustrations

1 Vought - Sikorsky OS2U-2 (BuNo. 2216) of the US Navy's Patrol Wing Two, Pearl Harbor, Hawaii, assigned to the seaplane tender USS Tangier (AV8) in 1941.

2 OS2U-1 (BuNo. 1691) in 'Command Plane' colours for the Commander-in-Chief, US Fleet, aboard the flagship USS Pennsylvania (BB38), 1941.

3 OS2U-2 of Inshore Patrol Squadron VS-5D4, Naval Air Station Cape May, New Jersey, 1942.

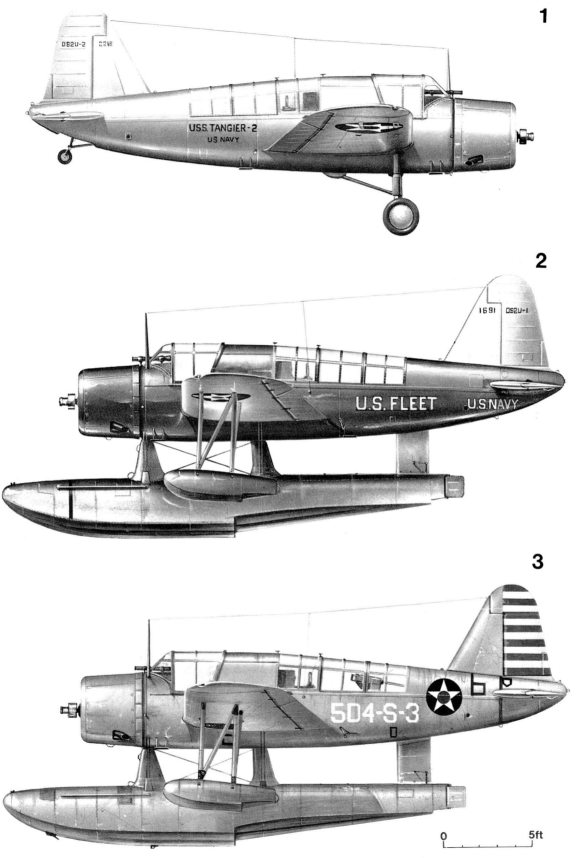

1

OS2U-2 2216

U.S.S. TANGIER-2
US NAVY

2

1691 OS2U-1

U.S. FLEET U.S. NAVY

3

5D4-S-3

0   5ft

Trim/Britton/Hadler/Johnson   © *Profile Publications Ltd.*

Subject of colour illustration No. 3 on the previous page, this OS2U-2 of Inshore Patrol Squadron VS-5D4 was based at NAS Cape May, NJ, in early 1942. This OS2U displays the rare combination of markings and paint scheme. Non-specular light-grey overall, white unit code letters and red and white tail stripes as directed by the Bureau of Aeronautics in January 1942 but some 2½ months after the grey-overall scheme had been abandoned.
(Photo: via Harry S. Gann)

Circuits and bumps. At Naval Air Station Pensacola, Florida, a training OS2U-1 with novel embarking ramp. Florida's famed sunshine is responsible for the smart headgear. In the background, two Consolidated P2Y-2 obsolescent patrol flying-boats used for training with VN-4D8 (Eighth Naval District).
(Photo: from colour transparency by Art Schoeni)

bombs instead of the lighter stores for which they had been designed—was in connection with the initial assault against the Japanese based on Attu in the Aleutians in the second half of 1942. 'With conspicuous success they came through in characteristic Vought style.'[1]

On July 15 1942, two Kingfishers (Ensigns Frank C. Lewis and Charles D. Webb) of VS-9D4, NAS Cherry Point, N. Carolina, assisted the Fleet Auxiliary, USS Unicoi (IX216) in sinking the German submarine U-576. The action took place off Diamond Shoals, east of Cape Hatteras —better known as 'The Graveyard of the Atlantic'.

Rescue Kingfishers

For the Kingfisher, and despite all its valuable combat rôles around the world, only one event was to bring it into dramatic public focus. Late in October 1942, a US Army Air Forces' Boeing B-17 Flying Fortress was forced to 'ditch' in the Pacific. For nearly three weeks, the US Navy carried out an unrelenting search for the eight missing airmen. One of those missing was Captain Eddie V. Rickenbacker, Congressional

Medal of Honor, America's highest-scoring World War One 'ace' and then (1942) virtually a household name. Enter 'The Bug'.

'The Bug' was an OS2U which had rolled-off the assembly line in mid-1941 and had been assigned to 'the veteran battlewagon of the Pacific Fleet',[1] the battleship USS Pennsylvania (BB38) first commissioned in 1916. At Pearl Harbor during the Japanese attack in December 1941, the OS2U escaped major damage. Rapidly effected repairs allowed 'The Bug' to take-off at dawn on December 8 in search of the Japanese Fleet. Without avail.

Eventually, 'The Bug' was transferred to another scouting squadron and when American forces occupied Ellice Islands, 'The Bug' was there. In a matter of weeks, 'The Bug' was searching the South Pacific for the missing B-17 crewmen. Then, on November 11 1942, success. Flying 'The Bug' was Lieutenant (jg) F. E. Woodward with the rear cockpit occupied by L. H. Boutte, AR/1c (Aviation Radioman First Class). They alighted near a spread of yellow marker dye and the rescue of the B-17's crew began with Captain W. T. Cherry and four others.

---

[1] Wings for the Navy—A history of Chance Vought Aircraft.

[1] Chance Vought's (1943) Wings for the Navy.

Just before nightfall on the next day, 'The Bug' had its best day. The raft with Eddie Rickenbacker and the two remaining crew was discovered. Volunteers to attempt an immediate rescue were sought and Lieutenant William F. Eadie won the assignment. Once again Radioman Boutte went along 'for the ride'. Unable to fly all three survivors back at one go, the decision was taken to taxi the OS2U back to the nearest land—40 gruelling miles distant— with Rickenbacker and one B-17 crewman lashed to the wings while the most seriously-ill second B-17 crewman was placed in the back seat on AR/1c Boutte's lap. With 1,100 flying hours already logged, 'The Bug' flew on—the most famous Kingfisher of the Pacific War.

Kingfisher in Major Actions

Kingfishers took part in all the major actions of the Pacific War. From Guadalcanal to the Marshalls, the Gilberts, the Marianas, the Philippines and on to Iwo Jima and Okinawa. They stalked the Japanese Fleet, and provided observation for ground troops as well as their own ships. They also acted out their 'guardian angel' rôle by rescuing many downed pilots from the Fast Carrier Forces.

At Tarawa, the OS2U was responsible for the neutralization of Bairiki Island. On November 21 1943, a Kingfisher dropped a bomb on the island. This scored a direct hit on a drum of gasoline which exploded and killed the entire 15-man occupation force on the island.

In April 1944, as the US Fleet was starting its assault on the Japanese stronghold of Truk, little resistance from enemy aircraft was found. However, the anti-aircraft fire from the island was intense. Kingfishers from the battleship USS *North Carolina* (BB55) had been assigned to rescue work.

On April 30, the second day of the bombardment, the two Kingfisher crews were alerted that a pilot from the USS *Enterprise* (CV6), had 'ditched' at sea. Within an hour the two OS2Us were circling over the pilot, Lieutenant (jg) Bob Kanze. One of the Kingfishers, flown by Lieutenant (jg) J. J. Dowdle with R. E. Hill in the rear seat, managed to alight and taxi over to Kanze. The water was rough. As Kanze grabbed the wing float, his raft was swept away. Almost immediately a wave pushed into the side of Dowdle's OS2U and, with Kanze's weight on the float, the Kingfisher capsized throwing Dowdle and Hill into the choppy sea as well.

The three men were able to recover the life raft as the second OS2U, piloted by Lieutenant (jg) John A. Burns (rear-gunner, Aubrey J. Gill) banked overhead. Burns had observed the situation and began to make the tricky approach to the choppy sea. Alighting successfully, he taxied over to the raft. Very carefully Burns and his gunner helped the men aboard. To balance the floatplane, Kanze was placed on one wing and Dowdle on the other while Hill hung on the

Subject of the colour 5-view on the following two pages, echelon to starboard of four OS2U-3s used for pilot training (no crewmen are aboard) at NAS Corpus Christi, on the Gulf of Mexico, Texas. (Photo: Navy Dept., National Archives, ref. 80-G-10554)

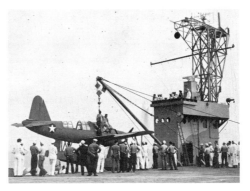

The escort carrier USS Charger (CVE30, ex-passenger/cargo MS Rio de la Plata, and as British Royal Navy name suggests, originally earmarked for RN but retained after Pearl Harbor), shows crew undergoing training in hoisting aboard an OS2U in June 1942, three months after commissioning. CVE30 was only employed for CVE training. (Photo: Navy Dept., ref. 28440 via H. S. Gann)

Atlantic convoy patrol by a US Coast Guard OS2U-3 in mid-1942. Note heavy depth charge under wing. (Photo: US Coast Guard, ref. 1655)

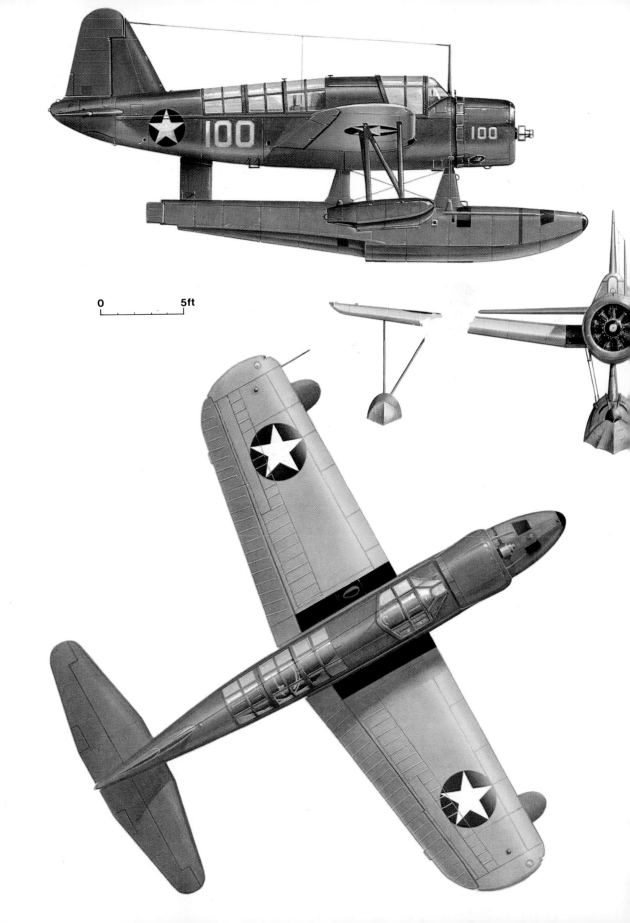

0   5ft

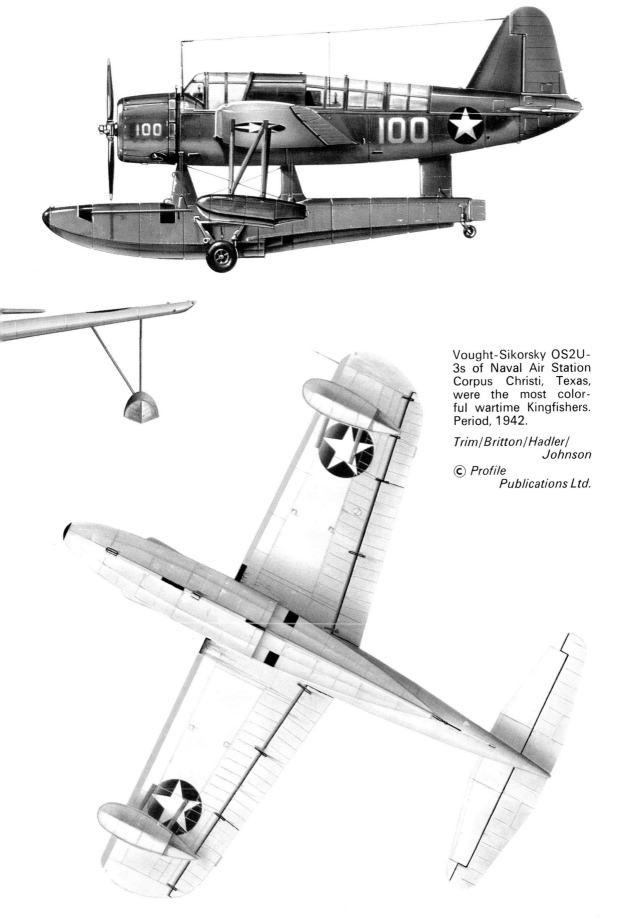

Vought-Sikorsky OS2U-3s of Naval Air Station Corpus Christi, Texas, were the most colorful wartime Kingfishers. Period, 1942.

Trim/Britton/Hadler/
Johnson

© *Profile*
Publications Ltd.

Rare bird. A standard OS2U-2 fuselage but with a difference. Experimental blunt-tipped wing incorporating 'Zap' narrow-chord, full-span flaps and wing-folding facility. New wing resulted in enlarged-area horizontal stabilizer or tailplane.
(Photo: Douglas, El Segundo, ref. 21691 via Harry S. Gann)

On patrol over the Caribbean in 1942, a Kingfisher of the US Marine Corps; in this case Marine Scouting Squadron Three (VMS-3) stationed at St. Thomas, Virgin Islands. Large depth charge is in evidence and rear crewman's 30-cal. Browning M-2 is in the stowed position.
(Photo: Defense Dept., USMC ref. 51927)

Wartime Kingfisher, with pre-war chevron marks on the wings, during exercises in late 1942. Aircraft number is repeated on cowling sides and top of cowling collector ring. (NB: Another fine view of this OS2U-3 appears on the last page of this Profile, but that one was not received by the British IWM until May 1944 from the US Office of War Information—Editor).
(Photo: via Lloyd S. Jones)

fuselage. With the increased load Burns was unable to take-off, so he taxied to the rescue submarine USS *Tang* (SS306) where he deposited his very soggy passengers. Dowdle's OS2U was then destroyed by SS306's guns to keep it from the enemy.

Burns was then directed to the east where another pilot was reported down. The *Tang* had also been directed to cover rescue operations in the eastern waters of the atoll.

Burns found the downed aviator, Lieutenant Robert T. Barbor from the Light carrier USS *Langley* (CVL27), and picked him up. Barbor sitting in the rear seat with Gill created too much weight for the OS2U to take-off in the rough sea. Burns decided to wait for the *Tang*, which had radioed that it was on the way. The three men in the Kingfisher sat and observed the carrier pilots from the Fleet continue their aerial assault on Truk.

As they watched, two Grumman TBM Avengers—piloted by Lt. Robert S. Nelson and Ensign Carroll L. Farrell—received hits from the anti-aircraft fire on Truk. The two TBMs had to 'ditch'. Burns decided he would try to reach the stricken Avengers' crews. He reached them in about 30 minutes. Finding Nelson's raft first, also with Joseph Hranek and Owen T. Tabrum aboard, Burns tossed them a life line. Towing the raft he then proceeded to the other raft containing Farrell and his crew, Robert W. Gruebel and James L. Livingston. After throwing them a line he attempted to tow both rafts to safety. This proved impractical because as soon as Burns started to increase his engine power, the backwash and spray soaked the six men. Also the weight produced tremendous drag on the aircraft.

Burns then transferred all six men to the Kingfisher, placing some on the wings and others on the fuselage to balance the load and keep the OS2U from capsizing. Burns then began taxiing his Kingfisher to the awaiting USS *Tang*. Before he reached the submarine there was an emergency call and the *Tang* disappeared

Another view of one of the two experimental OS2U-2s (BuNos. 2189 and 3075). Black area in tail cone is housing for test anti-spin parachutes. Both photographs show the Kingfisher's normally retracted footrests to advantage. (Photo: Vought Aeronautics via Art Schoeni)

beneath the waves.

After rescuing another pilot who had alighted close to shore, the submarine *Tang* returned to Burns' OS2U. The Kingfisher had started to take on water in the main float and was listing badly. All nine aviators were taken aboard the *Tang*. Before leaving the area, the submarine's guns had to destroy the Kingfisher that had worked so hard that day in picking-up no fewer than 10 downed American aviators.

Kingfisher v. Zero-Sen

The Kingfisher also was responsible for the downing of at least one Japanese Mitsubishi *Zero-Sen* fighter. On February 16 1945, three days before the landing on Iwo Jima, an OS2U from the heavy cruiser USS *Pensacola* (CA24), flown by Lt. (jg) D. W. Gandy, was spotting gunfire for the pre-invasion bombardment. At 1,500 ft. a *Zero-Sen* dived on the OS2U, fired a short burst and turned away. Lieutenant Gandy turned his Kingfisher to the left, then to the right, which placed him on the tail of the enemy fighter. He began firing on the *Zero-Sen* with his calibre 30 (0.300-in.) Browning M-2 forward-firing machine-gun. The fighter began to smoke and attempted to turn away from the onrushing OS2U. Gandy continued to fire into the smoking Zero until it

Revised national insignia shows to advantage in this photograph taken on June 8 1945 at Okinawa, aboard a US Navy Light cruiser (CL category). Embarkation ladder is in position but the 'at rest' securing struts are stowed alongside the catapult. Aft is a single 450 rounds-per-minute 20-mm. Oerlikon anti-aircraft machine-gun; Navy does not call it 'cannon'. (Photo: Defense Dept., USMC, ref. 125485)

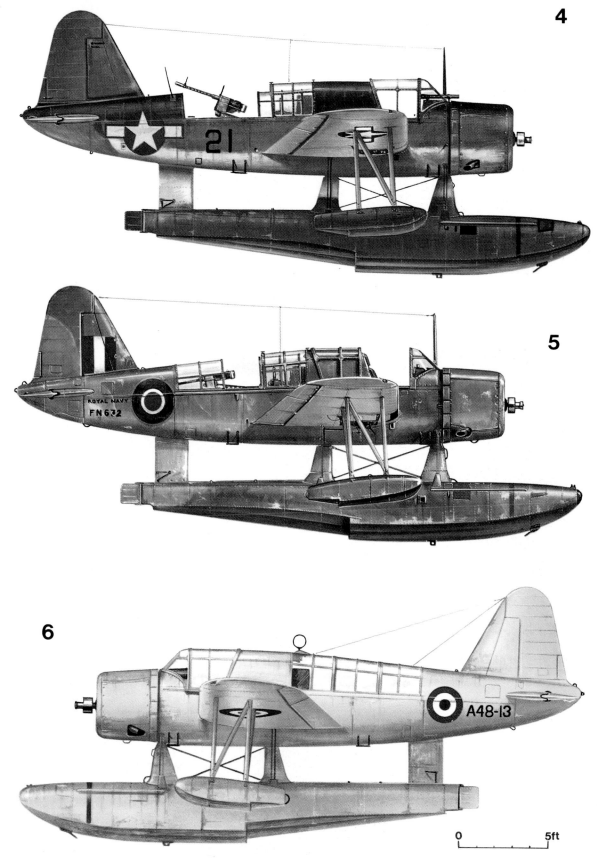

4

5

6

21

ROYAL NAVY
FN 632

A48-13

0   5ft

Trim/Britton/Hadler/Johnson   © Profile Publications Ltd.

burst into flames and crashed into an island bluff.

The Vought-Sikorsky OS2U Kingfisher had transversed the entire length of the US participation in World War Two. She had been in on the beginning at Pearl Harbor on December 7 1941 and she was aboard the battleship USS *Missouri* (BB63) when the surrender was officially signed in Tokyo Bay on September 2 1945. The Kingfisher served the Navy for only a short few months after the war, by 1947 the OS2U was only a memory in the US Fleet.

Kingfisher in the Royal Navy

The OS2U began its career in the Royal Navy in mid-May 1942. The Kingfisher was slated to re-equip certain light cruisers and Armed Merchant Cruiser Catapult Flights. These ships could not handle the heavier pusher amphibian Supermarine Walrus, the standard catapult aircraft of the RN, because they were fitted with a Light Series catapult capable of launching only

aircraft of up to 5,500 pounds.

The Kingfisher's predecessor, the British Fairey Seafox—comparatively fragile and under-powered—had no British replacement so two US Navy types were requested. The Ranger air-cooled inverted-Vee inline-powered Curtiss SO3C Seagull (RN: Seamew) and the Vought OS2U were evaluated. The Seamew failed completed as far as the Royal Navy was concerned and in early 1942 the Kingfisher made the team.

The first OS2Us were ferried to the United Kingdom aboard the aircraft carrier HMS *Furious* and in mid-May 1942, 703 Squadron was formed at Lee-on-Solent. This provided a headquarters unit for the Kingfisher Flights, the first of which was 703 *Fidelity* Flight. This Flight worked at Lee and then on the river Tay at Dundee with one Kingfisher.

On June 1 1942, *Ranpura* Flight was formed with two aircraft. Two months later, August, this Flight was re-assigned to *Cilicia* and redesignated accordingly. On August 15 1942, two more

Key to colour illustrations

4 The code '21' indicates that this 1945-period OS2U-3 was Plane No. 1 of Battle Division Two; it was assigned to USS *Tennessee* (BB43).

5 British Royal Navy Kingfisher I (serial FN672) which was attached to the catapult-aircraft training carrier HMS *Pegasus* (ex-*Ark Royal*) in 1942.

6 OS2U-3 Kingfisher I (A48-13), which took part in the Australian Antarctic Expedition of 1947–48.

Two excellent views of unit-unidentified OS2U-3s. Fin emblem (above) shows 'Donald Duck' in sailor's rig and holding a telescope. From paint weathering both OS2Us appear to have been long-service Kingfishers. The spinner (lower view) is non-standard. (Photos: via Lloyd S. Jones and Fred C. Dickey, Jr.)

Flights were formed; *Canton* and *Corfu*.

These Flights all saw service with Armed Merchant Cruisers. The *Fidelity* however, was classified a 'Special Service Vessel' and was used for a variety of special operations. *Corfu, Cilicia* and *Canton* were ex-P & O liners and saw service in the Indian and South Atlantic Oceans.

Two light cruiser Flights were formed in January 1943 for *Enterprise* and *Emerald*. Also during January two additional Armed Merchant Cruiser Flights came into being; one at Palisadoes, Jamaica, and the other at Wingfield, Capetown. These Flights were equipped with one Kingfisher each.

703 Squadron's *Fidelity* Flight met with misfortune during operations on December 28 1942. *Fidelity*'s Kingfisher was attempting a water take-off (*Fidelity* had no catapult) and in doing so flipped-over in the rough sea and was lost. Both aircrew survived. The *Fidelity* was lost off the Azores just three days after this luckless incident.

During the summer and autumn of 1942, *Canton, Cilicia* and *Corfu* were fitted with US Navy-type catapults. *Cilicia* operated in the South Atlantic from January 1943 until January 1944. *Canton* began operations in the same area in February 1943, but only stayed until the latter part of the following March. *Corfu* took over where *Canton* left off.

Rescue I. Nothing is known as to whether this was a genuine rescue re-enactment or merely a training exercise (the facial expressions suggest gloom!) or even where and when the photograph was taken. The non-specular white underside colour demarcation line is unusually high on the fuselage of this OS2U-3. (Photo: via Lloyd S. Jones)

Rescue II. This was a genuine rescue, one of the famous incidents described in this Profile. Seven rescued aviators are on the wings of Lieutenant (jg) John A. Burns' OS2U-3 at Truk Atoll, April 30 1944. (Photo: US Navy, ref. 15202 via Art Schoeni)

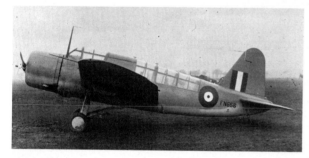

Operating in all types of weather, *Corfu* Flight flew 142 sorties in 10 months with no time lost due to damage to its Kingfishers.

Cilicia Flight compiled a total of almost 200 sorties in 11 months. Near the end of 1943, both *Cilicia* and *Corfu* Flights received an additional Kingfisher bringing their complement to three each.

Canton operated in the Indian Ocean throughout most of 1943 escorting troop convoys between Durban, Bombay, Colombo, Aden and Mombasa. It is worthy of note that during the months of July, August and September, 1943, the Eastern Fleet air strength consisted wholly of catapult-type floatplanes. During this time the Royal Navy could not spare an aircraft carrier for this area. Fifteen aircraft—three of them Kingfishers—carried the load.

Canton's Flight flew 120 sorties during the 13 months she served in the South Atlantic and Indian Oceans.

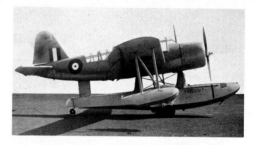

Royal Navy Kingfisher Is. Two views of landplane Royal Navy OS2U-3, serial FN656 (ex-BuNo. 5817) in England, April 1942. Red and blue B-type British roundels under wings are non-standard. Floatplane Kingfisher I of the same period is another OS2U-3, serial FN678 (ex-BuNo. 5839). Orthochromatic film gives false reading to outer yellow circle of red, white and blue fuselage roundel. Side view of FN656 reveals a Hawker Hurricane Mk. I (W9187) in the background. (Photos: IWM, refs. A.10847C and B:FN656 and A.10848E and F:FN678)

Canton Flight departed the Eastern Fleet in February 1944. *Emerald* Flight remained in the area until the end of April 1944 when it returned to Dundee and was disbanded. By the end of April 1944, catapult aircraft had been phased-out of service in the Royal Navy—and 703 Squadron was decommissioned in the same month. Forty of the 100 Kingfishers allocated to Britain were used by 703 Squadron. The remaining Kingfishers were used by 749 Squadron at Piarco, Trinidad, for observer training duties from late 1942 to the spring of 1945. In South Africa, a Fleet Requirements Squadron—726—used two Kingfishers for target-towing, com-

munications, radar calibration and various other tasks from September 1943 to early 1945. Twenty Kingfishers were returned to the USA shortly before the end of World War Two in Europe thus ending OS2U service in the Royal Navy. The Kingfisher won a certain measure of acceptance in British service especially when compared with the Seafox. Overall, the Royal Navy favourite was the Supermarine Walrus which, with the Kingfisher, shared the unique experience of being the only shipborne air cover in the Indian Ocean in mid-1943. Both rightly deserve their honoured niche in naval aviation history.

'Donald Duck' Royal Navy-style, HMS Pegasus (ex-Ark Royal seaplane tender of World War One) served in World War Two as an aircrew and deck-handling crews' catapult training ship. These two photographs of the same Kingfisher I (serial FN672, ex-BuNo. 5833, delivered in March 1942) were issued to the Press in October 1942. Photo above shows the Disney character of Donald Duck astride a ship painted on the motor cowling. This view also shows to advantage the sling hoist and canted radio mast for crane operation. It can be observed that fore and aft footrests were installed on both sides of the fuselage.
(Photos: IWM, refs. A.12043X and A.12046WK)

Museum theme. Top and bottom photographs show an OS2U which, in 1971, was beautifully restored by retired employees of Vought Aeronautics Division of LTV Aerospace Corporation at Dallas, Texas. The Kingfisher had crashed into a hillside on Calvert Island, British Columbia in 1944, the remains being recovered in 1963. Six years later USS North Carolina Battleship Commission negotiated for the wreck so that it could be rebuilt and exhibited on the fantail of USS North Carolina (BB55) now moored in the harbour of Wilmington, NC. The memorial OS2U-2 has been given the BuNo. serial 3073. The May 12 1941 photograph (centre) is of a genuine OS2U-2, light-grey overall and inscribed 'North Carolina' on the rear fuselage.
(Photos: Vought Aeronautics)

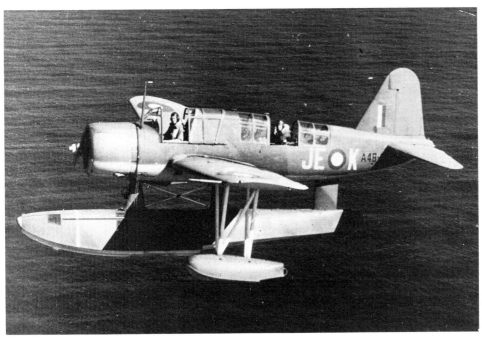

Originally destined for the Naval Air Service of the Netherlands East Indies, the events of the Pacific War resulted in the diversion of at least 18 of the 24 ordered to Australia. These were allocated to the Royal Australian Air Force and given the serial numbers A48-1 to A48-18. Seven were delivered in April and eleven more in June 1942. This OS2U-3 arrived at No. 1 Aircraft Depot on May 6 1942 and was subsequently assigned to No. 107 Squadron (code JE) at Rathmines, Sydney NSW.
(Photo: via Vought Aeronautics/Art Schoeni)

An August 1943-released photograph of a US Navy Kingfisher showing the contemporary colours and markings 'through a cloud of spray at a (British) East Coast port' to quote from the official caption.
(Photo: IWM PL.290E)

Museum pieces. (Right) At Quintero Air Base, north of Valparaiso, a currently preserved Chilean Air Force US2U-3 (CAF serial 314). In addition to the OS2U aboard USS North Carolina, two other memorial battleships have OS2Us, the USS Massachusetts (BB59) and (below) the USS Alabama (BB60) at Mobile, Ala. The last-mentioned has the curious serial, namely of the XOS2U-1 (BuNo. 0951) whereas it was originally a landplane OS2U-3 located in Mexico. (Photos: CAF 314 via Juan-Carlos Gumicio and (0951) from colour prints by Norman B. Wiltshire)

Kingfisher Contemporaries

Mention in this Profile is made of the British Fairey Seafox (above) and the Kingfisher's predecessor, the Curtiss SOC Seagull (left). Unlike the redoubtable but older Fairey Swordfish torpedo biplane, the Seafox suffered a disappointing career. On the other hand, the SOC Seagull was a worthy OS2U predecessor.

The Seagull depicted scouts for the Fleet during the attack on the atoll of Wotje, Marshall and Gilbert Islands, February 1 1942. (Photos: Air-Britain archives and Curtiss-Wright Corp.)

But not a Kingfisher. (Right and below) Superficially resembling the OS2U-1 was the confusingly designated XSO2U-1 (BuNo. 1440) which was photographed as a landplane on July 26 1939 and as a floatplane on December 28 1939. Only one prototype and not proceeded with, the XSO2U-1 had the novelty of an air-cooled inverted-vee inline Ranger XV-770-4 offering 450 h.p. at 3,000 r.p.m. The NACA-designed low-beam-to-length float was evolved to lessen water and aero-dynamic drag but turned in a disappointing performance in docking and recovery manoeuvres. Span, 38 ft. 2 in.; length 24 ft. 2 in. (land), 36 ft. 1 in. (sea). Note cowlings differ. (Photos: Vought Aeronautics-Art Schoeni)

COMPARATIVE DATA: ALL KINGFISHER MODELS

Model	Powerplant (Pratt & Whitney 'Wasp Junior')	Max. Output (h.p.)	Gross Weight (lb.)	Max. Speed (m.p.h.)	Service Ceiling (ft.)
XOS2U-1	R-985-4	450	4,611	177	20,300
OS2U-1	R-985-48	450	4,542	184	19,500
OS2U-2	R-985-50	450	4,542	182	20,000
OS2U-3	R-985-AN-2	450	4,560	183	20,100
OS2N-1	R-985-AN-2/8				

Dimensions: For all models—Span, 36 ft. 0 in.; length, 30 ft. 1 in.; height, 12 ft. 11 in.

OS2U KINGFISHER BUREAU NUMBER ASSIGNMENTS

Model	Bureau Number	Quantity	Comments
XOS2U-1	0951	1	Prototype
OS2U-1	1681–1734	54	Entire production of OS2U-1
OS2U-2	2189–2288	100	First production of OS2U-2
OS2U-2	3073–3130	58	Second production of OS2U-2
OS2U-3	5284–5941	658	First production of OS2U-3
OS2U-3	5942–5972	31	Assembled by the Naval Aircraft Factory
OS2U-3	5973–5989	17	
OS2U-3	5990–6289	(300)	Cancelled
OS2N-1	01216–01515	300	Same as OS2U-3 but built by Naval Aircraft Factory
OS2U-3	09393–09692	300	

Total number of Kingfishers built: 1,519

KINGFISHERS DELIVERED TO COUNTRIES NOT UNDER THE LEND LEASE AGREEMENT

Model	Bureau Number	Quantity	Comments
OS2U-3	Unknown	3	To Dominican Republic
OS2U-3	Unknown	6	To Mexico

OS2U KINGFISHERS DELIVERED TO OTHER COUNTRIES

Model	Bureau Number	Quantity	Comments
OS2U-3	5811–5840	30	And later 09513–09582 total 100 to British Royal Navy; serials FN650–749, (Lend Lease)
OS2U-3	5911–5925	15	To Chile, (LL)
OS2U-3	5926–5931	6	To Uruguay, (LL)
OS2U-3	5932–5940	9	To Argentina, (LL)
OS2U-3	5966–5989	24	To Netherlands East Indies. After fall of NEI, these OS2Us were sent to Australia. Only 18[1] of the 24 are accounted for; the fate of six is not known
OS2U-3	09513–09582	70	To Britain, (LL). Twenty later returned to US Navy

Total number of OS2U-3s delivered under Lend Lease: 154
[1] RAAF serial nos. A48-1 to 18, received April–June 1943.

Acknowledgements

The authors take this opportunity of expressing their deep appreciation of the invaluable assistance given to them by the US Navy, government agencies and private individuals. As usual, American Aviation Historical Society members have given generously including William A. Riley, William T. Larkins, Harry S. Gann, Lloyd S. Jones, John W. Caler; and Bunny d'E. C. Darby of the A.H.S. of New Zealand. For the above lists and many photos, special thanks to Art Schoeni of Vought Aeronautics.

Series Editor: CHARLES W. CAIN

(Left) *Floatplane training for Royal Navy Kingfisher observers took place at Royal Naval Air Station Piarco, Trinidad, of which this OS2U-3 coded BL3P is an example.*
(Photo: via the authors)

Rex B. Beisel

On February 2 1972, the man who designed the OS2U Kingfishers—and the Navy's F4U Corsair fighter which first flew on May 29 1940— died aged 78 at Sarasota, Florida. Born in San Jose, California on October 23 1893, Rex Buran Beisel began a lifelong association with naval aviation by serving from 1917 to 1923 as an engineer and draughtsman with the Navy Dept., Washington DC. When he retired in 1949 he had been general manager of Vought-Sikorsky for seven years.
(Photo: Vought Aeronautics)

OS2U-3s awaiting delivery at the plant on November 6 1941. The light-grey overall finish blends well with the misty winter's sunlight.
(Photo: Vought Aeronautics-Art Schoeni)

Another view of '43' illustrated on an earlier page of this Profile. *The wings and tail surfaces show evidence of the spray created by sea alighting and 10-kt taxiing.*
(Photo: IWM, ref. EN.22052)

Coming home to roost. Ordnance expended A-6A of VA-85 Black Falcons, CVW-11 (NH) in the groove and ready for recovery aboard USS Kitty Hawk during Vietnam operations in 1966. Wing tip speed brakes are deployed and hook is down.
(Photo: Grumman 66741)

Grumman A-6A/E Intruder; EA-6A; EA-6B Prowler

by Kurt H. Miska

'The Grumman A-6 family comprises the most modern, combat-ready, all-weather attack aircraft available on the free world inventory.'

Consider the proven facts. Armed with 15,000 pounds of ordnance, attack versions of the A-6 Intruder can be launched in pitch-black conditions from the flight deck of a carrier, can be navigated hundreds of miles through bad weather to seek out and attack a non-visual target, and can return to the 'moving airfield' of the aircraft carrier without recourse to any external reference. To date, only one other aircraft type—the land-based

General Dynamics F-111 of the US Air Force—has superior capability. But the F-111's combat career is brief enough against the A-6's nearly eight years to make any comparative assessment unfair.

The A-6 Family

Despite a fine combat record under every conceivable condition and the unique capabilities of the A-6 and its variants, in 12 years the total production of new airframes has barely exceeded 500 units. At the time of writing, the only services to operate the A-6 are the US Navy and the

US Marine Corps. Interest by the US Air Force has been token only and no foreign sales have been announced.

Navy A-6 inventory comprises the A-6A, A-6B, A-6C, KA-6D, A-6E and EA-6B Prowler and the Marines fly the A-6A, KA-6D and EA-6A. Both services operate the TC-4C flying classroom for A-6 crew training.[1]

The A-6 is equally suitable for operations either from carriers of the *Midway*-class and bigger, or from land bases.

Numerous Variants Prosper

The Grumman A-6 Intruder family, with exception of the EA-6B Prowler, is a series of two-place, all-weather attack aircraft powered by two turbojets. Utilitarian, unflattering lines have earned it a number of nicknames, of which only 'Mighty Tadpole' seems to have gained currency among knowing Fleet personnel.

Currently, six variants of the A-6 are in operation, as follows:

A-6A (488 airframes). This is the basic aircraft, which first flew in April 1960, and is currently powered by two, non-afterburning Pratt & Whitney J52-P-8 engines rated at 9,300 pounds thrust each. Empty weight is 26,066 lb., ordnance capacity is nearly 18,000 lb. and range is transoceanic. Maximum speed is 540 knots (623 miles per hour) and cruise is 400 kt (460 mph).

A-6B (19 aircraft; no new airframes). All aircraft (a/c.) are conversions of A-6As and are electronically configured as missile carriers in three different sub-variants offering from limited- to full-strike capability.

A-6C (12 a/c.; no new airframes). All are conversions of A-6As under the US Navy's TRIM (Trails, Roads, Interdiction, Multisensor) Programme. The A-6C is configured with electro-

optical sensors to aid in carrying out strikes against non-radar significant targets.

KA-6D (51 a/c.; no new airframes). Feasibility of an A-6 air-to-air refuelling tanker was first shown in April 1966. But it was not until the summer of 1970 that the Navy began to procure the KA-6D tanker in quantity. All are rebuilt A-6As prior to c/n 250 (BuNo. 152941).

A-6E (36 a/c. through Fiscal Year 1972). With completion of the A-6A contract in FY 1969, the Navy ordered an advanced all-weather A-6 using multimode radar, solid state avionics and numerous reliability improvements. Externally the A-6E is the same as the A-6A.

A-6(—). This is a projected version of the A-6 which will incorporate electro-optical sensors in the A-6E. The programme is known as Target Recognition Attack Multisensor (TRAM).

EA-6A (27 aircraft). Concurrent with initial production of the A-6A, the Marine Corps ordered this electronic countermeasure version of the A-6. This model retains partial attack capability.

EA-6B Prowler (47 a/c. through FY 1973). This four-seat variant of the A-6 is an electronic warfare aircraft used by the Navy. The first three test aircraft were A-6A conversions, followed by five prototypes and then series production. This model carries no armament.

Development—Long and Thorough

Genesis of the all-weather attack aircraft goes back to the Korean War but the necessary technology was lacking at that time. However, progress was made in radar, navigation systems and cockpit displays and, in 1956, the Navy was able to issue requests for proposals for a new all-weather attack aircraft. It was to fill the void between the Douglas A-1 Skyraider[2] and A-4 Skyhawk[3] light attack and the Douglas A-3 Skywarrior and North American A-5 Vigilante heavy attack aircraft.

The Navy wanted the new aircraft to be able to fly long distances at low altitude by night, find and attack moving and stationary targets and

With initial smaller rudder, the first Intruder, BuNo. 147864 in landing configuration reveals tilting tailpipes to good advantage. This and next three A-6As (BuNos. 147865–7) had hydraulically tilting tail pipes arranged to swivel down 23° to improve short field and carrier capability by reducing take-off and landing speed by about 11 mph. However, no real improvement was noted and the system was deactivated early in the programme.
(Photo: Grumman 60654)

---

[1] For consistency and uniformity, all variant references to early Intruders conform to the Unified Nomenclature System, adopted in November 1962, before which the A-6A was A2F-1 and the EA-6A was A2F-1H.

Similarly, although the TC-4C (which is Grumman G-159 Gulfstream I-based) pilot and bombardier/navigator trainer is an integral part of the A-6 community, comprehensive coverage is outside the scope of this *Profile*.—Author

[2] See *Aircraft Profile No. 60*; [3] see *Profile No. 102*.

return to its land or carrier base without aid of external navigational references. Nuclear capability against land targets was also part of the request. Indeed a tall order.

Response came from Martin, Douglas, Vought and Boeing with two designs each and Bell, Grumman, Lockheed and North American with one design each. Noteworthy entries were Boeing's response with one subsonic (turboprop) and one supersonic design and Bell's vertical-take-off-and-landing (VTOL) proposal. On the very last day of 1957, Grumman Design 128 was selected the winner. Design 128 was subsequently USN-designated A2F-1.

Subsequent to Grumman's victory in the design competition, significant milestones were recorded in May 1958 with formal signing of the development contract and 11 months later with award of a $101-million incentive fee development and production contract. Construction of the first A-6A (BuNo. 147864, the USN serial no.) proceeded and the aircraft made its first flight out of Grumman's Calverton Field on April 19 1960 with Bill Smyth at the controls. Four days prior the company had announced that the name Intruder had been selected after a company-wide contest, which drew 4,000 names in 1,000 entries.

Other milestones on the road to Fleet deployment were the first flight of a fully configured A-6A in November 1960 and the Navy Preliminary Evaluation (NPE) in September 1961.

On December 15 1961 the range of the A-6A was impressively demonstrated for the first time when class desk officer Lieutenant Commander C. P. (Bud) Ekas, USN, flew BuNo. 148617 (c/n 7) from Naval Air Station North Island, California, to Calverton, NY. The non-stop 2,583-mile flight took 4 hours 30 minutes and was accomplished on internal fuel only.

Recommendations made during the September 1961 NPE had been incorporated and another NPE was held in December 1962. By November 1962, airframe BIS (Board of Inspection and Survey) had also begun at Naval Air Test Center (NATC) Patuxent River, Maryland. By then Fleet introduction was less than two months away. Thus, on February 7 1963, Vice-Admiral Frank O'Beirne, Commander US Forces Atlantic, took formal delivery of two A-6As for Attack Squadron Forty-Two (VA-42) 'Green Pawns'. The squadron then began training of aircrews for future A-6A squadrons.

A-6—General Description

All models of the Intruder share a common basic geometry, though the EA-6B has an extended fuselage.

The basic A-6 design is a mid-wing configuration with 25° sweepback at the quarter chord. Wing span is 53 feet 0 inches (25 ft. 4 in., with wings folded); area is 528.9 square feet. Wing thickness range is 9 to 6% from root to tip and the aerofoil is a modified NACA 64A009 section at station 33, modified 64A005.9 at the tips and

64A008.4 at the fold joint. The wing has a negative dihedral of one degree and is mounted with a zero degree angle of incidence.

The continuously variable wing flaps are 30% chord surfaces of the semi-Fowler slotted type and these are set to 30° for take-off and 40° for landing. Flap area is 52 sq. ft. per wing. The wing leading-edge slats are also continuously variable from zero to 27.5°. A third set of wing control surfaces are 'flaperons' (flap + aileron) for lateral control and these travel up to a maximum of 51°. To decrease landing roll during short field operations, the flaperons pop up to 42°, provided both throttles are retarded and the aircraft has set on its landing gear. Finally, there are wing tip speed brakes (BuNo. 149940 and subsequent) which open to an included angle of 120° and have an area of 24.24 sq. ft.

The horizontal tail comprises two one-piece slab surfaces of 117 sq. ft. swept 30° at the quarter chord. They are mounted at 0° dihedral and their deflection ranges from +1.5° leading-edge 'up' to −24° leading-edge 'down' in landing and spin recovery configuration.

The vertical tail or fin and rudder has an area of 79.25 sq. ft., of which 16.32 sq. ft. is rudder. Rudder deflections are 4° left and right when the aircraft is clean and 35° left and right with flaps down or for spin recovery. Sweep at the quarter chord is 28°.

The original fuselage speed brakes have now been deactivated on A-6As prior to c/n 310

Camouflage trial. Between March and May 1966, VA-65 and VA-85 evaluated three different camouflage schemes, but did not adopt any. Here is BuNo. 151822 of VA-65 Tigers at NAS Atsugi, Japan. Flaps and slats are deployed and single centre-line fuel store is in use. (Photo: I. Yatsuhashi)

Brand new. A-6E of VA-65 Tigers, CVW-7 (AG), at NAS Albany, Ga. in July 1972. White nose radome became standard with all A-6s subsequent to BuNo. 155628. Markings are vivid orange. (Photo: Ken Buchanan)

(BuNo. 154170) and were deleted during production on those subsequent to shop 310. Since they do not have wing tip brakes, EA-6As retain the fuselage brakes.

Maximum length of the A-6 is 54 feet 9 inches, and maximum height is 16 ft. 2 in. Height, while folding wings, 21 ft. 11 in.

Airframe, powerplants and avionics

The Intruder is essentially an aluminium aircraft powered by conventional turbojet engines and employing avionics that reflect the 'state of the art' of the late 1950s. There have been hundreds of engineering changes to the airframe. Similarly, engine changes have taken place; while on the A-6E, a major avionics innovation has been introduced. From an operating systems standpoint, the A-6 is essentially a hydraulic aircraft.

The wing is divided into five major subassemblies: centre-section and left and right or port and starboard inner and outer panels. The centre-section has a continuous box beam passing through the fuselage and both inner panels are spliced to this section. All five subassemblies contain integral fuel tanks.

The inner and outer panels use multi-beam construction and are covered by machined skins with integral ribs. Each wing fold joint uses four steel hinges and hydraulically-driven locking pins.

The aluminium fuselage is of semi-monocoque construction except for the lower half, where a deep structural keel beam of steel and titanium is used between the engines and non-structural doors that enclose the engine compartment. Aluminium honeycomb panels are used for structural covers over the fuselage fuel cells.

The horizontal stabilizer or tailplane is of multi-beam construction, with machined aluminium

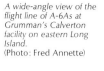

A wide-angle view of the flight line of A-6As at Grumman's Calverton facility on eastern Long Island.
(Photo: Fred Annette)

Up, up and away! A-6A of VA-85 Black Falcons, CVW-11, (NH) leaves from angle deck of USS Kitty Hawk in South China Sea. Ordnance is on outer and centre pylons. 1966.
(Photo: Grumman 66740)

Maintenance. A-6A of VA-75 Sunday Punchers, CVW-7 (AG), with all systems down. Avionics 'birdcage' open below fuselage, starboard engine is out and ram air turbine on top of inside starboard wing is deployed. NAS Oceana 1964.
(Photo: Grumman 64820)

skins and an aluminium honeycomb trailing-edge. The stabilizers are retained on a steel tube that is mounted in bearings in the fuselage.

Rudder, flaps and slats have conventional leading-edges and aluminium honeycomb trailing-edges. The fin is also multi-beam construction with aluminium honeycomb skin and a glass fibre tip cap.

Design limit load factor within the flight design envelope is +6.5 g at 32,526 lb.; and, for asymmetrical flight manoeuvres, the limit is +5.2 g. Strength is sufficient to withstand 20.3 feet per second sink speed at design landing gross weight of 33,637 lb.

The A-6's landing gear is a conventional tricycle arrangement with addition of the catapult tow link to the nose strut. The main gear uses 36 × 11 wheels and tyres and also features an anti-skid system. The nose gear uses dual 20 × 5.5 wheels and tyres.

The A-6 has two completely independent 3,000 pounds per square inch hydraulic systems. One is the flight system using one 14 US gallons per minute pump on each engine to power the primary flight controls. The other is the combined system which also uses a 14-gal./min. pump on each engine; and it powers the primary flight controls and general utility items. Loss of flight hydraulic pressure limits the use of the combined system pressure to the longitudinal, lateral and directional control surfaces and the speed brakes.

Engines and Fuel System

In 1972, P&WA—Pratt & Whitney Aircraft Division of the United Aircraft Corporation—ran an advertisement for the 11,200 pounds thrust J52-P-408 turbojet, two of which are being installed in the newest and heaviest Navy A-6, the EA-6B Prowler. The bold headline message read: 'How can a hotshot of 6 years ago have 12 even better years ahead?'. The body copy went on to answer the question by stating that since 1959, the J52 has grown 50% in thrust. As the J52-P-408, the unit offers 23% boost in the Intruder/Prowler's power—without any significant change in engine size, shape or weight. P&WA's advertisement ended on the confident note that 'the J52 can grow still more—enough to power the A-6 series well into the 1980s.'

In fact, A-6s built have been powered by variants of the J52. Intruder production prior to c/n 136 (BuNo. 152583) had the 152-P-6 units installed; thereafter the J52-P-8 turbojets of 9,350 pounds thrust (700 pounds greater output over the P-6) was employed. Although the EA-6B, with its heavier all-up weight, uses the P-408 (BuNo. 158544 and subsequent Prowlers), a 1963 proposal to install the turbofan P&WA TF30 was dropped when it became obvious that the change would involve extensive airframe modifications.

Two self-sealing fuel cells and one fuselage fuel bladder cell (9,016 lb.), three integral wing cells (6,923 lb.) and assorted equipment comprise the A-6 fuel system. All store stations can carry 300 US gallon capacity external tanks (8,160 lb.); additionally, a 300-gal. refuelling store (2,040 lb.) may be carried on the centreline store station. This brings the maximum fuel for an A-6A or A-6E tanker mission to 26,139 pounds weight or 3,844 US gallons of JP-5 fuel. (Capacities and capabilities of the KA-6D tanker will be found under its description later in this *Profile*).

NAS Whidbey Island in 1964. VAH-123 (NJ) still had responsibility for A-6A replacement air crew training. This task was taken over by VA-128 Golden Intruders of RCVW-12 (NJ). RCVW-12 was decommissioned in 1970 and code NJ assigned directly to VA-128 and other former RCVW-12 units—VA-122 (A-7s) and VF-121 (F-4s). (Photo: Unknown)

Flight line of A-6As at Grumman's Calverton facility on eastern Long Island. (Photo: Grumman)

DIANE

Without the Digital Integrated Attack and Navigation Equipment, or DIANE, the A-6A's attack capability would be limited at best. However, using DIANE and sub-systems the crew can fly against preselected targets, and targets of opportunity, with a variety of ordnance loads, over any kind of terrain, and under varying tactical conditions, without the crew needing to look outside the cockpit from launch to recovery.

Automatic navigation, requiring only selection of operating mode, and manual insertion of pertinent navigation data and flight control may be varied from non-automatic to fully-automatic 'hands off' mode. But, in all modes, the pilot is provided with an instant display of the immediate tactical situation by means of the analog 'highway in the sky' display.

The attack function is fully implemented by DIANE for acquiring and tracking the target, solving the ballistic equations and generating weapons release signals. This frees the pilot from non-essentials and he may devote his full attention to immediate tactical decisions and simply monitoring the flight.

The complexity of the DIANE system can be appreciated by a brief description of the many sub-systems and components that constitute its make-up.

AN/ASQ-61 ballistics computer is a digital computer which supplies flight pattern data, navigation cruise commands and data to aid in selection, fuzing and delivery of weapons.

AN/ASW-16 automatic flight control system (AFCS) is the aircraft's three-axis autopilot.

CP-729A, -863/A or -864/A air data computer supplies altitude, static pressure, Mach number and airspeed data to the AFCS, vertical display, ballistics computer and conventional flight instruments and displays.

AN/ASN-31 inertial navigation system (INS) is an automatic aid to navigation which is independent of outside references. The INS provides information on aircraft heading, attitude, and horizontal and vertical velocities. The data is derived from accelerometers mounted along three axis on a gyro-stabilized platform.

AN/APQ-92 search radar provides the pilot with capabilities for navigation to and from the target area, search and detection of stationary and moving targets, all-weather low-level attack, automatic and rate-aided manual tracking.

AN/APQ-112 track radar tracks moving and prominent stationary targets and maps terrain ahead of the aircraft.

AN/AVA-1 vertical display is a TV-like display to aid the pilot and give him terrain clearance and elevation scan.

AN/APN-141 radar altimeter is a low altitude (5,000 ft.) electronic altimeter with precise readouts at very low altitudes, such as are encountered during carrier approach.

AN/APN-153 radar navigation set (Doppler) supplies ground speed and drift angles to the ballistics computer.

AN/ASQ-57 integrated electronic control and **AN/AIC-14** intercommunications system provides communications systems, navigation and identification (IFF) functions. Navigation functions take the form of TACAN and ADF.

The main bulkhead at the nose radome

hinge-line constitutes the reference mounting surface for the INS gyroscope and search and track radar antennae. Other avionic equipment is mounted on the bulkhead to simplify maintenance. The aft equipment compartment houses units of the Doppler radar, radar recorder, air data computer and integrated electronic control. The Doppler radar antenna and other equipment is mounted on the extensible equipment platform, sometimes known as the 'birdcage'. This platform is hinged to the fuselage so that it can be lowered for equipment accessibility. Lowered, it provides a ladder to enter the aft equipment compartment.

There were many anxious moments during the initial deployment of the A-6A, involving concern as to whether or not it would ever make the grade. Many A-6As flew with 'partial' systems, that is, not everything was working. At times, a staggering 60 mmh/fh (maintenance man-hours per flight-hour) was once the rule but that has improved markedly by now.[1] Maintenance time is still high for the avionic systems, but when it all works there is no question in respect of the Intruder's success in all-weather attack.

Major Model Changes
Since the first A-6A rolled-out, six variants have been built and deployed to Fleet units. Several other models have been proposed but not built.
A-6B—The first A-6B proposal and contract was for an A-6A 'stripped' of its all-weather avionics and used for visual attack but this contract was cancelled.

The A-6B now in operation exists in three different (modified) configurations: Mod. '0'; Mod. '1'; and PAT/ARM (Passive Angle Tracking). Each version uses the USAF-developed General Dynamics AGM-78 Standard ARM (anti-radiation missile) in SAM (Surface-to-Air Missile) suppression. All three configurations represent a different approach to the same mission. Little additional information is available because of military security requirements. Externally this model is the same as the A-6A.
A-6C TRIM—In early 1968 a modified A-6A (BuNo. 147867) with large wing-mounted pods took to the air for the first flight of simulated electro-optical sensors. It was the beginning of a programme called TRIM (Trails, Roads, Interdiction Multisensor). TRIM was an outgrowth of a Southeast Asia requirement for an aircraft with increased daylight capability.

The A-6C was the Navy's answer and the Martin/General Dynamics B-57G[2] was USAF's answer. The A-6C supplements A-6A all-weather capability with forward looking infra-red (FLIR) and low light level television (LLL-TV) systems. Because these sensors are mounted in a turret

underneath the fuselage that particular store station is no longer available. A third element in TRIM is the direction finder which notes presence of targets by means of a video display. All of these are 'real time' systems. The FLIR and LLL-TV are regarded as complementary to one another. Much of this programme is also veiled in secrecy but it is known that the A-6C has been successfully deployed to Southeast Asia.
KA-6D Tanker—Using the A-6A's generous payload capacity to carry extra fuel was demonstrated by Grumman in April and May 1966. An A-6A (BuNo. 149937; shop 23) was converted to tanker configuration for demonstration purposes. By May 27 1966 all tests were completed; an A-6A and a McDonnell Douglas F-4 Phantom[1] had been refuelled by the demonstration tanker.

However, it was not until the latter part of 1969 that contract negotiations were finished to proceed with a production tanker, then designated KA-6D. It was an austerity programme. No new airframes or static test articles were specified; aircraft in the pre-200 (BuNo. 152891) (c/n) series were to be selected for conversion.

Initially four A-6As were flown to Calverton and conversion began at once. On April 16 1970, Grumman's Chuck Sewell completed the production tanker's (BuNo. 151582) first flight. After the first four KA-6Ds were completed, the programme shifted to Grumman's Stuart, Florida, facility.

Conversion involves removal of the avionics 'birdcage' in the aft fuselage and associated all-weather cockpit displays not needed for the tanker mission. In place of the 'birdcage' is a hose-and-reel assembly which transfers fuel at rates up to 350 gallons per minute. As in the A-6A, the fuel supply is contained in wing and and fuselage tanks, augmented by five 300-gal. external fuel tanks. This gives the KA-6D a total of 3,844 gal. of fuel, of which just about 3,000 gal. are transferable. A McDonnell Douglas D-704 'Buddy Mission' refuelling store, in place of the centreline 300-gal. tank, can be used as a back-up.

The KA-6D has retained daylight visual attack capability, but plans to equip it with four 20-mm. cannon in the nose have been dropped through lack of funding. This refuelling version of the A-6 Intruder is a replacement for the McDonnell Douglas KA-3B Skywarrior tanker. In the course of company evaluation some drogue spit-out problems arose, but once cured, the KA-6D demonstrated its ease of refuelling all in-flight refuellable Navy aircraft.
A-6E—On February 27 1970, yet another milestone in the A-6 programme came and went with little fanfare. On that day the prototype A-6E (BuNo. 155673; A-6A airframe 404) completed its first flight with Grumman pilot Joe Burke and B/N (Bombardier/Navigator) Jim Johnson at the controls.

[1] For the USN A-7A Corsair II, the manufacturer's contract guarantee was set at 11.5 mmh/fh—see *Aircraft Profile No. 239 LTV (Vought): A-7A/E Corsair II.*—Editor

[2] *Profile No. 247: Martin B-57 A/G & RB-57F.*

[1] *Profile No. 208.*

Key to colour side views
1 A-6A Intruder of the US Navy's Attack Squadron Fifty-Two or VA-52 (calling themselves the 'Knight Riders'). Tail code letters NL identify Carrier Air Wing or CVW-15. Period, 1968.

2 A-6C of VA-165, the 'Boomers' (on the tail and sandwiching NG for CVW-9 is the unit's stylized boomerang). Ventral centre-line turret contains FLIR and LLL-TV equipments. Period, 1970.

3 KA-6D in-flight tanker refueller of VA-115 (the 'Chargers') bearing CVW-5's code letters NF. Period, 1972.

4 A-6E of VA-65, the 'Tigers' with code letters AG denoting CVW-7. Period, 1972.

5 EA-6B Prowler of VAQ-131, a Tactical Electronics Warfare Squadron. Period, 1972.

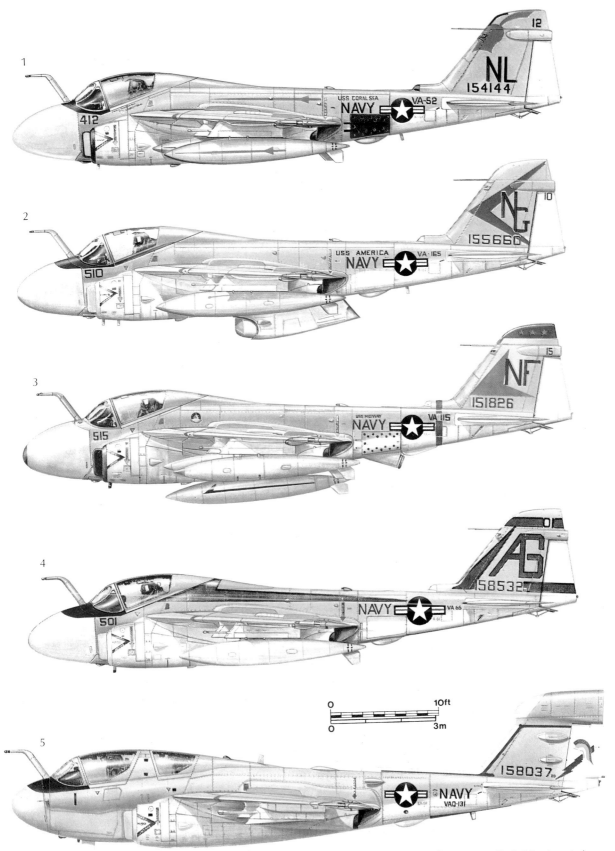

M. Trim/T. Hadler/D. Palmer ©Profile Publications Ltd

The A-6E is a true second generation Intruder. All changes are avionic and the external appearance remains the same as the A-6A.

Proposal of Design 128S or an A-6E goes back to July 1967. The A-6A utilizes 1950s' state-of-the-art avionics which, in an aircraft as complex as the A-6A, compounds maintenance and reliability problems. The A-6E proposal contained plans for (1) a new general purpose computer, (2) multimode radar and (3) a new weapons release system. Authorization to proceed with sub-systems procurement came in 1969 and the A-6E prototype was provisionally accepted in December 1969.

When the prototype began flight tests in March 1970, it was to evaluate the IBM AN/ASQ-133 solid-state digital computer already proven in the EA-6B Prowler, A-7 Corsair II and the USAF's General Dynamics F-111. By August 1970 the weapons release system was under flight test. The new system features solid-state design and new switching circuits combined with increased self-test capability. Last to fly (November 1970) was the Norden AN/APQ-148 multi-

Massive nose landing gear. Tow link on front of nose strut must withstand substantial forces when A-6 weighing 60,000 lb. is launched. Drag brace is equally massive. Steering actuator is in middle and lights on gear door are (left to right) anti-collision, taxi and angle of attack.
(Photo: Author)

Wide stance. Main gear track is 11 ft. 0.3 in., giving good stability on pitching carrier decks. Speed brakes 'bleed' open when aircraft hydraulic system is not pressurized.
(Photo: Author)

Project Stormfury. That's the marking on the rudder of this VMA(AW)-224 A-6A at MCAS Cherry Point, N.C. during 1970. Stormfury is annual hurricane research and modification programme.
(Photo: D. Kasulka)

mode radar, replacing separate track and search radars of the A-6A. The new radar performs the detection, tracking and terrain clearance functions simultaneously. There are no airframe or engine changes.

In 1972 Grumman was awarded a contract for long leadtime items which will be used in a major retrofit programme to update the A-6As now in Fleet service. In 1973 36 A-6As will be modified. This work is in addition to FY 1970, '71 and '72 contracts for production A-6Es.

In a further move to enhance capability of some A-6Es, the Navy plans to outfit them with FLIR systems (see A-6C) to detect, identify and attack enemy targets in darkness. The programme is known as TRAM and is an outgrowth of the A-6C TRIM programme. In the new aircraft (A-6 suffix not yet announced) the B/N will have FLIR and radar displays. The radar will detect the target at relatively long range and

once the target is fully recognizable on the FLIR display, tracking will be done with the detection and ranging system. The computer then works out the bombing run. The proposed system is expected to be very useful against non-significant (non-reflective) radar targets.

EA-6A—The A-6A was about one year from squadron service when the first variant, the EA-6A (formerly A2F-1H), was approved for production. The contract for the new tactical ECM (Electronic Counter Measures) aircraft was finalized in March 1962. Its primary ECM mission is to support strike aircraft and ground troops by suppressing enemy electronic activity and obtaining tactical electronic intelligence within a combat area. The carrier-suitable EA-6A features limited all-weather capability with conventional and special weapons.

The aircraft, which completed its first flight on April 26 1963, is currently only in service with

Fire-away! A-6A of USMC attack squadron VMA(AW)-242 Batmen fire USN Maxson Electronics AGM-12 Bullpup missile. Tail markings of USMC A-6s have become considerably more colourful since this photo was taken in 1966.
(Photo: Unknown)

One of VMA(AW)-533's Hawks comes home to roost at NAS Atsugi, Japan, in January 1971.
(Photo: H. Nagakubo)

The carrierborne Grumman EA-6A is equipped for ECM (Electronic Counter Measures) roles and is in service with the US Marine Corps. Code letters RM apply to the Marines First Composite Reconnaissance Squadron (VMCJ-1). This EA-6A was assigned to the Marine Corps Air Station at Iwakuni, Japan. Period, 1970.

M. Trim/T. Hadler/D. Palmer ©*Profile Publications Ltd*

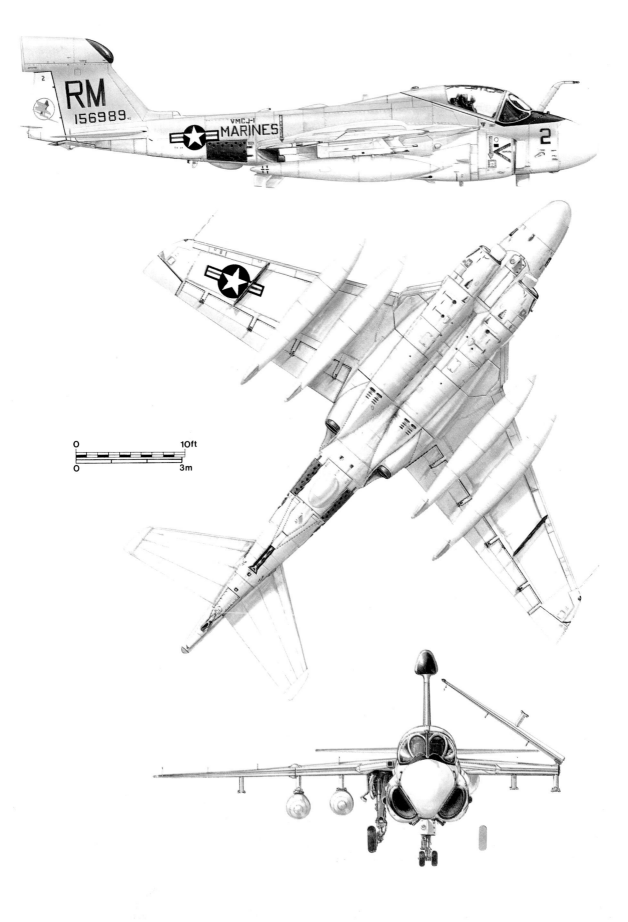

RM
156989
VMCJ-1
MARINES
2

0 ——————— 10ft
0 ——————— 3m

the US Marine Corps, where it replaced the Douglas EF-10B (originally the F3D Skyknight). Basic airframe and engines are as in the A-6A but wing pods containing electronic equipment and a large faired radome on top of the vertical fin give this model a very distinctive appearance.

Two contracts have been let for the EA-6A. To complete the first order for 12 aircraft, A-6As were taken off the assembly line and modified to the new configuration. A second contract for 15 EA-6As was awarded in December 1967. These constituted new airframes and were financed from FY 1968 appropriations.

EA-6B Prowler—This variant represents the most radical departure from the A-6A configuration in that it is an unarmed, four-seat aircraft solely configured for tactical electronic warfare; the Grumman designation is Model 1128.

Construction of the pre-production prototype EA-6B (BuNo. 149481; c/n M1) began in 1967 and was built from an A-6A (BuNo. 149481; c/n 15) by 'splicing-in' a 40-inch section forward of the cockpit. This prototype flew for the first time on May 25, 1968, with Grumman pilot Don King at the controls. A second EA-6B (c/n M2) was built by similar conversion of another A-6A (BuNo. 149479; c/n 13). C/N M1 and M2 are now designated NEA-6Bs. Yet a third, but non-flying, EA-6B prototype (BuNo. 148615) emerged

Safety revetments at Da Nang, Vietnam. A-6As of VMA(AW)-533 Hawks (ED) sit under the merciless sun and are also soaked in tropical humidity, not exactly the best environment for this complex aircraft. (Photo: Unknown)

Aboard USS Saratoga in 1964. Black and white test marked A-6A also carries markings of Weapons System Test (W), Service Test (S) and Flight Test (chevron). (Grumman 64446)

'Loaded for bear!' A-6A (BuNo. 147618) loaded with 500-lb. bombs has nose wheel off the deck as NATC-assigned aircraft leaves USS Saratoga during 1964 BIS Trials. (Photo: Grumman)

'Oh, my achin' back!' Heavily loaded A-6A (BuNo. 149483) of Weapons System Test Section of NATC Patuxent River, Md., is burdened by flat of starboard tyre. (Photo: AAHS L2301)

from Grumman's shops, designated as an electronic test article. This test A-6 was installed in an anechoic chamber for thorough testing of the proposed EA-6B electronic warfare systems—the chamber design preventing interference with local radio and TV reception.

The EA-6B differs from the A-6 airframe in various ways. For example, by the addition of a forward cockpit and equipment bay, by incorporation of a pod-shaped fairing on top of the vertical fin and by strengthening the airframe structure to assure adequate operational fatigue life at maximum gross weights.

The five external store stations are retained and can carry ECM jamming pods or fuel tanks. The EA-6B Prowler also retains the Pratt & Whitney J52-P-8A engine but the uprated J52-P-408 is being installed in EA-6Bs from BuNo. 158544 onwards. Other EA-6Bs will receive this engine during major overhaul. Two aft-hinged canopies are used, as are the proven Martin-Baker Aircraft ejection seats. There are no fuselage speed brakes.

At present the aircraft carries 8,000 pounds of avionics internally and accommodates another 950 lb. on each of the four wing pylons and along the fuselage centreline. With a gross weight of 51,000 lb., including pods, the EA-6B attains 510 knots (587 mph) at sea-level. It can manoeuvre at 5,5g and its range and altitude are compatible with the A-6A.

The multiple ECM roles the EA-6B can perform include those of a stand-off jammer, an ECM escort or protection penetration aircraft, depending on the desired mission. To date, the

Standard ARM missiles. A-6B carrying General Dynamics Standard Anti-Radar Missiles on inner wing pylons takes off from Lindbergh Field, San Diego, Calif. 'Pock marks' on nose radome are small antennas.
(Photo: General Dynamics)

A-6C Prototype. BuNo. 151568 at Grumman's Calverton Flight Test Facility in the Fall (autumn) of 1969. FLIR and LLL-TV are housed in centreline turret; large shutter covers mechanism when sensors are not in use.
(Photo: Grumman P306180)

A-6E prototype. BuNo. 155673 is A-6A (shop 404) and was used to evaluate new avionic systems destined for production A-6Es. A-6E marking on fin is Grumman-originated and coloured light blue.
(Photo: Grumman)

Long mission finished. Judging by the six-pylon fuel tanks, this EA-6A of VMCJ-1, MAW-1 (RM), has just completed a long mission. Centreline store is AN/ALQ-99 jamming system powered by air-driven generator. EA-6A is seen landing at Yokota Air Base, Japan in November 1970.
(Photo: H. Nagakubo)

6

A

TONKIN GULF
YACHT CLUB

B

00
AC
155631
VA-7

C

NMC
151591
E

D

50
NJ
152623

E

10
NG
152940
VA 35

F

3
CE
151798

G

10
AE
154129
VA-

H

3
DT
155687

I

04
AG
155634
VA-

J

05
WK
155652
E

K

00
VK
151593

L

08
EA
152895

M. Trim/T. Hadler/D. Palmer © Profile Publications Ltd

aircraft has successfully flown against actual captured and simulated Soviet radar threats.

Heart of the EA-6B's ECM systems is the AN/ALQ-99 tactical jamming system (TJS) that generates high power jamming signals through specially-designed, low-drag pods, each of which has its own turbine-driven, alternating current power source. Other ECM equipment includes a radar deception transmitter and the communications jamming system.

Besides the pilot, there are three naval flight officers (NFO) whose duties include operation of the ECM equipment. The senior NFO sits next to the pilot and operates or monitors one-half of the frequency coverage of the TJS. The second NFO, seated behind the first, handles the other half of the TJS. The third NFO is responsible for communications jamming.

The three pre-production prototypes (M1–M3) were followed by five prototypes, (P1-P5). These underwent the rigours of BIS Trials and carrier suitability tests aboard USS *Midway* during the spring and summer of 1970. Trials included flights against radar ranges at Eglin Air Force Base, Florida, in addition to extensive work at the Naval Air Test Center, NAS Patuxent River, Maryland.

Intruder Block Changes
Numerous major airframe and avionic changes have been made on the A-6 on the production line and during cyclic overhaul since entering production in 1960. Primarily, changes have been for increased reliability. Changes occurred at c/n 200, 246, 310, 359, 373, 451 and 476.
● C/N 200 (BuNo. 152891) includes canopy operation without having to operate either engine. Three search radar modifications and the pilot's vertical display.
● C/N 246 (BuNo. 152937) includes boresight weapons delivery mode, several changes to search and track radars as well as other reliability changes.
● C/N 310 (BuNo. 154170) changes were once again in the interest of reliability. At this point, Grumman also took the first steps toward elimination of the track radar, a sign of the coming A-6E. The search radar was modified to perform some tracking functions. Fuselage speed brakes were deleted and the heavier

nose wheel of the EA-6B was also included. The latter improves catapult characteristics and permits heavier gross takeoff loading.
● C/N 359 (BuNo. 155628) changes affect the external appearance of the aircraft. White Neoprene coatings replaced black material. This change is also incorporated during overhaul.
● C/N 373 (BuNo. 155642) aircraft include provisions for wing-mounted minigun pods, primarily for air-to-ground use but also with limited air-to-air capability.
● C/N 451 (BuNo. 155720) and block 476 (BuNo. 157017) changes incorporate a zero/zero Martin-Baker Aircraft rocket-powered ejection-seat, making ejection at zero air-speed/altitude possible.

Planned use of the EA-6B wing, with its additional hardpoints, did not materialize. The wing is also configured for addition of high-lift devices should improvement in carrier take-off and landing be required.

Not Proceeded With
A version of the A-6A that never proceeded beyond the study stage was a three-seat trainer, tentatively known as the TA-6A. The third seat was to have been aft of the existing two. However, this approach was not considered practical or cost-effective and therefore cancelled in 1964. Instead the Navy and Marine Corps procured the TC-4C based on the commercial Grumman Gulfstream I.

In 1966, Grumman proposed a variant which was company-designated 128NT—a long-range navigation trainer for the international (European) market. This derivative would have used the A-6A airframe, omitting those systems not required for the trainer mission and replace these with off-the-shelf navigation training equipment. No aircraft was built.

For the light attack (VAL) competition in 1962,[1] Grumman entered the fray with a single-seat version of the A-6A which retained the J52 engines rather than the suggested turbofan TF30. This model was designated 128G-12 and actually proceeded to the mock-up stage. It is of note that the G-12 featured folding horizontal

[1] Profile No. 239: A-7 Corsair II also provides details of this VAL competition.—Author

Key to colour side views

6 A-6A Intruder of VA-65, the 'Tigers'. For a short time in 1966, A-6s aboard USS Constellation had two-tone green camouflage to test for effectiveness in sorties over Viet Nam.

A: Wry humour; an unofficial badge circulating among crews engaged in Viet Nam operations.

B: A-6A of VA-75, the 'Sunday Punchers'. Period, 1972; letters AC denote Carrier Air Wing Three or CVW-3.

C: A-6B of NMC, the Naval Missile Center, Pt Mugu, California; mid-1972.

D: A-6A of VA-128, the 'Golden Intruders'; late 1967. Tail code NJ stands for units of (West Coast) Replacement Carrier Air Wing Twelve or RCVW-12.

E: A-6A of VA-35, the 'Panthers'. Period, 1969; code NG, CVW-9.

F: A-6A of VMA(AW)-225, the 'Vagabonds'. Code letters CE, unlike USN, are applicable solely to the squadron; Marine Attack (All Weather) Squadron 225, First Marine Air Wing.

G: A-6A of VA-85, the 'Black Falcons'; period, 1968. Code AE for CVW-6.

H: A-6A of Marine Squadron VMA(AW)-242, the 'Batmen'; period, 1970.

I: A-6A of VA-65, the 'Tigers'; AG stands for CVW-7. Period, mid-1971.

J: A-6A of VMA(AW)-224 at MCAS, Cherry Pt, NC; period, 1969.

K: A-6A of VMA(AW)-121, the 'Green Knights'; period, 1969.

L: A-6A of VMA(AW)-332, the 'Polka Dots'; period, mid-1969.

EA-6A of VMCJ-2, MAW-2 (CY), at MCAS Cherry Point, N.C. VMCJs are composite reconnaissance squadrons that also operate McDonnell Douglas RF-4B photographic aircraft.
(Photo: D. Kasulka)

stabilizers in an effort to place 139 of these aboard a *Forrestal*-class carrier. Two Mk. 12 20-mm. cannon were to have been contained in the lower portion of the nose. Grumman's whole proposal was based on the fact that this aircraft could be delivered almost immediately, since it drew so heavily from the A-6A. However, this did not appear to influence the evaluators and they chose the A-7A Corsair II.

Attack Missions
In its primary role as an all-weather, low-altitude attack aircraft, the A-6 is used in close air support of ground forces or in long-range delivery of conventional or special weapons. Some typical missions are now quoted.

The close support mission (CAS) calls for loiter-on-station at 5,000 feet and uses high altitude cruising between base and combat area. One-hour loiter is possible 635 nautical miles from base with internal fuel while carrying four Bullpup AGM-12 missiles. With 30 × 500-lb. bombs, a 330-mile radius is attainable with about 1-hr. loiter. If maximum time on station is required, the A-6 can carry three 300-gal. external tanks for 5-hr. loiter at an 8-mile radius; 2 × 1,000-lb. bombs are carried.

For most CAS missions, take-off over a 50-ft.

Feasibility study. An A-6A (BuNo. 149937) was converted to tanker configuration in April 1966. Tests proved that KA-6D would be practical replacement for KA-3 tankers and finally beat out KA-7F in vigorous competition. (Photo: Grumman)

Assembly line at Grumman. Complex backbone of A-6A reveals numerous hydraulic lines, cables and pneumatic lines. Highest production rate of Intruder was in Fiscal Year 1967 with 122 aircraft. (Photo: Grumman)

Detached to CVW-17. In April 1971 several VMCJ-2 EA-6As were assigned to CVW-17 (AA) aboard the USS Forrestal for Mediterranean cruise. USMC adopts USN marking when aboard ship. (Photo: J. Sullivan)

Aboard USS Kitty Hawk in 1966. EA-6A (BuNo. 148618) carries Navy Flight Test NATC markings during carrier qualifications. Large pods on folded wing panel are ECM countermeasure equipment as are the pods with the wind-driven generators (at fold joint). Horizontal and vertical black stripes are for photographic reference. (Photo: Grumman)

obstacle requires 2,900 to 3,000 ft. Rocket-assisted take-off will reduce this distance to less than 2,000 ft.

A typical long-range mission might be to a target nearly 1,000 miles from base with 285-kt. (330-mph) cruise in and out at sea-level. In-flight refuelling can easily add another 500 miles of range. For high altitude weapons delivery, the A-6 provides a mission radius capability of about 1,500 miles with one store and four 300-gal. external tanks.

There are countless variables influencing mission capability; suffice to say that payload, range to target, availability of in-flight refuelling service and weather conditions are just a few of these variables.

Intruder Deployments

A period of just over five years elapsed from first prototype flight to production Intruders in combat. Since then, from July 1965 onwards, countless sorties have been flown over Southeast Asia. Intruders also continue to constitute a strong force in the Mediterranean as part of the US Sixth Fleet. All models of the A-6 family have seen combat with exception of the A-6E.

After Attack Squadron Seventy-Five, VA-75 ('Sunday Punchers') graduated as the first fully-trained A-6A unit in 1964, they joined the Fleet. On July 1 1965, they were launched from USS *Independence* to attack key highway bridges at Bac Bong and other targets in the area about 80 to 125 miles south of Hanoi. There was also a night attack against the power generating plant at Thanh Hoa, some 80 miles s. of Hanoi. This mission was significant because the target was located by radar—graphic evidence that no target was secure from night attack. For 96 days VA-75 deployed before being relieved by VA-85

('Black Falcons') aboard the USS *Kitty Hawk*.

The Black Falcons flew against Viet Cong strongholds north of Saigon and unleashed heavy night strikes. The A-6As approached the targets at low altitude and high speed before climbing to altitude before beginning the attack. But often they would operate alone or in pairs, to make radar detection more difficult. The effectiveness of the A-6A must have left its mark on the North Vietnamese because after one spectacular night raid they announced that the Americans had escalated the war by sending B-52s[1] into the Haiphong area—an unexpected tribute to the A-6A's payload capability.

Not to be left out, the US Marines ferried VMA(AW)-242 and VMCJ-2 across the Pacific in 1966 in order to support their ground troops in Vietnam. By 'island-hopping' they arrived in Da Nang on November 1 1966, and began flying strikes two days later.

The A-6A build-up in Southeast Asia continued. VA-35 flew off the USS *Enterprise* and the Marines also sent VMA(AW)-224 and VMCJ-1. As squadrons and carriers left the line, others came to take their place in the relentless pounding of Viet Cong and North Vietnamese invaders. The seemingly never-ending rotation of squadrons came to an end on November 1 1968, when President Johnson ordered bombing of the North to be stopped. By then, the A-6 had been proven.

Endorsements came from all quarters. Typical is one lieutenant's comments: 'We prefer "goo", or darkness, as it means less enemy fire over the target'. Commander Ron Hayes, former Commanding Officer of VA-85, noted: 'The A-6A airframe is rugged and reliable. When the

---

[1] *Profile No. 245: Boeing B-52A/H Stratofortress.*

Variety of stores. In outer ring are 500-lb. Mk. 82 (behind) aircraft and 250-lb. Mk. 81 (left and right) general purpose (GP) bombs, with Grumman universal multiple bomb racks in foreground. Second ring includes Mk. 79 fire bombs (behind aircraft), 1000-lb. Mk. 83 GP bombs (left and right), LAU-10/A rocket launchers and 4 of the 5-in. Zuni rockets which they fire (right foreground), AERO 7D rocket launchers and 19 2.75-in. FEAR Mighty Mouse projectiles (left foreground) and some special weapons in front. Immediately behind A-6, left, are 2,000-lb. Mk. 84 GP bombs and, right, AERO 8A practice bomb containers. In front of wings, left, are 4 Sidewinder IC missiles and a 300-gal. refuelling store. In front of wings, right, are 5 Bullpup missiles and 5 300-gal. tanks are on aircraft. (Photo: Grumman 62213)

P-303339

Intruder among Prowlers . . .
A-6A with markings of
VAQ-129 New Vikings, who
are assigned task of training
replacement aircrews for the
other VAQ or tactical
electronic warfare squadrons
at NAS Whidbey Island.
(Photo: Unknown)

Golden Intruders, VA-128,
are flying this A-6A which
still has original fuselage
speed brakes panels; the
brakes no longer operate as
is evidenced by paint that
remains unburned.
(Photo: Bob Labuoy)

Grumman TC-4C trainer
accommodates one A-6
pilot trainee, four B/N
trainees and two instructors.
Aircraft is equipped with
simulated A-6 cockpit,
complete attack-nav system
and four B/N consoles.
Shown is one of VA-42's
TC-4Cs. VA-128 and
VMAT(AW)-202 also use it.
Nine were built; BuNos.
155722 to 155730.
(Photo: Author)

Camouflage evaluation,
spring 1966. Upper surfaces
were dark (almost black)
green and deep blue while
under surfaces remained
flat white. National insignia
was reduced in size. A-6A
(BuNo. 151819) was assigned
to VA-65 Tigers. Photo at
NAS Lemoore, Calif.
(Photo: Unknown)

Formation of Marine Intruders. Carrying 300-gal. fuel stores these A-6As of VMA(AW)-224 are on a training flight out of their home base MCAS Cherry Point, N.C. Fuselage speed brakes are readily seen. (Photo: US Marine Corps)

situation dictates, the airplane can be muscled around within a "g" envelope comparable to that of a fighter. Even with heavy bomb loads the A-6 is still fleet footed.'

In 1968, Vice-Admiral Thomas Connolly, then Deputy CNO (Air)[1], said: 'This aircraft has been superlative. During the past five months, since November 1967, the Vietnamese weather, from a standpoint of being able to see targets, has been miserable. The A-6A has carried the load, both with respect to missions and quantitity delivered. It has measured up to our highest expectations.'

In 1970, the A-6C and KA-6D tanker joined operational squadrons VA-165 and VA-176, respectively. The A-6C spent the summer of that year flying from USS America in pursuit of moving targets on the Ho Chi Minh Trail. The A-6C was not without teething problems but enough was learned to realize that electro-optical sensors have a bright future.

The considerably less complex KA-6D reached Vietnam in early 1971 but enthusiasm for it was tempered by a 3-g airframe limit. The limit was imposed to extend aircraft life because several of them already had over 1,500 hrs. on the airframe. However, squadrons allocated the KA-6D praised its tanking capability and exploited the field carrier landing practice it provided and used it for numerous other training tasks. Visual bombing and air combat manœuvering are ruled out by the 3-g acceleration limit.

In early 1971, the EA-6B Prowler also joined the A-6 community when it arrived at NAS Whidbey Island. There it joined VAQ-129, the EA-6B aircrew replacement squadron. As training progressed, more EA-6B squadrons formed up. Then VAQ-132 had the distinction of being the first squadron to go aboard ship and deploy to Southeast Asia, sailing on USS America in the summer of 1972.

And finally, the A-6E, having completed NPE and BIS, also joined the A-6 community. As in the case of the A-6A, VA-42 was assigned the job of training A-6E replacement aircrews; they received the first A-6E in December 1971. The first Fleet squadron to transition to the second generation Intruder was VA-85, also at NAS Oceana, in early 1972.

---

[1] Deputy Chief of Naval Operations (Air).

159

TABLE I: A-6/EA-6B Airframe Production

A-6A Airframes

Fiscal Year	Qty.	Serial Numbers
1959	4	147864–147867
1960	4	148615–148618
1961	12	149475–149486
1962	24	149935–149958
1963	43	151558–151600
1964	48	151780–151827
1965	64	152583–152646
1966	33	152891–152923
1967	31	152924–152954
	48	154124–154171
	43	155581–155643
1968	82	155644–155725
1969	32	156998–157029
Total	488	

A-6E Airframes

1970	12	158041–158052
1971	12	158528–158539
1972	12	158787–158798
1973	21	—

EA-6A Airframes

Contractual requirements for the first dozen EA-6As were fulfilled by conversion of 12 A-6A airframes and therefore their serial numbers are carried over to the EA-6As. These are as follows:

Fiscal Year	Qty.	Serial Numbers
1959	1	147865
1960	2	148616 and 148618
1961	3	149475, 149477 and 149478
1962	none	
1963	6	151595–151600
1968	15	156979–156993
Total	27	

EA-6B Airframes

1969	5	156478–156482
1970	12	158029–158040
1971	8	158540–158547
	3	158649–158651
1972	10	158799–158810
1973	6	158811–158817

A-6B, A-6C and KA-6D Airframes

Contractual requirements for these airframes were fulfilled by random conversion of existing A-6A airframes. It is not possible to establish sequential serial numbers for any of these aircraft.

A-6B   10 Mod. '0' conversions in Fiscal Years 1962 and 1963; six Mod. '1' conversions in FY 1962 to 1965 and three PAT/ARM conversions in FY 1967.

A-6C   12 conversions in FY 1968.

KA-6D   51 aircraft between shop (block) numbers 28 and 243.

TABLE II: SPECIFICATIONS, A-6 FAMILY

Dimensions: Wing span, 53 ft. 0 in.; folded, 25 ft. 4 in. (all); overall length, 54 ft. 7 in. (A-6A); 55 ft. 3 in. (EA-6A); 59 ft. 1 in. (EA-6B); overall height, 15 ft. 7 in. (A-6A); 16 ft. 3 in. (EA-6A and EA-6B).

Weights: Empty, 26,350 lb. (A-6A); 28,643 lb. (EA-6A); 32,971 lb. (EA-6B). Max. take-off gross, 60,626 lb. (A-6A); 58,833 lb. (EA-6A); 63,177 lb. (EA-6B). Max. payload, 18,000 lb. (all).

Performance: Min. take-off distance, 1,940 ft. (A-6A); 3,280 ft. (EA-6A); 4,100 ft. (EA-6B). Take-off over 50 ft. obstacle, 2,610 ft. (A-6A); 4,090 ft. (EA-6A); 4,890 ft. (EA-6B). Service ceiling, 47,000 ft. (A-6A); 40,000 ft. (EA-6A); 38,000 ft. (EA-6B). Max. speed, 625 mph (A-6A); 563 mph (EA-6A); 571 mph (EA-6B). Cruise speed, 461 mph (A-6A); 450 mph (EA-6A); 466 mph (EA-6B). Stall speed (landing), 95 mph (A-6A); 104 mph (EA-6A); 118 mph (EA-6B). Ferry range, 3,160 n.mi. (A-6A); 2,790 n.mi. (EA-6A); 2,360 n.mi. (EA-6B). Note: performance based on full internal fuel, no-load condition, standard reserve fuel included.

ACKNOWLEDGEMENTS

The author is grateful for assistance rendered by D. A. (Dave) Anderton; Hal Andrews; Richard Dunne and Norman Gandia of Grumman; Captain W. E. Scarborough, USN(Ret), and all the photographers who contributed so generously of their work.

TABLE III: A-6/EA-6A/EA-6B Squadrons

A-6 Attack Squadrons, US Navy

VA-34	Blue Blasters	NAS Oceana
VA-35	Panthers	NAS Oceana
VA-42	Green Pawns	NAS Oceana
VA-52	Knight Riders	NAS Whidbey Island
VA-65	Tigers	NAS Oceana
VA-75	Sunday Punchers	NAS Oceana
VA-85	Black Falcons	NAS Oceana
VA-95	Sky Knights	NAS Whidbey Island
VA-115	Chargers	NAS Whidbey Island
VA-128	Golden Intruders	NAS Whidbey Island
VA-145	Swordsmen	NAS Whidbey Island
VA-165	Boomers	NAS Whidbey Island
VA-176	Thunderbolts	NAS Oceana
VA-196	Main Battery	NAS Whidbey Island

A-6 Attack Squadrons, US Marine Corps

VMA(AW)-121	Green Knights	MCAS Cherry Point
VMA(AW)-224		MCAS Cherry Point
VMA(AW)-225	Vagabonds	MCAS El Toro
VMA(AW)-242	Batmen	MCAS El Toro
VMA(AW)-332	Polka Dots	MCAS Cherry Point
VMA(AW)-533	Hawks	MCAS Iwakuni
VMAT(AW)-202		MCAS Cherry Point

EA-6A Composite Reconnaissance Squadrons, US Marine Corps

VMCJ-1		MCAS Iwakuni
VMCJ-2		MCAS Cherry Point
VMCJ-3		MCAS El Toro

EA-6B Tactical Electronic Warfare Squadrons, US Navy

VAQ-129	New Vikings	NAS Whidbey Island
VAQ-130	Zappers	NAS Whidbey Island
VAQ-131		NAS Whidbey Island
VAQ-132	Scorpions	NAS Whidbey Island
VAQ-133	Wizards	NAS Whidbey Island
VAQ-134		NAS Whidbey Island
VAQ-135		NAS Whidbey Island

Miscellaneous and Deactivated Squadrons

VX-5	Vampires	Operational Test and Evaluation Force
VAH-123		Flew A-6As prior to formation of VA-128 and is now deactivated.

US Marine Corps Unit Code Letters

VMA(AW)-121	VK	VMAT(AW)-202	KC
VMA(AW)-224	WK	VMCJ-1	RM
VMA(AW)-225	CE	VMCJ-2	CY
VMA(AW)-242	DT	VMCJ-3	TN
VMA(AW)-332	EA		
VMA(AW)-533	ED		

TABLE IV: LIST OF COMMON ABBREVIATIONS

AN/	US Air Force—US Navy joint inventory classification
BIS	Board of Inspection and Survey
B/N	Bombadier/Navigator
BuNo.	Navy Bureau of Aeronautics assigned serial number
ECM	Electronic Countermeasures
FLIR	Forward Looking Infra-Red system
FY	Fiscal Year
LLL-TV	Low Light Level Television system
MCAS	Marine Corps Air Station
NAS	Naval Air Station
NATC	Naval Air Test Center
NPE	Navy Preliminary Evaluation
PAT/ARM	Passive Angle Tracking—Anti-Radiation Missile
TRAM	Target Recognition Attack Multisensor
TRIM	Trails, Roads, Interdiction, Multisensor (Navy)
VA	Attack Squadron (Navy)
VAQ	Tactical Electronic Warfare Squadron (Navy)
VMA(AW)	Attack Squadron (All-Weather) (Marine Corps)
VMAT(AW)	Attack Training Squadron (All-Weather) (Marine Corps)
VMCJ	Composite Reconnaissance Squadron (Marine Corps)

Series Editor:
CHARLES W. CAIN